I0837212

POEMS

BY

GERALD MASSEY.

POEMS

BY

GERALD MASSEY.

A NEW EDITION,
REVISED AND GREATLY ENLARGED.

FIFTH EDITION.

BOSTON:
TICKNOR AND FIELDS.
M.DCCC.LXVI.

To J. T. FIELDS.

My dear Fields: — Will you let me inscribe this new Book of mine with your name, as a little memento of our brief but pleasant intercourse on a certain summer day in England. I have all Leigh Hunt's feeling with regard to a pocket edition of poetry. It was through a pocket edition I first got at poetry. In a pocket edition I first read the poetry of Longfellow, Bryant, Whittier, Lowell, (why don't he write more?) Holmes, (Happy Autocrat! I dare say he does not need me to tell him that his latest Book is one of the most charming that ever crossed the sea, on either passage,) and the Essays of Emerson, (what a capital Book is that "English Traits;" I read it more than most in these days.) But of all pocket editions I think yours the choicest and am proud to find myself in its goodly company. The Blue and Gold are true colors also to sail under in crossing the Atlantic, and I desire to thank your firm for their fair and generous dealing with myself, and for their manner of getting up a bonny little book. In this volume will be found some one hundred and thirty to one hundred and forty pages of new matter. The series of "Christie's Poems," "England and Louis Napoleon," "Burns," and "Appendix," are mainly new. The rest are scattered through the various other sections. The old matter has undergone a thorough revision. I should have preferred to leave a good deal out, but it was thought best to retain the earlier poems as they are. You must let me use my English privilege and have one grumble at your previous title of "Poetical Works," as too presumptuous in its challenge. As yet I am a Man of Faith — for the future — rather than of Works.

And so I remain,

Faithfully yours,

GERALD MASSEY.

Brantwood, Coniston. — Lake Country.
May, 1860.

CONTENTS.

POEMS FOR CHRISTIE.

ONLY A DREAM.

ENGLAND AND LOUIS NAPOLEON.

THE MOTHER'S IDOL BROKEN.

LYRICS OF LOVE.

THE BRIDEGROOM OF BEAUTY.

GLIMPSES OF THE CRIMEAN WAR.

MISCELLANEOUS POEMS.

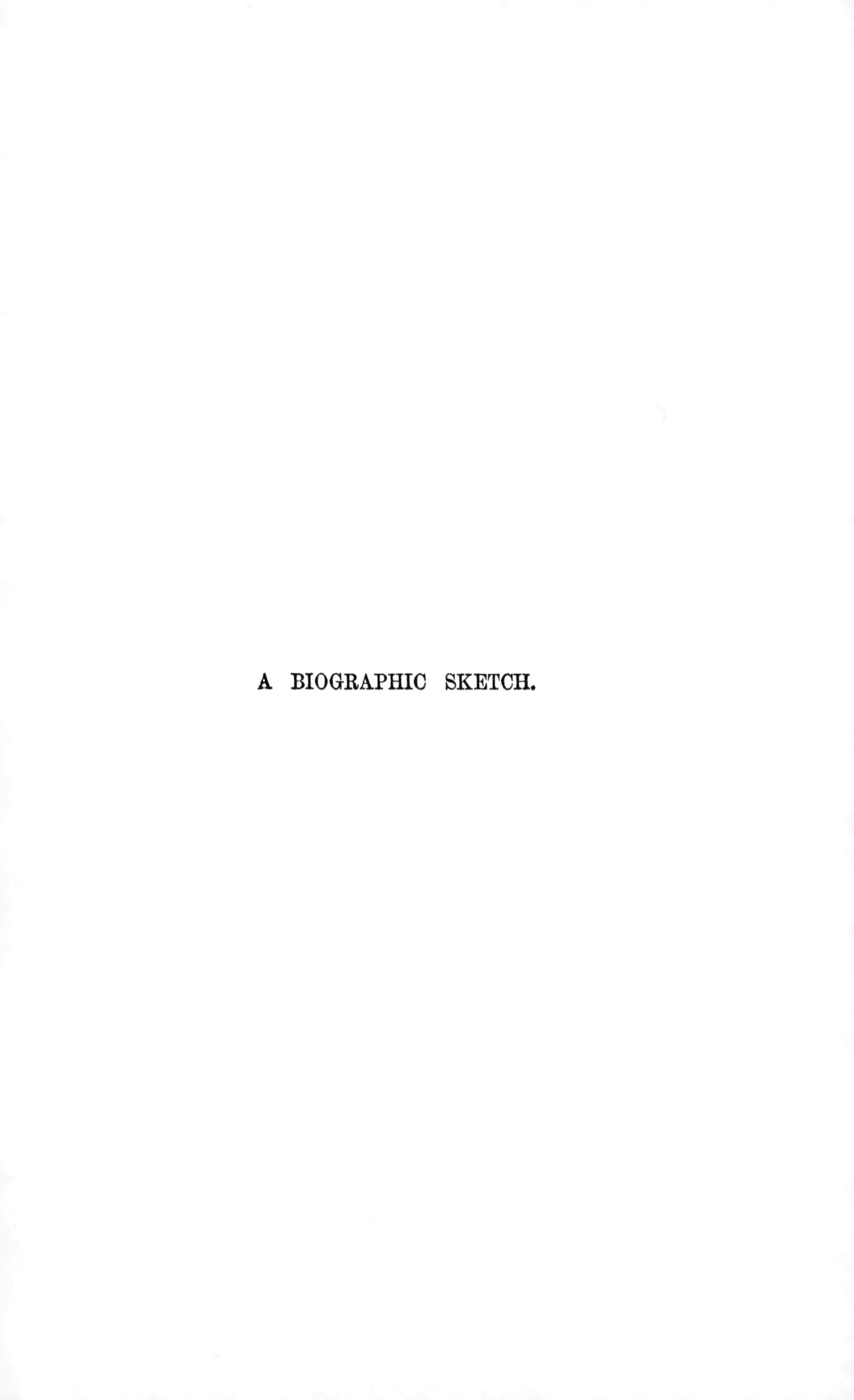

A BIOGRAPHIC SKETCH.

A BIOGRAPHIC SKETCH.

The reader of the miscellaneous literature of the day has doubtless met with the name of Gerald Massey attached to poems strikingly beautiful in language and intensely passionate in feeling. These poems have heretofore been published chiefly in journals which are yet in a great measure *tabooed* in what are regarded as "respectable literary circles." The "Spirit of Freedom," a cheap journal, started in 1849, and written exclusively by working-men, contained a large number of them; and others have since appeared in the "Christian Socialist," a cheap journal conducted by Clergymen of the Church of England; and many others also, of great beauty, have been published in the "Leader," a remarkably able journal conducted by Thornton Hunt, the son of the poet.

You see at once that the writer is a man of vivid genius, and is full of the true poetic fire. Some of his earlier pieces are indignant expostulations with society at the wrongs of suffering humanity; passionate protests against those hideous disparities of life which meet our eye on every side; against power wrongfully used; against fraud and oppression in their more rampant forms; mingled with appeals to the higher influences of knowledge, justice, mercy, truth, and love. It is always thus with the poet who has worked his way to the light was no bread in the cupboard, except what was purchased by the labor of the elder children, some of whom were early sent to work in the neighboring silk-mill. Disease, too, often fell upon the family, cooped up in that unwholesome hovel: indeed, the wonder is, not that our peasantry should be diseased, and grow old and haggard before their time, but that they should exist at all in such lazar-houses and cesspools.

None of the children of this poor family were educated, in the common acceptance of the term. Several of them were sent for a short time to a penny school, where the teacher and the taught were about on a par; but so soon as they were of age to work, the children were sent to the silk-mill. The poor cannot afford to keep their children at school, if they are of an age to work and earn money. They must help to eke out their parents' slender gains, even though it be only by a few pence weekly. So, at eight years of age, Gerald Massey went into the silk manufactory, rising at five o'clock in the morning, and toiling there till half-past six in the evening; up in the gray dawn, or in the winter before the daylight, and trudging to the factory through the wind or in the snow; seeing the sun only through the factory windows; breathing an atmosphere laden with rank oily vapor, his ears deafened by the roar of incessant wheels: —

'Still all the day the iron wheels go onward,
Grinding life down from its mark;
And the children's souls, which God is calling sunward,
Spin on blindly in the dark."

What a life for a child! What a substitute for tender prattle, for childish glee, for youthful play-time! Then home, shivering under the cold, starless sky, on Saturday nights, with 9*d.*, 1*s.*, or 1*s.* 3*d.*, for the whole week's work, for such were the respective amounts of the wages earned by the child-labor of Gerald Massey.

But the mill was burned down, and the children held jubilee over it. The boy stood for twelve hours in the wind and sleet and mud, rejoicing in the conflagration which thus liberated him. Who can wonder at this? Then he went to straw-plaiting, — as toilsome, and, perhaps, more unwholesome than factory-work. Without exercise, in a marshy district, the plaiters were constantly having racking attacks of ague. The boy had the disease for three years, ending with tertian ague. Sometimes four of the family and the mother lay ill at one time, all crying with thirst, with no one to give them drink, and each too weak to help the other. How little do we know of the sufferings endured by the poor and struggling classes of our population, especially in our rural districts! No press echoes their wants, or records their sufferings; and they live almost as unknown to us as if they were the inhabitants of some undiscovered country.

And now take, as an illustration, the child-life of Gerald Massey. "Having had to earn my own dear bread," he says, "by the eternal cheapening of flesh and blood thus early, I never knew what childhood meant. I had no childhood. Ever since I can remember, I have had the aching fear of want, throbbing in heart and brow. The currents of my life were early poisoned, and few, methinks, would pass unscathed through the scenes and circumstances in which I have lived; none, if they were as curious and precocious as I was. The child comes into the world like a new coin with the stamp of God upon it; and in like manner as the Jews sweat down sovereigns, by hustling them in a bag to get gold-dust out of them, so is the poor man's child hustled and sweated down in this bag of society to get wealth out of it; and even as the impress of the Queen is effaced by the Jewish process, so is the image of God worn from heart and brow, and day by day the child recedes devilward. I look back now with wonder, not that so few escape, but that any escape at all, to win a nobler growth for their humanity. So blighting are the influences which surround thousands in early life, to which I can bear such bitter testimony."

And how fared the growth of this child's mind the while? Thanks to the care of his mother, who had sent him to the penny school, he had learnt to read, and the desire to read had been awakened. Books, however, were very scarce. The Bible and Bunyan were the principal; he committed many chapters of the former to memory, and accepted all Bunyan's allegory as *bonâ fide* history. Afterwards he obtained access to "Robinson Crusoe," and a few Wesleyan tracts left at the cottage. These constituted his sole reading, until he came up to London, at the age of fifteen, as an errand-boy; and now, for the first time in his life, he met with plenty of books, reading all that came in his way, from "Lloyd's Penny Times," to Cobbett's Works, "French without a Master," together with English, Roman, and Grecian history. A ravishing awakenment ensued, — the delightful sense of growing knowledge, — the charm of new thought, — the wonders of a new world. "Till then," he says, "I had wondered why I lived at all, — whether

> 'It was not better not to be,
> I was so full of misery.'

Now I began to think that the crown of all desire, and the sum of all existence, was to read and get knowledge. Read, read, read! I used to read at all possible times, and in all possible places; up in bed till two or three in the morning, —

nothing daunted by once setting the bed on fire. Greatly indebted was I also to the bookstalls, where I have read a great deal, often folding a leaf in a book, and returning the next day to continue the subject; but sometimes the book was gone, and then great was my grief! When out of a situation, I have often gone without a meal to purchase a book. Until I fell in love, and began to rhyme as a matter of consequence, I never had the least predilection for poetry. In fact, I always eschewed it; if I ever met with any, I instantly skipped it over, and passed on, as one does with the description of scenery, &c., in a novel. I always loved the birds and flowers, the woods and the stars; I felt delight in being alone in a summer-wood, with song, like a spirit, in the trees, and the golden sun-bursts glinting through the verdurous roof; and was conscious of a mysterious creeping of the blood, and tingling of the nerves, when standing alone in the starry midnight, as in God's own presence-chamber. But until I began to rhyme, I cared nothing for written poetry. The first verses I ever made were upon 'Hope,' when I was utterly hopeless; and after I had begun, I never ceased for about four years, at the end of which time I rushed into print."

There was, of course, crudeness both of thought and expression in the first verses of the poet, which were published in a provincial paper. But there was nerve, rhythm, and poetry; the burthen of the song was, "At even-time it shall be light." The leading idea of the poem was the power of knowledge, virtue, and temperance, to elevate the condition of the poor, — a noble idea truly. Shortly after he was encouraged to print a shilling volume of "Poems and Chansons," in his native town of Tring, of which some 250 copies were sold. Of his later poems we shall afterwards speak.

But a new power was now working upon his nature, as might have been expected, — the power of opinion, as expressed in books, and in the discussions of his fellow-workers.

"As an errand-boy," he says, "I had, of course, many hardships to undergo, and to bear with much tyranny; and that led me into reasoning upon men and things, the causes of misery, the anomalies of our societary state, politics, &c., and the circle of my being rapidly out-surged. New power came to me with all that I saw and thought and read. I studied political works, — such as Paine, Volney, Howitt, Louis Blanc, &c., which gave me another element to mould into my verse, though I am convinced that a poet must sacrifice much if he write party-political poetry. His politics must be above the pinnacle of party zeal; the politics of eternal truth, right, and justice. He must not waste a life on what to-morrow may prove to have been merely the question of a day. The French Revolution of 1848 had the greatest effect on me of any circumstance connected with my own life. It was scarred and blood-burnt into the very core of my being. This little volume of mine is the fruit thereof."

But, meanwhile, he had been engaged in other literary work. Full of new thoughts, and bursting with aspirations for freedom, he started, in April, 1849, a cheap journal, written entirely by working-men, entitled, "The Spirit of Freedom:" it was full of fiery earnestness, and half of its weekly contents were supplied by Gerald Massey himself, who acted as editor. It cost him five situations during a period of eleven months, — twice because he was detected burning candle far into the night, and three times because of the tone of the opinions to which he gave utterance. The French Revolution of 1848 having, amongst its other issues, kindled the zeal of the working-men in this country in the cause of association, Gerald Massey eagerly joined them, and he has been recently instrumental in giving some impetus to that praiseworthy movement, — the object of which is to permanently elevate the condition of the producing classes, by advancing them to the status of capitalists as well as laborers.

A word or two as to Gerald Massey's recent poetry. Bear in mind that he is yet but a youth; — at twenty-three a man can scarcely be said fairly to have entered his manhood; and yet, if we except Robert Nichol, who died at twenty-four, we know of no English poet of his class, who has done anything to compare with him. Some of his most beautiful pieces originally appeared in the columns of the "Leader." They give you the idea of a practised hand — one who has reached the full prime of his poetic manhood. Take, for instance, his "Lyrics of Love," so full of beauty and tenderness. Nor are his "Songs of Progress" less full of poetic power and beauty.

Gerald Massey is a teacher through the heart. He is familiar with the passions, and leans towards the tender and loving aspect of our nature. He takes after Burns more than after Wordsworth, Elliot rather than Thomson. He is but a young man, though he has crowded into his twenty-three years already the life of an old man. He has won his experience in the school of the poor, and nobly earned his title to speak to them as a man and a brother, dowered with "the hate of hate, the scorn of scorn, the love of love."

Extract from an Article written by Dr. Samuel Smiles, in "Eliza Cook's Journal," 1851.

PREFACE TO THE THIRD EDITION

OF

BABE CHRISTABEL.

I DO not think a volume of verse should need a Preface. But as my Book has reached a Third Edition, and as almost as much has been said about myself as about my Book, perhaps I may be excused, even by the Preface-hater, if I do take this opportunity of saying a few words. I have been considerably censured for the political opinions which it contains, — as I expected to be. Before printing, I was advised not to include the political pieces, as, it was urged, they would prove an obstacle to the success of my Poetry, and close the drawing-room door against me. And if I had looked on the success of my Book in a poetical light alone, I should not have printed the greater portion of the political verses. But that was not the sole point of view. Those verses do not adequately express what I think and feel now, since they were written some five or six years ago: yet they express what I thought and felt then, and what thousands beside me have thought and felt, and what thousands still think and feel. They were the outcome of a peculiar and marked experience. I printed the "Memoir," so that they might be read in the light, or gloom, of that experience, and the Book contain its own excuse. They have not read me aright, who have not thus interpreted it. I have been blamed for the rebellious feelings to which the political pieces give utterance; but they were perfectly natural under the circumstances. Indeed, I look upon those same rebellious feelings as my very deliverance from a fatal slough. There are conditions in which many of the poor exist, where humanity must be either rebel or slave. For the slave, degradation and moral death are certain; but for the rebel there is always a chance of becoming conqueror; and the force to resist is far better than the faculty to succumb.

It is not that I seek to sow dissension between class and class, or fling firebrands among the combustibles of society; for when I smite the hearts of my fellows, I would rather they should gush with the healing waters of love, than with the fearful fires of hatred. I yearn to raise them into loveable beings. I would kindle in the hearts of the masses a sense of the beauty and grandeur of the universe, call forth the lineaments of Divinity in their poor worn faces, give them glimpses of the grace and glory of Love and the marvellous significance of Life, and elevate the standard of Humanity for all. But strange wrongs are daily done in the land, bitter feelings are felt, and wild words will be spoken. It was not for myself alone that I wrote these things: it was always the condition of others that so often made the mist rise up and cloud my vision. Nor was it for myself that I have uncurtained some scenes of my life to the public gaze, but as an illustration of the lives of others, who suffer and toil on, "die, and make no sign;" and because one's own personal experience is of more value than that of others taken upon hearsay.

So I keep my political verses as memorials of my past, as one might keep some worn-out garment because he had passed through the furnace in it, nothing doubting that in the future they will often prove my passport to the hearts and homes of thousands of the poor, when the minstrel comes to their door with something better to bring them. They will know that I have suffered their sufferings, wept their tears, thought their thoughts, and felt their feelings; and they will trust me.

I have been congratulated by some correspondents on the uses of suffering, and the riches I have wrung from Poverty: as though it were a blessed thing to be born in the condition in which I was, and surrounded with untoward circumstances as I have been. My experience tells me that Poverty is inimical to the development of Humanity's noblest attributes. Poverty is a never-ceasing struggle for the means of living, and it makes one hard and selfish. To be sure, noble lives have been wrought out in the sternest poverty. Many such are being wrought out now, by the unknown heroes and martyrs of the Poor. I have known men and women in the very worst circumstances, to whom heroism seemed a heritage, and to be noble a natural way of living. But they were so in spite of their poverty, and not because of it. What they might have been if the world had done better by them, I cannot tell; but if their minds had been enriched by culture, the world had been the gainer. When Christ said, "Blessed are they who suffer," he did not speak of those who suffer from want and hunger, and who always see the Bastille looming up and blotting out the sky of their future. Such suffering brutalizes. True,—natures ripen and strengthen in suffering; but it is that suffering which chastens and ennobles,—that which clears the spiritual sight,—not the anxiety lest work should fail, and the want of daily bread. The beauty of Suffering is not to be read in the face of Hunger.

Above all, Poverty is a cold place to write Poetry in. It is not attractive to poetical influences.

The Muses do not like entertainment which is not fit for man or beast. Nor do the best fruits of Poetry ripen in the rain and shade and wind alone: they want sunshine, warmth, and the open sky. And should the heart of a poor man break into song, it is likely that his poverty may turn into hailstones that which might have fallen on the world in fructifying rain. A poor man, fighting his battle of life, has little time for the rapture of repose which Poetry demands. He cannot take Poetry like a Bride to his heart and home, and devote a life to her service. He can only keep some innermost chamber of his heart sacred for her, from whence he gets occasional glimpses of her wondrous beauty, when he can steal away from the outward strife, like some child who has found a treasure, and steals aside to look on it in secret and alone, lest rude and importunate companions should snatch it from the possessor's hands. Considering all things, it may appear madness for a poor man to attempt Poetry in the face of the barriers that surround him. So many hearts have been broken, so many lives have been wasted, so many lions are in the way of the Gate Beautiful, and so many wrecks lie by the path! And so it is, — a diseased madness, or a divine one. If the disease, then there is no help for a man: if the divine, then there is no hinderance for him.

Who would not pity the poor versifier at the outset of his career? But who would not also rejoice with him in the end, when the world crowns him a Poet with pæans of acclaim? And, in spite of all things, there will be Poetry in the midst of poverty. Even as there is scarcely a space in the world so barren but some plot of natural richness will be running all to flowers, — some type of loveliness will be starting up from Earth's inner Sea of Beauty, even in waste and wilderness, on rock and ruin, in Alpine snows and sandy solitudes, — so is it with Poetry, the Flower of Humanity. It will continually be springing, in its own natural way, in the most bleak and barren by-ways of the world, as well as in the richest and most cultivated pastures. The winds of heaven, or the birds of God, will drop the seed, and the flower will follow, even though sown amid the bushes and brambles of the obscurest hamlet, or in the crevices of the city pavement. Not that the wilderness, or the rock, or the snows, are the fittest places to rear flowers of the most exquisite fragrance and beauty; neither are Poverty and Penury, with their hell of torture, and daily wrestle with grim Death, the fittest soil to grow and perfect the flower of Poetry. The greatest original Genius can only develop itself according to the circumstances which environ it. It needs food to nourish it, and time and opportunity to unfold it. If it lack these, it must remain dwarfed and stunted, and perhaps wither and die.

Besides, it is not while the fight is raging, and the struggle is sore, that the Poet can sing. He must first do battle and overcome, climb from the stir and strife, and be able to watch from his mountain where he dwells apart. The fullest and rarest streams of Poetry only flow through a mind at peace. The mirror of the Poet's soul must be calm and clear: else it will give forth distorted reflections and false imagings.

Had I known, when I began to write verses, what I know now, I think I should have been intimidated, and not have begun at all. So many and so glorious are the luminaries already up and shining, that one would pause before hoisting a rushlight. But I was ignorant of these things. And as I have begun, and conquered some preliminary difficulties, — as I have been sweated down to the proper jockey-weight at which I can ride Pegasus with little danger of spraining his wings, —

and as a purpose has gradually and unconsciously grown upon me,—I dare say I shall go on, making the best of my limited materials, with the view of writing some songs that may become dear to the hearts of the people, cheering them in their sorrows, voicing their aspirations, lighting them on the way up which they are groping darkly after better things, and saluting their triumphs with hymns of victory!

I cannot conclude without thanking those Critics who have given me so generous a welcome. And I would also thank those who have not spared my faults, or dwelt tenderly on my failings. They, also, have done me good, and I am grateful for it. Friendly praise is somewhat like a warm bath,—apt to enervate, especially if we stay in too long; but friendly censure is like a cold bath, bracing and healthful, though we are always glad to get out of it. Some of the Critics have called me a "Poet;" but that word is much too lightly spoken, much too freely bandied about. I know what a Poet is too well to fancy that I am one yet. It is a high standard that I set up myself, and I do not ask it to be lowered to reach my stature; nor would I have the Poet's awful crown diminished to mete my lesser brow. I may have that something within which kindles flame-like at the breath of Love, or mounts into song in the presence of Beauty; but, alas! mine is a "jarring lyre." The dearth of Poetry should be great in a country where we hail as Poets such as have been crowned of late.

For myself, I have only entered the lists, and inscribed my name: the race has yet to be run. Whether I shall run it, and win the Poet's crown, or not, time alone will prove, and not the prediction of friend or foe. The crowns of Poetry are not in the keeping of Critics. At most they can only give us paper credit. There have been many who have given some sign of promise, — just set a rainbow of hope in the dark cloud of their life, — and never fulfilled their promise; and the world has wondered why. But it might not have been matter of wonder if the world could have read what was written behind the cloud. Others, again, are songful in youth, like the nightingales in spring, who soon cease to sing, because they have to build nests, rear their young, and provide for them; and so the songs grow silent, — the heart is full of cares, and the dreamer has no time to dream. I hope that my future holds some happier fate. I think there is a work for me to do, and I trust to accomplish it.

GERALD MASSEY.

April, 1854.

THE

BALLAD OF BABE CHRISTABEL.

THE

BALLAD OF BABE CHRISTABEL.

WHEN Danaë-Earth bares all her charms,
And gives the God her perfect flower,
Who, in the sunshine's golden shower,
Leaps warm into her amorous arms !

And all the kindled greenery glows,
While from her emeraldine sea
Spring rises up rejoicingly,
And life hath richest overflows :

When young Maids feel Love stir i' the blood,
And wanton with the kissing leaves
And branches, and the quick sap heaves,
And dances to a ripen'd flood ;

Till, blown to its hidden heart with sighs,
Love's red rose burns in cheeks so dear,
And, as sea-jewels upward peer,
Love-thoughts melt through their swimming eyes :

When Beauty walks in bravest dress,
And, fed with April's mellow showers,
The earth laughs out with sweet May-flowers,
That flush for very happiness :

And Spider-Puck his wonder weaves
O' nights, and nooks of greening gloom
Are rich with violets that bloom
In the cool dark of dewy leaves :

When Rose-buds drink the fiery wine
Of Dawn, with crimson stains i' the mouth,
All thirstily as yearning Youth
From Love's hand drinks the draught divine;

And honey'd plots are drowsed with Bees:
And Larks rain music by the shower,
While singing, singing hour by hour,
Song like a Spirit sits i' the Trees!

When fainting hearts forget their fears,
And in the poorest Life's salt cup
Some rare wine runs, and Hope builds up
Her rainbow over Memory's tears!

It fell upon a merry May morn,
I' the perfect prime of that sweet time
When daisies whiten, woodbines climb,—
The dear Babe Christabel was born.

All night the Stars bright watches kept,
Like Gods that look a golden calm;
The Silence dropt its precious balm,
And the tired world serenely slept.

The birds were darkling in the nest,
Or bosom'd in voluptuous trees:
On beds of flowers the happy breeze
Had kist its fill and sank to rest.

All night beneath the Cottage eaves,
A lonely light, with tremulous Arc,
Surged back a space the sea of dark,
And glanced among the glimmering leaves.

Without! the quiet heavens above
The nest of life, did lean and brood!
Within! the Mother's tears of blood
Wet the Gethsemane of her love!

And when the Morn with frolic zest,
Lookt through the curtains of the night,
There was a dearer dawn of light,
A tenderer life the Mother's prest!

Ah! bliss to make the brain reel wild!
The Star new-kindled in the dark—
Life that had flutter'd like a Lark—
Lay in her bosom a sweet Child!

How she had felt it drawing down
Her nesting heart more close and close,—
Her rose-bud ripening to a Rose,
That she should one day see full-blown!

How she had throbb'd with hopes and fears,
And strain'd her inner eyes till dim,
To see the coming glory swim
Through the rich mist of happy tears;

For it, her woman's heart drank up,
And smiled at, Sorrow's darkest dole:
And now Delight's most dainty soul
Was crusht for her in one rich cup!

And then delicious languors crept,
Like nectar, on her pain's hot drouth,
And feeling fingers—kissing mouth—
Being faint with joy, the Mother slept.

Babe Christabel was royally born !
    For when the earth was flusht with flowers,
    And drencht with beauty in sun-showers,
She came through golden gates of Morn.

No chamber arras-pictured round,
    Where sunbeams make a gorgeous gloom,
    And touch its glories into bloom,
And footsteps fall withouten sound,

Was her Birth-place that merry May-morn ;
    No gifts were heapt, no bells were rung,
    No healths were drunk, no songs were sung,
When dear Babe Christabel was born :

But Nature on the darling smiled,
    And with her beauty's blessing crown'd :
    Love brooded o'er the hallowed ground,
And there were Angels with the Child !

And May her kisses of love did blow
    On amorous airs, that came to her
    With gifts of Frankincense and Myrrh,
As came the Magi long ago

To worship Bethlehem's baby-King :
    Spring-Birds made welcoming merriment,
    And all the Flowers for welcome sent
The secret sweetness of the Spring.

In glancing light and shimmering shade,
    With cheeks that toucht and ripelier burn'd,
    May-Roses in at the lattice yearn'd
A-tiptoe, and Good Morrow bade.

No purple and fine linen might
    Be hoarded up for her sweet sake :
    But Mother's love shall clothe and make
The little wearer bravely dight !

And worlds of worship are their eyes,
    Their loyal hearts are worlds of love,
    Who fondly clasp the stranger Dove,
And read its news from Paradise.

Their looks praise God — souls sing for glee:
    They think if this old world had toil'd
    Through ages to bring forth their child,
It hath a glorious destiny.

O HAPPY Husband! happy Wife!
    The rarest blessing Heaven drops down,
    The sweetest blossom in Spring's crown,
Starts in the furrows of your life!

God! what a towering height ye win,
    Who cry, "Lo my beloved Child!"
    And, life on life sublimely piled,
Ye touch the heavens and peer within!

Look how a star of glory swims
    Down aching silences of space,
    Flushing the Darkness till its face
With beating heart of light o'erbrims!

So brightening came Babe Christabel,
    To touch the earth with fresh romance,
    And light a Mother's countenance
With looking on her miracle.

With hands so flower-like soft, and fair,
    She caught at life, with words as sweet
    As first spring violets, and feet
As faëry-light as feet of air.

The Father, down in Toil's mirk mine,
    Turns to his wealthy world above,
    Its radiance, and its home of love;
And lights his life like sun-struck wine.

The Mother moves with queenlier tread:
    Proud swell the globes of ripe delight
    Above her heart, so warm and white
A pillow for the baby-head!

Their natures deepen, well-like, clear,
    Till God's eternal stars are seen,
    For ever shining and serene,
By eyes anointed Beauty's seer.

A sense of glory all things took, —
    The red Rose-Heart of Dawn would blow,
    And Sundown's sumptuous pictures show
Babe-Cherubs wearing their Babe's look!

And round their peerless one they clung,
    Like bees about a flower's wine-cup;
    New thoughts and feelings blossom'd up,
And hearts for very fulness sung

Of what their budding Babe should grow,
    When the Maid crimson'd into Wife,
    And crown'd the summit of some life,
Like Phosphor, with morn on its brow!

And they should bless her for a Bride,
    Who, like a splendid saint alit
    In some heart's seventh heaven, should sit,
As now in theirs, all glorified!

But O! 'twas all too white a brow
    To flush with Passion that doth fire
    With Hymen's torch its own death-pyre, —
So pure her heart was beating now!

And thus they built their Castles brave
    In faëry lands of gorgeous cloud;
    They never saw a little white shroud,
Nor guess'd how flowers may mask the grave.

SHE grew, a sweet and sinless Child,
    In shine and shower, — calm and strife;
    A Rainbow on our dark of Life,
From Love's own radiant heaven down-smiled!

In lonely loveliness she grew, —
    A shape all music, light, and love,
    With startling looks, so eloquent of
The spirit burning into view.

At Childhood she could seldom play
    With merry heart, whose flashes rise
    Like splendour-wingéd butterflies
From honey'd hearts of flowers in May:

The fields in blossom flamed and flusht,
    The Roses into crimson yearn'd,
    With cloudy fire the wall-flowers burn'd,
And blood-red Sunsets bloom'd and blusht, —

And still her cheek was pale as pearl, —
    It took no tint of Summer's wealth
    Of colour, warmth, and wine of Health: —
Death's hand so whitely pressed the Girl!

No blush grew ripe to sun or kiss
    Where violet-veins ran purple light,
    So tenderly thro' Parian white,
Touching you into tenderness.

A spirit-look was in her face,
That shadow'd a miraculous range
Of meanings, ever rich and strange,
Or lighten'd glory in the place.

Such mystic lore was in her eyes,
And light of other worlds than ours,
She lookt as she had gathered flowers,
With little maids of Paradise.

Her brow — fit home for daintiest dreams —
With such a dawn of light was crown'd,
And reeling ringlets shower'd round,
Like sunny sheaves of golden beams:

And she would talk so weirdly-wild,
And grow upon your wonderings,
As tho' her stature rose on wings!
And you forgot she was a Child.

Ah! she was one of those who come
With pledged promise not to stay
Long, ere the Angels let them stray
To nestle down in earthly home:

And, thro' the windows of her eyes,
We often saw her saintly soul,
Serene, and sad, and beautiful,
Go sorrowing for lost Paradise

Our Lamb in mystic meadows play'd:
In some celestial sleep she walkt
Her dream of life, and low we talkt,
As of her waking heart-afraid.

In Earth she took no lusty root,
Her beauty of promise to disclose,
And round into the Woman-Rose,
And climb into Life's crowning fruit.

She came — like music in the night
    Floating as heaven in the brain,
    A moment oped, and shut again,
And all is dark where all was light.

She came, — as comes the light of smiles
    O'er earth, and every budding thing
    Makes quick with beauty — alive with Spring;
Then goeth to Hesperian Isles.

MIDNIGHT was trancéd solemnly
    Thinking of dawn: Her Star-thoughts burn'd!
    The Trees like burden'd Prophets yearn'd,
Rapt in a wind of prophecy:

When, like the Night, the shadow of Woe
    On all things laid its hand death-dark,
    Our last hope went out as a spark,
And a cry smote heaven like a blow!

We sat and watcht by Life's dark stream,
    Our love-lamp blown about the night,
    With hearts that lived as lived its light,
And died as died its precious gleam.

In Death's face hers flasht up and smiled,
    As smile the young flowers in their prime,
    I' the face of their gray murderer Time,
And Death for true love kist our child.

She thought our good-night kiss was given,
    And like a lily her life did close;
    Angels uncurtain'd that repose,
And the next waking dawn'd in heaven.

WITH her white hands claspt she sleepeth; heart is husht, and lips are cold;
Death shrouds up her heaven of beauty, and a weary way I go,
Like the sheep without a Shepherd on the wintry norland wold,
With the face of Day shut out by blinding snow.

O'er its widow'd nest my heart sits moaning for its youngling fled
From this world of wail and weeping, gone to join her starry peers;
And my light of life 's o'ershadow'd where the dear one lieth dead,
And I'm crying in the dark with many fears.

All last night-tide she seemed near me, like a lost beloved Bird,
Beating at the lattice louder than the sobbing wind and rain;
And I call'd across the night with tender name and fondling word;
And I yearn'd out thro' the darkness, all in vain.

Heart will plead, "Eyes cannot see her: they are blind with tears of pain;"
And it climbeth up and straineth for dear life to look and hark
While I call her once again: but there cometh no refrain,
And it droppeth down, and dieth in the dark.

In this dim world of clouding cares,
    We rarely know, till wildered eyes
    See white wings lessening up the skies,
The Angels with us unawares.

And thou hast stolen a jewel, Death!
    Shall light thy dark up like a Star,
    A Beacon kindling from afar
Our light of love, and fainting faith.

Thro' tears it streams perpetually,
    And glitters thro' the thickest glooms,
    Till the eternal morning comes
To light us o'er the Jasper Sea.

With our best branch in tenderest leaf,
    We've strewn the way our Lord doth come;
    And, ready for the harvest-home,
His Reapers bind our ripest sheaf.

Our beautiful Bird of light hath fled:
    Awhile she sat with folded wings —
    Sang round us a few hoverings —
Then straightway into glory sped.

With sense of Motherhood new-found
    The white-winged Angels nurture her,
    High on the heavenly hills of myrrh,
And all Love's purple glory round.

Thro' Childhood's morning-land, serene
    She walkt betwixt us twain, like Love;
    While, in a robe of light above,
Her better Angel walkt unseen,

Till Life's highway broke bleak and wild;
    Then, lest her starry garments trail
    In mire, heart bleed, and courage fail,
The Angel's arms caught up the child.

Her wave of life hath backward roll'd
To the great ocean ; on whose shore
We wander up and down, to store
Some treasures of the times of old :

And aye we seek and hunger on
For precious pearls and relics rare,
Strewn on the sands for us to wear
At heart, for love of her that 's gone.

O weep no more ! there yet is balm
In Gilead ! Love doth ever shed
Rich healing where it nestles, — spread
O'er desert pillows, some green Palm !

Strange glory streams thro' Life's wild rents,
And thro' the open door of Death
We see the heaven that beckoneth
To the beloved going hence.

God's ichor fills the hearts that bleed ;
The best fruit loads the broken bough ;
And in the wounds our sufferings plough,
Immortal Love sows sovereign seed.

SONGS FOR SINGING

A NATIONAL ANTHEM.

God bless our native Land,
Glorious, and grave, and grand,
God bless our Land!
God bless her noble face,
God bless her peerless race,
Great heart, and daring hand,
God bless our Land.

God love our Saxon Land,
Make her for ever grand,
God love our Land!
Robe her with righteousness,
Crown her with gifts of grace,
Throne her at Thy right hand,
God love our Land.

If secret foes should band
To strike our dear old Land,
God aid our Land!
Be Thou her strength and stay,
God, in the battle day!
Strew them ashore like sand,
God aid our Land.

Few are we, Sword in hand,
All Sword in soul we stand,
Around our Land!
And when her blood shall flow,
Green make her glory grow,
Lead her in triumph grand,
Our leal old Land.

2

Here pray we hand in hand,
Tears in our eyelids stand,
God save our Land!
Thy Watch-tower on the Sea,
Venger of Right is she,
Long let old Fear-not stand,
God save our Land.

OLD ENGLAND.

There she sits in her Island-home,
Peerless among her Peers!
And Liberty oft to her arms doth come,
To ease its poor heart of tears.
Old England still throbs with the muffled fire
Of a Past she can never forget:
And again shall she banner the World up higher;
For there 's life in the Old Land yet.

They would mock at her now, who of old lookt forth
In their fear, as they heard her afar;
But loud will your wail be, O Kings of the Earth!
When the Old Land goes down to the war.
The Avalanche trembles, half-launcht, and half-riven,
Her voice will in motion set:
O ring out the tidings, ye Winds of heaven!
There 's life in the Old Land yet.

The old nursing Mother 's not hoary yet,
There is sap in her Saxon tree;—
Lo! she lifteth a bosom of glory yet,
Thro' her mists, to the Sun and the Sea.
Fair as the Queen of Love, fresh from the foam,
Or a star in a dark cloud set;

Ye may blazon her shame,— ye may leap at her
name,—
But there 's life in the Old Land yet.

Let the storm burst, it will find the Old Land
Ready-ripe for a rough, red fray!
She will fight as she fought when she took her stand
For the Right in the olden day.
Rouse the old royal soul, Europe's best hope
Is her sword-edge by Victory set!
She shall dash Freedom's foes down Death's bloody
slope;
For there 's life in the Old Land yet.

LONG, LONG AGO.

OLD friend of mine, you were dear to my heart,
Long, long ago, long ago.
Little did we think of a time we should part,
Long, long ago, long ago.
Hand claspt in hand thro' the world we would go.
Down our old untrodden path the wild weeds grow!
Great was the love 'twixt us; bitter was the smart:
Old friend of mine long ago.

Patient watch I kept for you many, many a day,
Long, long ago, long ago;
Waited and wept for you far, far away,
Long, long ago, long ago.
Merry came each May-tide, green leaves would
start:
Never came my old friend back to my heart.
Lonely I went on my weary, weary way,
Old friend of mine long ago.

Oft as I muse at the shadowy nightfall
Over the dear Long Ago,

Borne on tears arises the dark, dark pall,
Fallen on my heart long ago.
Love is not dead, tho' we wander apart;
How I could clasp you, old friend, to my heart!
Barriers lie between us, but God knoweth all,
Old friend of mine long ago.

THAT MERRY, MERRY MAY.

AH! 't is like a tale of olden
Time, long, long ago;
When the world was in its golden
Prime, and love was lord below!
Every vein of Earth was dancing
With the Spring's new wine!
'T was the pleasant time of flowers,
When I met you, love of mine!
Ah! some spirit sure was straying
Out of heaven that day,
When I met you, Sweet! a-Maying
In that merry, merry May.

Little heart! it shyly open'd
Its red leaves' love-lore,
Like a rose that must be ripen'd
To the dainty, dainty core.
But its beauties daily brighten,
And it blooms so dear, —
Tho' a many Winters whiten,
I go Maying all the year.
And my proud heart will be praying
Blessings on the day,
When I met you, Sweet! a-Maying,
In that merry, merry May.

TO-DAY AND TO-MORROW.

HIGH hopes that burn'd like Stars sublime,
Go down i' the Heavens of Freedom;
And true hearts perish in the time
We bitterliest need 'em!
But never sit we down and say
There 's nothing left but sorrow:
We walk the Wilderness To-day,
The Promised Land To-morrow.

Our birds of song are silent now,
There are no flowers blooming!
Yet life is in the frozen bough,
And Freedom's Spring is coming!
And Freedom's tide comes up alway,
Tho' we may strand in sorrow:
And our good Bark, a-ground To-day,
Shall float again To-morrow.

Thro' all the long, dark night of years
The People's cry ascendeth,
And Earth is wet with blood and tears:
But our meek sufferance endeth!
The Few shall not for ever sway,
The Many moil in sorrow:
The Powers of Hell are strong To-day,
But Christ shall rise To-morrow.

Tho' hearts brood o'er the Past, our eyes
With smiling Futures glisten!
For, lo! our day bursts up the skies:
Lean out your souls and listen!
The world rolls Freedom's radiant way,
And ripens with her sorrow:
Keep heart! who bear the Cross To-day,
Shall wear the Crown To-morrow.

O Youth! flame-earnest, still aspire,
  With energies immortal!
To many a heaven of Desire,
  Our yearning opes a portal!
And tho' Age wearies by the way,
  And hearts break in the furrow,
We 'll sow the golden grain To-day,—
  The Harvest comes To-morrow.

Build up heroic lives, and all
  Be like a sheathen sabre,
Ready to flash out at God's call,
  O Chivalry of Labour!
Triumph and Toil are twins: and aye
  Joy suns the cloud of Sorrow;
And 't is the mârtyrdom To-day,
  Brings victory To-morrow.

THE KINGLIEST KINGS.

Ho! ye who in a noble work
  Win scorn, as flames draw air,
And in the way where Lions lurk,
  God's image bravely bear;
Tho' trouble-tried, and torture-torn,
The kingliest Kings are crown'd with thorn.

Life's glory, like the bow in heaven,
  Still springeth from the cloud;
Soul ne'er out-soar'd the starry Seven,
  But Pain's fire-chariot rode.
They 've battled best who 've boldliest borne,
The kingliest Kings are crown'd with thorn.

The Martyr's fire-crown on the brow
  Doth into glory burn;

And tears that from Love's torn heart flow,
  To pearls of spirit turn.
Our dearest hopes in pangs are born,
The kingliest Kings are crown'd with thorn.

As beauty in Death's cerement shrouds,
  And Stars bejewel Night,
God-splendours live in dim heart-clouds,
  And suffering worketh might.
The mirkest hour is mother o' Morn,
The kingliest Kings are crown'd with thorn.

OUR NATIVE LAND.

This is our Mother Country!
    The dearest land;
    The rarest land.
Round which the sea keeps sentry,
    Or Ships are manned;
    Or Ships are manned.
Nothing but Heaven above her!
    And here 's my hand;
    And here 's my hand.
We are Brothers all who love her,
    Our Native Land;
    Dear Native Land.

Afar and near they hail her,
    With greetings warm;
    With greetings warm.
The famous old brave sailer,
    That rode the storm;
    Ay, many a storm.
Who would not die to save her,
    Shall bear the brand;
    The Coward's brand.

Our love must never waver
For Native Land;
Dear Native Land.

No matter where our place is,
We may go forth;
We may go forth.
And turn dead frozen faces
Home from the North;
Home from the North.
Or sink 'neath orient Heaven,
In burning sand;
Waste, desert sand.
Our lives shall still be given
For Native Land;
Dear Native Land.

And long may such life nourish
The old land on;
This dear land on.
And long, long may she flourish,
When we are gone;
All dead and gone.
Long may the Sea caress her,
As great and grand;
As great and grand.
Thou God in Heaven bless her!
Our Native Land;
Dear Native Land.

Ofttimes the foe beheld us,
All torn apart;
All torn apart.
Altho' a blow would weld us
All one at heart;
All one at heart.
Now trust we in each other,
A little band;
A happy band.

The Children of one Mother!
        Our Native Land;
        Dear Native Land.

Some new heroic story
        The world shall learn;
        The world shall learn.
If we who keep her glory
        Are true and stern;
        All true and stern.
Come wild and warring weather,
        We ready stand;
        All ready stand.
To fight or fall together
        For Native Land;
        Dear Native Land.

A LOVER'S FANCY.

SWEET Heaven! I do love a maiden,
Radiant, rare, and beauty-laden:
When she 's near me, heaven is round me,
Her dear presence doth so bound me!
I could wring my heart of gladness,
Might it free her lot of sadness!
Give the world, and all that 's in it,
Just to press her hand a minute!
Yet she weeteth not I love her;
  Never dare I tell the sweet
Tale, but to the stars above her,
  And the flowers that kiss her feet.

O! to live and linger near her,
And in tearful moments cheer her!
I could be a Bird to lighten
Her dear heart, — her sweet eyes brighten:

Or in fragrance, like a blossom,
Give my life up on her bosom!
For my love 's withouten measure,
All its pangs are sweetest pleasure:
Yet she weeteth not I love her;
  Never dare I tell the sweet
Tale, but to the stars above her,
  And the flowers that kiss her feet.

THE CHIVALRY OF LABOUR.

Uprouse ye now, brave brother-band,
With honest heart, and working hand:
We are but few, toil-tried, and true,
Yet hearts beat high to dare and do:
And who would not a champion be
In Labour's lordlier Chivalry?

We fight! but bear no bloody brand,
We fight to free our Fatherland:
We fight that smiles of love may glow
On lips where curses quiver now!
Hurrah! hurrah! true Knights are we
In Labour's lordlier Chivalry.

O! there be hearts that ache to see
The day-dawn of our victory:
Eyes full of heart-break with us plead,
And Watchers weep, and Martyrs bleed:
O! who would not a Champion be
In Labour's lordlier Chivalry?

Work, Brothers mine; work, hand and brain;
We 'll win the Golden Age again:

And Love's Millennial morn shall rise
In happy hearts, and blessed eyes.
Hurrah! hurrah! true Knights are we
In Labour's lordlier Chivalry.

O LAY THY HAND IN MINE, DEAR!

O LAY thy hand in mine, dear!
  We're growing old, we're growing old;
But Time hath brought no sign, dear,
  That hearts grow cold, that hearts grow cold.
'T is long, long since our new love
  Made life divine, made life divine;
But age enricheth true love,
  Like noble wine, like noble wine.

And lay thy cheek to mine, dear,
  And take thy rest, and take thy rest;
Mine arms around thee twine, dear,
  And make thy nest, and make thy nest.
A many cares are pressing
  On this dear head, on this dear head;
But Sorrow's hands in blessing
  Are surely laid, are surely laid.

O lean thy life on mine, dear!
  'T will shelter thee, 't will shelter thee.
Thou wert a winsome vine, dear,
  On my young tree, on my young tree:
And so, till boughs are leafless,
  And Song-birds flown, and Song-birds flown,
We'll twine, then lay us, griefless,
  Together down, together down.

SONG.

METHOUGHT to bear her branches crowned
With fruit, my virgin vine:
Another fills her arms; around
Another life they twine!
So I lost the day,
And all the night I wake,—
Bird-like singing sad sorrow away,
Until my heart shall break.

While others gleaned Life's field for gold,
With Flowers I made a crown:
Till, looking up alone, behold,
The deepening night came down!
So I lost the day,
And all the night I wake,—
Bird-like singing sad sorrow away,
Until my heart shall break.

Poor me! I claspt a reed, and missed
My sweetest Syrinx fled!
Poor me! my tenderest music 's kist
From lips of dear love dead.
I have lost the day,
And all the night I wake,—
Bird-like singing sad sorrow away,
Until my heart shall break.

LOVE'S FAIRY RING.

WHILE Titans war with social Jove,
My own sweet Wife and I,
We make Elysium in our love,
And let the world go by!

O never hearts beat half so light
With crownéd Queen or King!
O never world was half so bright
As is our fairy-ring,
Dear love!
Our hallowed fairy-ring.

Our world of empire is not large,
But priceless wealth it holds;
A little heaven links marge to marge,
But what rich realms it folds!
And clasping all from outer strife
Sits Love with folden wing,
A-brood o'er dearer life-in-life,
Within our fairy-ring,
Dear love!
Our hallowed fairy-ring.

Thou leanest thy true heart on mine,
And bravely bearest up!
Aye mingling Love's most precious wine
In Life's most bitter cup!
And evermore the circling hours
New gifts of glory bring;
We live and love like happy flowers,
All in our fairy-ring,
Dear love!
Our hallowed fairy-ring.

We 've known a many sorrows, Sweet!
We 've wept a many tears,
And often trod with trembling feet
Our pilgrimage of years.
But when our sky grew dark and wild,
All closelier did we cling:
Clouds broke to beauty as you smiled,
Peace crown'd our fairy-ring,
Dear love!
Our hallowed fairy-ring.

Away, you Lords of Murderdom;
 Away, O Hate, and Strife!
Hence, revellers, reeling drunken from
 Your feast of human life!
Heaven shield our little Goshen round,
 From ills that with them spring,
And never be their footprints found
 Within our fairy-ring,
 Dear love!
 Our hallowed fairy-ring.

But, come ye who the Truth dare own,
 Or work in Love's dear name;
Come all who wear the Martyr's crown —
 The Mystic's robe of flame!
Sweet souls a Christless world doth doom
 Like Birds made blind to sing!
For such we'll aye make welcome room
 Within our fairy-ring,
 Dear love!
 Our hallowed fairy-ring.

THERE'S NO DEARTH OF KINDNESS.

There's no dearth of kindness
 In this world of ours;
Only in our blindness
 We gather thorns for flowers!
Outward, we are spurning —
 Trampling one another!
While we are inly yearning
 At the name of "Brother!"

There's no dearth of kindness
 Or love among mankind,

But in darkling loneness
  Hooded hearts grow blind!
Full of kindness tingling,
  Soul is shut from soul,
When they might be mingling
  In one kindred whole!

There's no dearth of kindness,
  Tho' it be unspoken,
From the heart it sendeth
  Smiles of heaven in token
That there be none so lowly,
  But have some angel-touch:
Yet, nursing loves unholy,
  We live for self too much!

As the wild-rose bloweth,
  As runs the happy river,
Kindness freely floweth
  In the heart for ever.
But if men will hanker
  Ever for golden dust,
Best of hearts will canker,
  Brightest spirits rust.

There's no dearth of kindness
  In this world of ours;
Only in our blindness
  We gather thorns for flowers!
O cherish God's best giving,
  Falling from above!
Life were not worth living,
  Were it not for Love.

MY LOVE.

My Love is true and tender,
  Her eyes are rich with rest;
Her hair of dappled splendour,
  The colour I love best;
So sweet, so gay, so odorous warm,
  She nestles here, heart-high,
A bounteous aspect, beauteous form,
  But—just a wee bit sly.

My Love is no light Dreamer,
  A-floating with the foam;
But a brave life-sea swimmer,
  With footing found in Home.
My winsome Wife, she 's bright without,
  And beautiful within;
But—I would not say quite without
  The least wee touch of sin.

My Love is not an Angel
  In one or two small things;
But just a wifely woman
  With other wants than wings.
You have some little leaven
  Of earth, you darling dear!
If you were fit for Heaven,
  You might not nestle here.

THE GOLDEN WEDDING-RING.

With a white hand like a lady,
  And a heart as merry as Spring,

I am ripe and I am ready
  For a golden wedding-ring;
  Heigho, for a wedding-ring.

This old world is scarce worth seeing,
  Till Love wave his purple wing,
And we gauge the bliss of being,
  Thro' a golden wedding-ring;
  Heigho, for a wedding-ring.

Would you draw far Eden nearer,
  And to earth the Angels bring;
You must seek the magic mirror
  Of a golden wedding-ring;
  Heigho, for a wedding-ring.

As the earth with sea is bounded,
  And the winter-world with spring,
So a Maiden's life is rounded
  With a golden wedding-ring;
  Heigho, for a wedding-ring.

I have known full many a Maiden,
  Like a white rose withering,
Into fresh ripe beauty redden
  Thro' a golden wedding-ring;
  Heigho, for a wedding-ring.

As the crescent Moon rings golden,
  Her full glory perfecting,
Womanly beauty is unfolden
  In a golden wedding-ring;
  Heigho, for a wedding-ring.

Fainting spirits oft grow fearless,
  Sighing hearts will soar and sing,
Tearful eyes will laugh out tearless,
  Thro' a golden wedding-ring;
  Heigho, for a wedding-ring.

There 's no jewel so worth wearing,
That a Lover's hands may bring, —
There 's no treasure worth comparing
With a golden wedding-ring;
Heigho, for a wedding-ring.

Ah! when hearts are wildly beating,
And when arms all glowing cling,
Think, Love's circle wants completing
With a golden wedding-ring;
Heigho, for a wedding-ring.

NO JEWELLED BEAUTY IS MY LOVE.

No jewell'd Beauty is my Love,
Yet in her earnest face
There 's such a world of tenderness,
She needs no other grace.
Her smiles, and voice, around my life
In light and music twine,
And dear, O very dear to me,
Is this sweet Love of mine.

O joy! to know there 's one fond heart
Beats ever true to me:
It sets mine leaping like a lyre,
In sweetest melody:
My soul up-springs, a Deity!
To hear her voice divine;
And dear, O very dear to me,
Is this sweet Love of mine.

If ever I have sigh'd for wealth,
'T was all for her, I trow;
And if I win Fame's victor-wreath,
I 'll twine it on her brow.

There may be forms more beautiful,
  And souls of sunnier shine,
But none, O none, so dear to me,
  As this sweet Love of mine.

NOW AND THEN.

O Love will make the leal heart ache
  That never ached before;
And meek or merry eyes 't will make
  With solemn tears run o'er.
In tears we parted tenderly,
  My Love and I langsyne;
And evermore she vowed to be
  Mine own, aye mine, all mine!

Sing O the tree is blossoming,
  But the worm is at the root;
And many a darling flower of Spring
  Will never come to fruit.
We meet now in the streets of life;
  All gone, the old sweet charms;
At my side leans a loving Wife;
  She — passes Babe-in-arms.

SONG.

Like leaves from Autumn's bough, Old Friend,
  Our ripest hopes depart;
There 's little left us now, Old Friend,
  To cheer the Patriot's heart.
The Altars where we knelt, Old Friend,
  Grow desolate and cold,

And faint is the faith we felt, Old Friend,
  I' the valiant days of old.

In bloody shrouds they sleep, Old Friend,
  Who could not live as slaves:
The living only weep, Old Friend,
  Above their Martyrs' graves!
Freedom hath many a wound, Old Friend,
  And, ring'd by hounds of hell,
She wraps her purple round, Old Friend,
  To fall as Cæsar fell.

The men of blood prevail, Old Friend,
  And, stricken in the night,
The people's weeping wail, Old Friend,
  Goes praying for the light.
And yet their day shall come, Old Friend,
  Though we may never hear
The shouts of Harvest-home, Old Friend,
  Nor see the golden year.

BRIDAL SONG.

Gaily the Sun woos the Spring for his Bride,
  With kisses all warm and golden;
Till the life at her heart she no longer may hide,
  And the wealth of her love is unfolden.

The wrinkled old Sea sidles up the sands,
  And lavishes kisses in showers
On the Earth, till the Gray-beard's young darling stands
  All dress'd in her bridal flowers!

With kisses, sweet kisses, the mellow Rains start
  The virgin flowers a-blossom,

And ripen their beauty till fragrant lips part,
  And Love's jewel gleams rich in their bosom.

Faint with love wingeth the wantoning Wind,
  And yearns as its heart were a-breaking,
And kisses sweet kisses, till buds be untwined,
  And the young leaves all are awaking.

And there 's nothing so dainty-sweet in life
  As to kiss the Maid glowing and tender,
Till the heart of the Wife giveth up in the strife,
  Full-flowering in Love's splendour.

LULLABY.

Softly sink in slumbers golden,
  Warm as nestled Birdlings lie,
Safe in Mother's arms enfolden,
  While I sing thy lullaby.
Lullaby, lullaby, lullaby, lullaby,
Sweet one, sleep to my Lullaby.

Tho' the night doth darken, darken,
  Light will Mother's slumbers lie;
Still my heart will hearken, hearken,
  Lest my wee thing wake and cry.
Lullaby, lullaby, lullaby, lullaby,
Sweet one, sleep to my Lullaby.

At thy golden gates of slumber,
  Stands my spirit tiptoe high,
Filled with yearnings without number,
  In thine inner heaven to fly.
Lullaby, lullaby, lullaby, lullaby,
Sweet one, sleep to my Lullaby.

In that world of mystic breathing,
  Spirit Sentinels, stand by!
Winnow, winnow, o'er my wee thing,
  Wings of Love that hover nigh.
Lullaby, lullaby, lullaby, lullaby,
Sweet one, sleep to my Lullaby.

Sleep! and drink the dew delicious!
  Sleep! till the morrow dawn is high!
Sleep with Mother near her precious,
  Wake! with Mother waiting nigh.
Lullaby, lullaby, lullaby, lullaby,
Sweet one, sleep to my Lullaby.

THE TWO ROSES.

SOFTLY stept she over the lawn,
    In vesture light and free;
A floating Angel might have drawn
Her hair from heaven in a glory dawn,
    And her voice rang silverly.
Then up she rose on her tiny tiptoes,
Her white hand catches, her fingers close;
You are tall and proud, my dainty Rose!
    But I have you now, said She.

O so lightly over the lawn,
    Step for step went he!
Thinking how, from His hiding-place,
The war of Roses in her face,
    Dear Love would laugh to see!
Two arms suddenly round her he throws,
Two mouths, turning one way, close;
You are tall and proud, my dainty Rose!
    But I have you now, said He.

SONG.

"FAREWELL, Sweet! may you find a nest
Of home in haven dearer;
And safelier rest upon the breast
Of truer love and nearer!
May favours fall, and blessings flow
For you, and cares come never!
But kiss me, dear, before you go,
And then shake hands for ever."

Her very heart within doth melt,
And gather while she lingers
A weeping warmth, as tho' it felt
A wee Babe's feeling fingers:
The minutes pass, they do not part,
And vain was all endeavour;
A touch had closed them heart to heart,
And hands WERE claspt for ever.

HUGH MILLER'S GRAVE.

BEFORE the grim Grave closes, let me drop
My few poor flowers upon his Coffin lid!
I loved the man: his taking roughness too
I liked; it was the Sword-hilt rough with gems.
I loved him living, not with that late love
Which asks for rootage in the dead man's grave,
And must be writ in Marble to endure.
To many he seemed stern, for he could guard
His tongue with his good teeth: to some he showed
Rough as the Holly's lower range of leaves,
His prickly humour all alive with spears:
But if you climbed to the serener height,
You found a life in smooth and shining leaf,
And crowned with calm, and lying nearer heaven

Low lies the grandest head in all Scotland.
We 'll miss him when there 's noble work to do!
We 'll miss him coming thro' the crowded street,
Like plaided Shepherd from the Ross-shire Hills,
Stalwart and iron-gray and weather-worn;
His tall head holding up a lonely light
Of steadfast thought still burning in his eyes,
Like some masthead-light lonely thro' the night;
His eyes, that rather dreamed than saw, deep-set
In the brow's shadow, looking forward, fixed,
On something which we saw not, solemn, strange!

He was a Hero true as ever stept
In the Forlorn Hope of a warring world:
And from opposing circumstance his palm
Drew loftier stature, and a lustier strength.
From the far dreamland height of youthful years
He flung his gage out mid the trampling strife,
And fought his way to it with spirit that cut
Like a scythed Chariot, and took up his own.
Once more Childe Roland to the dark tower came,
Saw bright forms beckon on the battlements,
And stormed thro' fighting foes, true steel to steel;
Slow step by step he won his winding way,
And reached the top, and stood up Victor there;
And yet with most brave meekness it was done.

His life-tree fair of leaf, and rich in fruit!
We could not see it mouldering at the heart.
We knew not how in nights of pain he groped,
And groped with bleeding feel down the dark Crypts
Of consciousness, to find the buried sense;
When the faint flame of being flickering low,
Made fearful shadows spectral on the walls;
And beckoning terrors muttered in the dark;
Old misery-mongers moaned along the wind;
The lights burned blue as Death were breathing near,
And dead hands seemed to reach and drag him down.
The powers of Evil often have a hand
With human Lots in the dim urn of Fate.

The awful Dark flung over him a pall
Of pain, hot hands of hell were on his eyes,
And Devils drew him thro' the cold night-wind;
But while they held the helpless body bound,
The spirit broke away. That rent was death!
The iron will wherewith he cleft his path
From the stone-quarries to the heights of fame,

Still strove for freedom when the leap was death.
But, never doubt God's Children find their home
By dark as well as day. The life he lived,
And not the death he died, was first in judgment.
It is the writing on the folded scroll
Death sends, and not the seal, that God will judge.

I love to think the Spirit of Cowper caught
Hold of his poor weak wandering hands in help,
As at the dark door he in blindness groped.
How it would touch that tender soul to read
The earthly memories written in his face!
Such memories as ope the gates of heaven:
And he who soothed him with last words on earth
Might whisper his first welcome in the heavens,
And lead him thro' cool valleys green where grow
The leaves of healing by the river of life,
Where tears and travel-stains are wiped away,
All troubled thoughts laid in ambrosial rest,
And there is no more pain.

Then as they bowed
Before His throne who sitteth in the Heavens,
Perchance the pleading Poet prayed that he
Might sit beside him at th' eternal feast.
The fancy flower-like from his coffin grew
Even while I lookt. He lay as Death did seem
Only a dream he might have dreamed before;
All peaceful as the face of Sabbath morn:
The meekened witness of another world.
That stern, white stillness had a starry touch,
As his last look had caught the first of heaven.
The battle-armour of a soldier soul
Lay battered, but still bright from many blows,
Upon the field; and such as few could wear.

The ghosts of last year leaves, that last night rose
And rustled in their spectral dance of death,
Are laid and silent in a shroud of snow!

The day is dark above the long, dark host!
The sad husht heavens seem choked, but cannot
    weep!
Many pale faces, many tristful eyes,
With dumb looks pleading for the kindly rain
That comes not when the heart can only cry
With unshed tears, close round his wintry grave!
The lonely men whose lives are still a-light
And shining when the tired toilers sleep,
To whom Night brings the larger thoughts like
    Stars.
I marvel if among them there is one
Who shudders when men speak of such a death
As if they named His — who has longed to pluck
Death's cool hand down upon the burning brain,
But chokes the secret in his heart as though
He crusht a hissing serpent in his hand,
Lest it scream out, and his white face be known!

Ah! come away, for sorrow is a child
That needs no nursing! And all seems so strange.
One last look, and then home to feel and feel
What we have lost; and when from the dark earth
A spring-tide dawn of leaf-light glistens green,
And Nature with her dewfall and her rain
Gives to our grief the last calm tender touch,
And makes the Heartsease grow from out his grave,
In those sweet days when hearts are tenderest
For those who never come back with the flowers,
Upon some balmy Eve so beautiful
We should not wonder if an Angel stood
Suddenly at our side; the silent march
Of all the beauty culminating thus!
Then let us come, dear friend, and spend an hour —
While Nature kneeleth in all places lowly,
God's blessing resting on a time so holy —
At the communion table of His tomb.

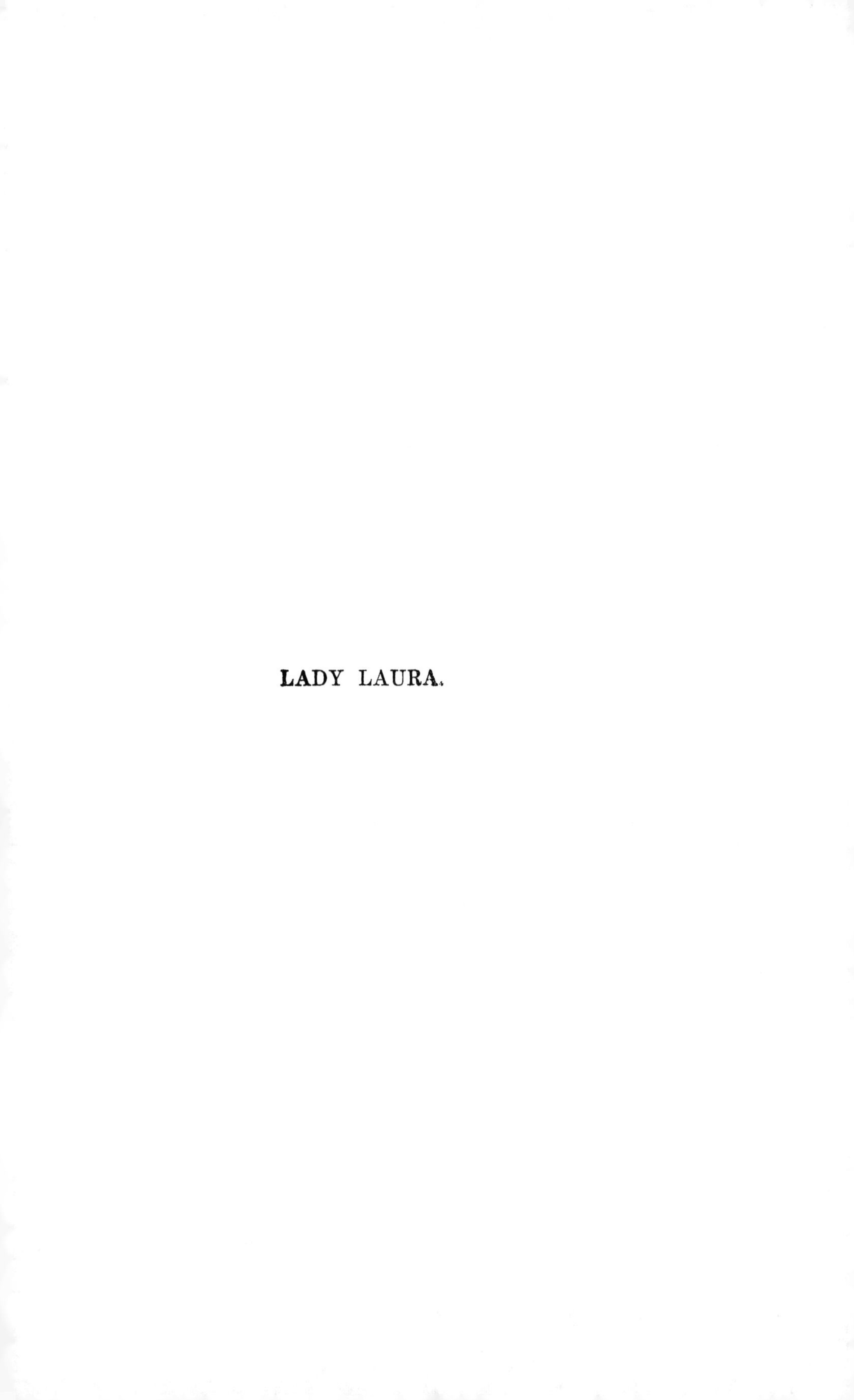

LADY LAURA.

LADY LAURA.

I.

THE Rainbow! lo, its living arch
    Of glory spans the sparkling green,
    Like Spirit Bridge that all unseen,
We passed thro' on the midnight march.

Midsummer Morn her silvery-gray
    Rain-veil uplifteth fold on fold;
    And purple-tinged, and topped with gold,
The white clouds kindle and float away

Across the violet-shadowed hills
    That take from heaven their soft attire;
    With fragrance and with sheeny fire
All the blue round of Ether fills.

Into rich flames of emerald break
    The woods against the ruddied light.
    A dance of radiance bickers bright
As laughter o'er a dimpling cheek;

In sapphire rain heaven ripples down:
    The sweet south-winds waft opened wide
    The glory-gates of Summer-tide;
A starry sweep of flowers is strown

Down the green meadows; white and gold,
    It laughs along the glowing ground:
    Such throng of blessings dances round
The old World's heart; lo, these unfold.

At faëry palace-portals peer
Quick eyes of Birds that sing i' the sun;
Their hearts with music overrun;
Listens each leafy forest-ear.

Wee cups of flowery wine brim high,
By the way-side, on brier and bush;
As lifted in a waiting hush
By unseen hands for passers by.

Her ripe cheek on the air, red Rose!
She leaneth from her fragrant bower;
Like lady from her latticed tower;
And by sweet force of beauty blows!

Bright-hearted with a golden dream,
The little daisy lifts its head;
Its wee lips glister wet and red;
Its look is thankful as a hymn.

The wildest weed the wind hath sown,
And commonest grass, are glorified,
Even as the Tulip in her pride;
The trumpet of her beauty blown.

All Life lies in a bath of balm,
Feeling the lavish glory flow;
With nought to do but thrill and grow
In strength, and joy, and luscious calm.

Now Love breathes dewier delight,
In cool green ways, and tender gloom;
Being hath such a dazzling bloom;
Its sun of bliss grows over-bright.

O balmy Morn! O tender type!
What tearful wooings of the May
Have brought about this bridal-day
Of Earth the rathe with June the ripe.

But, we must turn where Greed for Toil
Hath closed and claspt Morn's pictured book;
Where Nature hath a Gnome-like look,
And from her features dies the smile.

II.

Pleasantly rings the Chime that calls to the Bridal-hall or Kirk;
But the Devil might gloatingly pull for the peal that wakes the Child to work!
"Come, little Children," the Mill-bell rings, and drowsily they run,
Little old Men and Women, and human worms who have spun
The life of Infancy into silk; and fed, Child, Mother, and Wife,
The factory's smoke of torment, with the fuel of human life.
O weird white face, and weary bones, and whether they hurry or crawl,
You know them by the factory-stamp, they wear it one and all.
The Factory-Fiend in a grim hush waits till all are in, and he grins
As he shuts the door on the fair, fair world without, and hell begins!
The least faint living rose of health from the childish cheek he strips,
To run the thorn in a Mother's heart: and ever he sternly grips
His sacrifice; while Life's soiled waters turns his wildering wheels;
And shouts, till his rank breath thicks the air, and the Child's brain Devil-ward reels.

From cockcrow until starlight, very patiently they plod;
A sea of human faces turning sadly up to God.

O wan white winter world that hides no coloured dreams of Spring!
No summer sunshine brightens; no buds blossom; no birds sing.
In at the windows Nature looks, and sings, and smiles them forth,
To walk with her, and talk with her, and see the summering Earth;
And drink the air that cools the heart in pathways dim with dew;
While the miracle of Morning raises glorified life anew.
But they are shut from the heavenly largess; they must stint and moil,
Tho' Death stare ghastly in their face, and life is endless toil.
Did you mark how vacantly they eyed this land of loveliness,
The Flower of Sleep into their eyes, your heart would ache to press.
The moving glory of the heavens, their pomp and pageantry,
Flame in their shadowed faces, but no soul comes up to see.
They see no Angels lean to them; they stretch no spirit-hand;
Melodious Beauty sings to them; they cannot understand.

Yet here, where the sweet flower of life may hoard no precious dew,
To feed its heart of greenness, keep the glory of its hue;
Here, where the fingers of Work and Want are writing silent, slow,
Their warrant for the grave on many a Mother's darling's brow;
Here, where the Fiend doth trample out the soul-sparks day by day;

Here, where such seed of God is rotting in the killing clay;
Some Saviour-Seraph walks the waves of sorrow and of sin,
And some poor wrestler doth not sink the wrecking gulfs within;
And aye she rises with her charge in loving arms caressed,
As Morning rises out of night, her love-star on her breast.

III.

In a grand old Gothic Palace,
  The Lady Laura dwells:
It crowns the warm green valleys,
  High as the surge of summer swells.
There, with her emerald chalice, Spring
  Kneels, offering beauty's wine;
There, in a land of enchantment, sing
  The birds thro' shower and shine.
'T is a noble solitude serene,
  Where the sudden glory glows!
In a happy nook of nestling green,
  That virginal flower blows, —
Just in the sweetness of the bud,
  Brimming with brightness and balm;
The tenderest glimpse of Womanhood
  Golden, and sweet, and calm.
She is the Lily of the land;
  Born neither to spin nor toil:
She can rest her fair cheek on her dainty white hand,
  While the human honey-bees moil.
O the world of rich visions that peer in her eyes!
  Around her what fantasies dance!
As she leans in her air of paradise,
  And the bower of dalliance:
But her earnest life is sorrowfully
  O'ershadowed from above:

She feels the ache of Life's mystery,
  And she feels the hurt of Love.
The Lady Laura's soul is sad
  For the suffering under the sun:
She looks on the world, and is only glad
  For the duties to be done.
She might have moved by in the pageant grand,
  Sweet slip of a lordly line!
Nor soiled the glory of her white hand,
  And fairy fingers fine;
And swam in this world's wine and oil,
  With those who sink for the next,
Faint with delight, and plundered Toil
  With no strange thought perplext.
O the burnisht stream would have bravely borne
  Her, dancing down in its whirl;
And the dark wreck-kingdom have proudly worn
  On its bosom the pure queen-pearl.
But Sorrow hath toucht her young, young years,
  When their rose-light was smiling and fair;
And her eyes have wept the sharp, sharp tears,
  That pierce through all mirage of air.
Ah, the Poor! with her finer sense she hears
  How they moan in their cloud of care.
They will tell you down in the valleys
  What the Orphan Heiress hath done;
How the grand old Gothic Palace
  With Love's new wine doth run.
She is Dawn on the cold hill-tops that divide
  The poor from their neighbour Rank;
The first bright wave of a sluggish tide,
  That hath overleapt its bank.
And to Lady Laura by window and door,
  Hearts climb with the Roses up,
Their blessings to breathe, and their pride to pour,
  In many a crowning cup.
Rebel hindrance she treads queenly down,
  Where it stands in her Throne's high way.

O Factory-Fiend with the fearful frown,
She will bloom in your desert to-day.

IV.

THE lady Light hath Daughters seven,
In sovereign state sit smiling fair
On their cloud-throne ; but down the air
They float from arms of clasping Heaven :

For they their lofty home will leave,
To winnow, on their golden plumes,
Through ocean-bowers, and water-glooms ;
And wondrous spells of beauty weave

To clothe the sea-shells in their trance
So lone and cold, with coloured lights,
And jewel-flames ; till their dim Night 's
Alive with shapes of radiance.

On Alpine heights a little Flower
From its snow-cradle soft doth reach ;
And with its tiny hands beseech
Thy vesture-hem, Eternal Power !

Then straightway help of heaven descends,
And vital influences run
Down golden ladders of the sun,
And pleading life wins spirit-friends.

Thus souls in barrenest solitude
Oft bring the kindly powers down,
To lighten on them with a crown,
Or cheer them with immortal food.

And thus on one poor Worker's sight
Dawns Lady Laura through the mirk,
Much marvelling how there may lurk
A presence toucht with tender light.

His life stands still to hear what fate
Comes with the step of mystery;
And husht for some event to be,
In conscious calm the waters wait.

She sees a prayer for rest and air
In every face, but, in his eyes
Alone, are childish memories;
And his the only spirit there

That waves the Seraph-wand of fire,
To fright the Serpent flickering near.
One jewel in that dark Mine! and clear
It flashes as she brightens nigher.

And all beside how dull and grim!
O saintly show of maiden grace!
From out a golden mist, her face
Seems floating, floating on to him.

Daughter of Light! she seems to swim,
As on the wings of a mighty love;
Sad-smiling that blind world above;
Sunning that human forest dim.

She speaks to him; she takes his hand;
With such a gracious tenderness!
The tears up in his eyes will press;
Life's waste in sudden flower doth stand.

As when the spirit of Winter old
Passes away in a dream of spring,
The quick buds burst, and shimmering
All into fluttering wings unfold,

And wave so strong, and thrill so free,
As they the wakened world would wing
Along the warm way of the Spring,
Where they are drawn deliciously:

So from his life a burst of wings
  Is thrilling leaf-like for the light;
  And in that Splendour's wake of white,
They make melodious murmurings.

Light, Music, Fragrance, seem to kiss
  And swathe him in a bloom of fire;
  Make shining beauty his attire,
And bury his dead past in bliss.

At her soft touch ethereal dies
  The old dark, as Morning's spear of light
  Doth gently touch the dying night,
And from it Day, a white Spirit, doth rise.

V.

THE Lady Laura took him, in her kind and queenly way,
From out that cruel iron world, to the tender human day.
There all the folded bloom of life like a banner rich unfurled,
And waved luxuriant in the air of a glad and glorious world.

She fed his mind, she led his mind, thro' vistas strange and sweet;
Ah, blessèd boon to toil and lay the fruitage at her feet!
She took his widowed Mother; bless her full and flowing hand!
To rest her weary bones from toil, and live upon her land.

Their barren world of poverty with flowers she girdled round,
Till life that toiled with bleeding feet can walk on softer ground.

My Lady comes; my Lady goes; his being doth
rejoice,
A breaking sea of rapture; every wave uplifts a
voice.

Like dungeoned foe that seeth the King's daughter
walking nigh,
He blesseth the revealing dark for the beauty
thronéd high.
And in the beating of his heart, and flashing of his
eye,
A new life climbeth, — waving glory, — as she passeth by.

My Lady comes; my Lady goes; he can see her
day by day,
And bless his eyes with her beauty, and with blessings strew her way
My Lady comes; my Lady goes; she passes from
his sight,
As daylight dies into the skies, and at her gate
stands Night.

VI.

AH, little thinks my Lady
Of the subtle seedling sown;
But, fruitful was the silence
Where its secret life hath grown.
From human love's great ocean
It draws the nursing springs;
And 't is fed on hidden manna
That her fragrant beauty brings.

Ah, little thinks my Lady,
As the days and seasons roll;
How she took him by the hand,
To pass in to his soul.

There she lies in a light of smiles;
  And like a soft caress,
Her voice goes soothing, soothing
  With a kiss of tenderness.

O Love, tho' shut without, will laugh
  All barriers above;
And higher as they soar, still towers
  The stature of mighty Love.
And bud by bud, the climbing seed
  Into a tall tree springs!
Ah, little thinks my Lady
  What the Bird in the branches sings!

VII.

"SHE smiled on me, she smiled on me,
  And I walk in a glory now;
'T is writ on my cheek in a rose of pride;
  'T is read in a light on my brow.

"She smiled on me, she smiled on me,
  I think as I sit alone;
And my heart o'er its tender secret
  Is brooding with love's sweet moan.

"She smiled on me, she smiled on me,
  And that surging smile of light,
In a happy silence, thro' my life
  Goes circling out of sight.

"She smiled on me, she smiled on me,
  And my soul with bliss doth ache;
So many a clue to happiness,
  I know not which to take!

"She smiled on me, she smiled on me,
  And the human world goes by —
In a sound as of Angels talking,
  And a feel as if Heaven swum nigh.

"She stoopt to kiss me with her smile,
  Thro' the clouds where I darkly lay;

As she glided thro' my night, Sweet Moon!
  High on her heavenly way.

" She stoopt to kiss me with her smile,
  And life soared up in flame!
But, for my worship, not my kiss,
  The glorious phantom came.

" She smiled on me, she smiled on me ;
  Ah me, that in her smiles
My heart might break, in a wide love-wave,
  On her bosom's happy Isles! "

VIII.

As earliest flowers, the sweet first-love of Spring,
Are tenderest in their fragrance — saintliest pure,
Love's firstlings, budding in the heart, unfold
Most precious sweet of all the lusty year;
And all his life is with their fragrance filled
In shy and shady nooks he steals, to brood
O'er what his heart for worship lifteth up.

With a ripe flush in his warm face the Dawn
Uplifts the veil of dew-mist from the shape
Of Beauty sleeping on the lap of Earth:
So down into his secret soul he peers,
To see the veilèd Beauty thro' its mist,
And bows to bless her where she lies alight,
Unconscious of the reddening dawn of love.

A face, like nestling luxury of flowers;
Soft hair, on which Light drops a diadem;
A mouth of roses wet with damask wine:
The sweetest eyes, — ah, when in their far heaven
Shall Love rise up and beckon with the palm ? —
And all the beauty hid from mortal sight,
Like lily-bud in leaves of cool green light.

His happy eyes o'erflow with holy dew,
Gathered in the rich air of secret love.

Anon his heart goes wandering like a wind
That reels thro' meads of spice, o'er hills of myrrh,
Drunk with flower-fragrance, and the wine of love,
And making music at the lightest touch,
Till faint with sweets it wearies into rest.

IX.

Lady of the forest
  Is the Silver Birk;
Shimmering in the sunshine;
  Shivering at the mirk;
Rocking in her rapture;
  A dancing Psaltress slim!
Her hair a shower of beauty!
  Her motion a faëry-swim!
Or, when dewy Quiet
  Pours its chrism of balm,
And her tremulous tresses
  Are bound with a tender calm;
Rustling in her richness,
  A Glory in the land;
Veilèd when the gloaming
  Is gray with shadows grand;
'Mid the dance of colours,
  And semitones of green,
Gleams this daintier Spirit
  That in leafdom is the Queen.
Of all the trees o' the forest,
  He loves the Silver Birk,
Shimmering in the sunshine,
  Shivering at the mirk.
So like the Lady Laura
  In her purity and grace;
Dreaming in its shadow,
  Often rose her face!
And as when a Sunburst
  Goldens the green aisles,

The woodland water smileth,
So his heart within him smiles.

X.

"Just a smile i' the face of Nature;
Just a mirror of May-morn;
Is the shining, comely creature,
Worshipt by the peasant-born.

"Beauty has no rarer blossom,
Budding fain, or flowering fair;
Nestling to a Mother's bosom,
If a lover's hand should dare.

"She is graceful as the greenly
Waving boughs in summer wind;
And her beauty calm and queenly
Wears its royal crown of mind.

"Might I bear Love's shield above her;
Might I snood her silken hair;
How my heart would round her hover
On the tender wings of care!

"Ah, dear Heaven, all blessings shower
On her sweet life's balmy bud;
Till it lift immortal flower,
In the blooming fields of God."

XI.

A dazzling wonder in the dark of Dreams,
His heart-hid Jewel gleams;
And for a peerless richness it doth range
Thro' zones of radiant change.
Breathing soft hues the glorious thing doth shine,
With lustres Opaline.
The shifting Sapphire lovingly beguiles,
With dewy azure smiles.
The Ruby now with soul of crimson yearns,

Or like a blood-drop burns.
The Topaz in transparent hand doth hold
Imprisoned flame of gold.
Now twinkles from soft shade the Emerald tender,
A drop of cool green splendour.
Or, with love-drooping eye, the Pearl o' the deep
Melts in a sea of sleep.
And now, wide ope, it lights the inner night,
A starry Chrysolite.
And aye, for a peerless richness it doth range
The zones of radiant change.

XII.

One of the silent Poets of the world who find no word
To utter their dumb soul of love, so, like the shy night-bird,
They break their hearts in music; die in sorrow's solitude;
One Autumn eve he sat beneath the white Grace of the Wood;
Where Birds of Thought so often brought his love ambrosial food;
When all the spirits of the flowers stole forth i' the hush of night,
And all the greeny silence slumbered in a dream of light.

The world lay in a purple calm, and tenderness of tears;
In every pulse of being lived the tenderness of years.
He had wrestled with his passion, — caught up in its wild caress —
Voluptuous as a Bride of Fire, with arms as pitiless.
He had wept his pain in a fiery rain, and a calm came o'er his tears,

As a vision of sweet Peace comes treading down
War's cruel spears.
Then in a trembling confidence of love to himself
he talkt,
And sang above his whispering heart, that felt what
Spirit walkt.

"We cannot lift the wintry pall
From buried life; nor bring
Back, with Love's passionate thinking, all
The glory of the Spring.
But soft along the old green way
We feel her breath of gold;
Her radiant vesture ripples gay, —
She comes! and all is told.

"So in Her absence Memory
Aye strives, but cannot paint
The Vision of sweet Majesty;
The beauty of my Saint.
She comes! like dawn in spring her fame!
My winter-world doth melt;
The thorns with flowers wave a-flame!
She smiles! and all is felt."

Is it a vision! or the pure pale face
Of Lady Laura, coming thro' the trees?
Strange fire consumes the rich dew of her eyes!
Trembles her lip; her soul, tho' very calm,
Gleams like a naked sword from its soft sheath.
Ah, she has found his secret in its nest?
And will she crush him with her silent scorn?
He dare not know. She speaks; he scarcely hears
So loud the blood goes singing through his brain.
"I am no longer mistress at the Hall;
False friends usurp my title and my lands,
And keep them till the Law shall do me right.
I leave to-morrow morn. I think you have
The mounting spirit to rise where'er you fall,
And shall rejoice to mark your fortunes shine."

She paused; he raised his eyes to hers, and saw
The unuttered something that could not be told.

Her rustling robe thrilled all his life, and soft
Her fragrant footsteps died upon the night.

XIII.

Like one caught in the Tempest's arms unseen,
Dasht overboard unheard, and left all night
With the mad waves, blindfolded by the gloom,
All thro' that desolate dark he wrestled lone;
Tossing tumultuous in a storm of soul;
And lived his life o'er in the agony stern;
As on the drowning rushes all the past.

Again he saw her in the Silk-mill stand
Complete in beauty, crowned with meekest calm,
As missioned Angel down to Hell wings when
Some suffering spirit's time is up in Heaven.
He went with her among the Poor where fell
Her smile as sunshine on the harvest land;
And from the folded flowers of thorny life,
Her presence charmed a kindlier spirit forth;
He, hoarding up their blessings in his heart.

He saw her in the spring-dawns gliding down,
Like Morning on the world, to tend the flowers
That from her touch sprang thrilling with delight
Darkened into himself, he watcht, all eye,
Like Spirit that sees its mortal love go by,
Itself invisible.
In languorous noons
Of summer, when, a Shape of fragrant warmth,
Nature seems glowing thro' her sumptuous robe;
With all her beauty rounding tenderly;
And from behind the tapestry of flowers,
Her passion takes you with ambrosial breath;
He in the cool, green shadows would lie down,
O'er him the leaves a lowe of glimmering gold,

To kiss where the beloved foot had toucht,
With lip of crimson fire, and fondling cheek,
All tingling thro' and thro' with lightning life.

He saw the visible Divinity
O' the time and place, taking her twilight walk,
Starrily moving in an air of smiles;
The serious sea-blue dreaming in her eyes;
Her lofty beauty robed about with heaven;
And drank the wine of wonder as she went.
So tender hour by hour, love grew in his heart;
A dew-drop in the flower's cup held toward heaven.

Ah, happy times, when on the top of life
He saw her beauty's daily sunrise, heard
Her voice, and breathed the air made holy by her,
And in her presence cloud-like sunned himself,
With such sweet silent awe; while all his heart
With rich love trembled as 't would break for bliss;
Like shaken dews in jewelled cups of morn!

Ah, happy nights, and lustrous darks, in which
He watcht her casement when the house was mute,
And Silence took the place in loving arms,
Where the tall Chestnuts husht her beauty round,
Uplifting in their hands a light of flowers!
There with its speechless yearning strove his heart,
O'erflowing till the night was filled with love.

How often thro' the winter wind and rain,
His spirit fluttered to her, winged with blessings.
And he stood clothed and warmed with thoughts
of her;
And thro' the darkness and the cold, his love
Glowed like a watch-fire in a wilderness;
Or glistened upward in a light of tears;
Soul-diamonds of the purest water — tears
Trembling with tenderness, alive with light;

Such as the Angels wear for jewels in heaven.
Ah, happy times that wave their sad farewells,
To come no more, no more, O Nevermore!
To him, who, tasting the forbidden tree,
Now sat at Eden gates, and they were closed.

Sudden a thought struck new life thro' him as strikes
Land on the swimmer's feet who gives up lost!
He who could die for her, could he not live
For her, and help her win her rightful throne?
He sat not down on shore to mourn his wreck;
Not his the heart to wail when he might work.

That night hath passed; but from its death-bed rose
A Star, to sing and sparkle in his soul,
And light him to some crowned accomplishment.

XIV.

O MIGHTY mystery London, there be children still, who hold
Her palaces are silver-rooft, her pavements are of gold;
And blindly in that dark of fate, they grope for the golden prize,
For somewhere hidden in her heart the charméd treasure lies.
Such glory burning in the skies, she lifts her crown of light
Above the dark, we see not what we trample in the night.
O merry world of London! O aching world of moan,
How many a soul hath stoopt to thee, and lost its starry throne!

There Circe brims her sparkling ruby, dancing welcome, — laughs
All scruples down with wicked eye, and the crazed lover quaffs,
Until the fires of Hell have left white ashes on his lips;
And there they pass whose tortured hearts the worm that dies not grips.
The stricken crawl apart to die. There, many a bosom heaves
With merry laughters mournful as the dancing of dead leaves.
There griping Greed rich-heaps the yellow wealth of Bank and Shop,
As Autumn leaves grow goldenest when rotten-ripe to drop:
And many melt the marrow of their Manhood, burn its bloom,
In Passion's serpent arms, and with her kiss of fire consume:
And Vanity sideling seeks a mirror in each passing face.
But through the dark some luminous lives flash up and pray Heaven's grace.

All beauteous stand her Idols shining on their azure height,
And from their fairy heaven lean veiled Shapes, half-dim, half-bright;
They draw us with a dream delicious to the aching sight;
Armfuls of warm delight, white waists, ripe lips, and merry Brides;
Beds of lilies and roses! low sweet music, worlds besides!
And day by day, on each highway, from many a sunny shire,
The country life comes green to wither for the hungry fire.

All into London leaping, leaping flows the human sea,
Where, wreck at heart, or prize in arms, the waves flash merrily.
With a prayer to God on high, he sees the tumult, hears the strife,
And dives, from out the gulfs to snatch a nobler-crownéd life.
The Lady Laura leaneth like a bending heaven above,
And his life is safely steadied with the anchor of his love.

Three times into the City's heart there ran the news of Spring:
Sweet primrose-time is come again, and silver showers sing.
The cloudy imagery of heaven sails o'er him day by day,
He watches parching as the Palm when rain floats far away,
All thirsty, as the Hero's soul with glory's burning drouth!
And yearning, as the dying yearn for a death-bed in the South!
For Spring's warm breath, and bright caress, and pleasant feel of leaves,
And all her beauty wet with morn, his heart within him grieves.
The country memories rich inlaid, so fragrantly are stirred,
As spice-winds whisper something low, or sings a careless Bird.
The green-woods beckon spirit-like thro' dreams of azure sky;
All heaven looks out from a flower as from his Beloved's eye,
And visions of a lovelier-lighted life go glimmering by.

Above that wilderness o' the weary oft he sat alone,
Watching the surges of his soul, which, ever and anon,
Revealed the proud wave-wrestler Hope forever battling on!
And ever thro' the dark the Lady Laura smiling shone.
Ah, the dear night was all his own, life rose fantastic-towered;
Full-honeyed with its folded Spring, his shut heart bud-like flowered.
Upon the stream that pined all day, the calm of heaven doth rest;
Its Star of love, tho' far above, keeps bridal on its breast.
Pure, painéd, Loveliness! she walks a world of wrong and guile,
Yet nightly looketh in his face with the same sweet, patient smile.
While ever and forever goeth up to God for doom,
The City's breath of life and death, in glory or in gloom;
And there it rings each spirit round, of light or darkness woven,
And they shall wake and walk their self-unfolded hell or heaven.
Nightly a merry harvest-home the Devil in London drives,
And gathers on the shores of hell the wreck of human lives.
While God sits over all, in heaven, and in His hand doth hold,
The Flower of Silence shedding worlds like seed of sunny gold.

XV.

A LONELY life, a lonely lot;
He climbs his mountain day by day;
But finds beside the stoniest way
Love's wild rock-honey, and fainteth not.

He sees the Vision shine afar;
Sweet wedded lives in happy home;
And strains his eyes against the gloom,
Like Nuns that throb at prison-bar,

Wooed by a dear and dazzling dream,
When thro' the mirk Love's glory burns.
The hearth of Home warm welcome yearns;
His face is glowing with the gleam

And sparkle of their brimming cup,
Who round the home-altar dance and sing,
All in a golden marriage-ring,
And light with love Life's picture up.

They sit in nestling nook, and see
The ripening promise of the years;
The budding quicks, the springing ears;
Flowers honey-wet, and fruits to be.

As bridal-gifts from God above,
The Children bring their glad new spring;
Past joy's refrain their voices ring,
All loud with mirth, or lown with love.

Fine actions feed Love's holy fire,
Like sandal-wood of fragrant gold;
Till heavenward, glorious to behold,
It breaks, in many a splendid spire.

There, hand in hand, they reach across
A double range of rich delights;

And climb in safety where the heights
Of Life have many a chasm of Loss.

A happy soul goes singing aloft,
Ere closes their day-book of bliss,
So gently claspéd with a kiss,
While loving eyes grow still more soft.

"O blesséd Bird that soars and sings,
And moves in heaven on triumphing wings;
Then drops to rest
Within my breast,
And aye some balm of blessing brings.

"O Flower of mine, Life's stream may start
Thy trembling leaves, but cannot thwart
Love's calm below,
Where wed roots grow
In twin strength, smiling heart to heart.

"O crest of beauty on my brow;
O light of love upon my prow;
To the death-dark,
I row my bark;
You gild with glory as we go."

'T is merry to walk the deck of life,
Tho' billows beat, and the wild winds blow;
And proudly feel they rest below;
That precious freightage, weans and wife.

But, he drifts on, in lonely bark,
Past shining home, and singing isle.
Fine Apparition, with a smile
Like spirit-music! in the dark

Thy sudden beauty lightens near,
And bows him to the knees in prayer.
He needs long draughts of heavenly air,
Who dives to clutch a pearl so dear.

XVI.

To-DAY, with his work done, the Victor stands;
His brows are bound by Lady Laura's hands.
He conquered. To her feet he brought the prize
Twin worlds of bliss were throbbing in her eyes.
Sparkled her smiling soul like that of a child,
And smiling, all her life in love-light smiled.

She gloweth happy as the tender South,
When Spring doth kiss her on the flowery mouth.
The lilies white upon the stream of life
Stir with the sweet feel of its dancing strife.
If but one favouring breath of heaven move,
Into his bosom drops the fruit of love.

He lookt into the windows of her eyes
To see Love, sitting by the hearth, arise
And let him in, and lead him to his throne,
For love and worship thro' all worlds his own:
Then from the heart's heaven a sweet simple Grace
Came blushing all the secret in her face,
Dyeing her beauty daintier for embrace.

On her white holy hand the ring of gold
Exults its branch of glory to enfold.
Comes forth in greeting all the country side,
To welcome Lady Laura home, a Bride.
Ring, merry bells, ring, blithesome bridal bells!
To the tune of happy hearts your triumph swells.

Upon his life now leaneth dewily
The rose of her ripe beauty rare to see.
In honeyed light, and sweet with pleasant showers,
Lies all the land, a coloured flame of flowers;
And with a sidelong grace smiles of the sight;
Heaven shakes its bridal torch and laughs delight.

XVII.

"My life lay like a Sea-bud, dark upon the watery wold,
That feels when Spring is in the world, and striveth to unfold,
The breath of Love passed o'er me, and the Spring went laughing by,
Till on a sudden I was 'ware, Beloved, thou wert nigh!
The Bird of Love to my window came, and sang a strain divine.
Sweet Bird! he makes his nest, I said, 'neath other eaves than mine:
But many a day hath come and gone, and still he sits and sings
His song of happy futures, and of dear remembered things.

"My life went darkling like the Earth, nor knew it shone a Star
To that dear Heaven on which it hung in worship from afar.
O, many bared their bravery like flowers to the bee;
She might have ranged thro' sunny fields, but nestled down by me:
A King upon his Throne might have smiled her to his side;
But, with a lowly majesty she came to me, my Bride,
And grandly gave her love to me, the dearest thing on Earth,
Like one who gives a jewel, all unweeting of its worth.

"O, was it an Immortal Child, left by a fair Dream-Bride,
Seen in a world of vision with mine eyes stretcht spirit-wide?
Or was the Image pictured, by the sun of another life,
In secret soul, that I might know its living like my Wife?
I know not; but, when luminous she floated on to me,
Methought she flamed from out the mist of some far memory.
The hiding Love just stirring the spring-roses of her face;
The picture of sweet Saintliness; the glory and the grace.

'T was when the Earth her green lap spreads for Summer's gorgeous gifts;

And plump for kisses of the Sun, her ripened cheek uplifts;
When May among her flowers was caught in lusty arms of June;
She newly strung my harp of life, and played its sweetest tune.
O, I had been content to live in a cottage of the clay,
So I might see and bless her, when she chanced to pass that way;
But she came down from her heaven, with a look of glorious pride,
And I clasp my heart's sweet Vision; lo! a nestling human Bride."

XVIII.

CALM is their sheltered shore of life, caressed
By gentle tides of peace, whose murmurs are
Of storms at rest, and sorrows sanctified.
But not for them alone the honey-time,
And bliss of being! hearts were all too full
Of lusty longing for all human good,
And happiness was only meant to share.
That luminous revealer, hallowing Love,
Gave them the seeing eye, not drooping lid.
His chosen are but caught up into Heaven,
For wider vision of a suffering Earth.
Their lavish bliss ran over to make rich,
And kindle with a spring of joyful life
The poor world kneeling at the feet of theirs.
And not forgotten was that Factory-world,
Which like a doomed Ship far away i' the night
Pleaded — each port-hole lighted up for help!

Christ on the Cross for eighteen hundred years,
And still His Poor their long redemption wait —
Still tempted of the Devil in the Desert.
Still are they, crouching by the fireless hearth,
In the dead winter often driven to burn
The bravest hangings of their house of life,

To scare the gaunt wolf Hunger, whose eyes glare
In at the window lit with bloody lust!
Sometimes a cry runs throbbing thro' the night,
As tho' Creation quickened with the birth
Of new life strange and monstrous, in our world.
Then startled Fear from his high lattice looks,
With face as white as death-toucht Want's below·
There rage a people like a forest of fire!
Grim on the banner Labour's challenge flames,
"Leave to live working, or die fighting."
Fear
Sends forth his Guards, and to his pillow slinks.
Red Murder leaps up sudden in their midst;
The gathering of fierce suffering breaks in blood:
Begins again the old long agony,
And Order reigns! tho' many a day the Ghost
Of Revolution at his banquet sits,
And standeth Sentry at his door o' nights.

O hopeless Poor, and impotently Rich!
O hurrying host of battling enmities,
That, fighting, feel no earthquake rock the ground!
O human world, panting without the pale
Of harmony, the universal law,
Like Soul, with troublous wail, shut out of bliss!
Shall it not come, the time of which we dream,
To crown long years of strife, and blood, and tears,
When from the Book the Poet's thought shall step
Clothed on with human lineaments, and live?
And this Ideal of our hopeful Brave
Come down and dwell with us in daily life,
And Earth and Heaven lie in each other's arms?

They deem so, who, with visionary eyes,
Have held communion with that world to come;
Our wedded pair: their faith made quick by love
They look within — its Shadow comes that way.
And they will make their outer life a dial,
On which the inner light may rise and shine;

And touch with radiance soft some sullen spot
Where falls the Devil's shadow, till a smile
Is on its face as it turns up to God.
Ho for the New World and its golden age
Of delicate dream-work, and of rich romance!

They bought the Factory: turned its stream of toil
To a flood of Joy, on Lady Laura's lands.
There Life, whose dark and stagnant waters swarmed
With hideous things, in merry radiance runs;
Brightens with health, and breaks in frolic spray;
Peeps thro' a garland green, and laughs in light;
Its rest, blessèd as tho' the calm high heavens
Had lookt it into some transfiguring trance,
Then with light-hearted morrow sparkling on —
So to the dark arch Death, thro' which the stream
Will bicker or blacken for the shoreless sea.

They built their little world, wherein the Poor
Might grow the flower of Hope, and fruit of Love;
And human trees, with outstretcht arms of cheer,
Might mingle music, wreathe in bud and bloom,
And in their branches nest the birds of God,
That in immortal beauty whitely hover,
But come not down to build while boughs are bare.

They bought and sold, they ploughed, and sowed, and reapt.
Cheapness, Free Trade, and such Economy
As suck their strength from human blood and tears;
Feeding on Beauty's waste, and Childhood's spring
Shredding with wintry hand life's leafy prime;
They bowed not down to — Baal of the strife
That gives the Devil his own vantage-ground,
Where each man's hand is at his brother's throat;
The knight in golden mail combats the naked!
And hearts must run with never-tiring wheels!
The weak go down; the Victors merciless

Still wield the Sword of Selfish interest,
To win their crown of Individual gain,
And throne of Isolation cold and lone.

Not this, but life of freedom, law of love;
The wine-press trod by each, the cup for all;
In this serener world — this morning star
That rises out of chaos and the night,
Like throbbing heart of some Millennial Day.
Here, life is no soul-sickening round of toil;
No need to blink the Spirit's longing sight.
Here, simple Childhood opens vernal eyes,
And young blood dances thro' the veins of Age.
White Cottage homes rise from the sea of green,
Like clouds where happy spirits sit and sing.

The old wild-brier, Labour, from which spring
The radiant Roses of a warmer world,
With kindlier nurture blossoms forth anew,
A glory of Flowers, and wears immortal green;
Breaks the stern granite, sparkling into beauty,
And precious jewels glow from common stones:
Soft white hands smoothe the brow of wrinkled Wrath;
The gentle balm of Love makes hard eyes soft,
And melted hearts to swim thro' woe-worn looks,
With sweet and delicate human tenderness.
The trampled battle-field of sin-scarred faces
Is healéd with the harvest of ripe love;
Its frowning furrows crowned with ridgéd smiles.

Over their World where Passion hurtled down
Burning instead of beauty, as its sun,
And all around was black eternal night;
Love's radiant shadow sheds an atmosphere
Of soft celestial brightness, calm, and peace.
And Life goes hand in hand with happy things;
In lovely shadow-lands with spirits talks;
There with all gracious Shapes of Beauty walks,

And wins their motion, majesty, and mien;
And rears his temple rich for God, inlaid
With precious jewels and colours fair, and cries,
"Behold how good and joyful a thing it is
To dwell together in peace and unity."

Thus Lady Laura and her peasant lord
Built o'er the dead past their proud monument,
That signals to far times their word of love:
And God was with them smiling on their work.
They wrought not without hindrance, sorrow and pain:
Who work for Freedom win not in an hour:
Their cost of conquest never can be summed!
They toil and toil thro' many a bitter day,
And dark, when false friends flee, and true ones faint.
The seed of that great Truth from which shall spring
The forest of the future, and give shade
To those who reap the harvest, must be watcht
With faith that fails not, fed with rain of tears,
And walled around with life that, fighting, fell.

POEMS FOR CHRISTIE.

FOR CHRISTIE'S SAKE.

Upon us falls the shadow of night,
  And darkened is our day!
My Love will greet the morning light
  Four hundred miles away.
God love her! torn so swift and far
  From hearts so like to break!
And God love all who are good to her;
    For Christie's sake.

I know whatever spot of ground
  In any land we tread —
I know the eternal arms are round;
  That heaven is overhead;
And faith the mourning heart will heal,
  But many fears will make
Our spirits faint, our fond hearts kneel,
    For Christie's sake.

Good-bye Dear! be they kind to you
  As tho' you were their ain!
My Daisy opens to the dew,
  But shuts against the rain!
Never will New Moon glad our eyes
  But offerings we shall make
To old God Wish! and prayers will rise
    For Christie's sake.

Four years ago we struck our tent;
  O'er homeless Babes we yearned;
Our all — three darlings — with us went,
  But only two returned!
While life yet bleeds into Her grave

Love ventures one more stake;
Hush, hush, poor Hearts.! if big, be brave,
For Christie's sake.

Like Crown to most ambitious brows
Was Christie to us given;
To make our Home a holy house,
And nursery of heaven!
O softer was her bed of rest,
Than lily's on the lake;
Peace filled so deep each billowy breast,
For Christie's sake.

To music played by Harps and Hands
Invisible, were we drawn
O'er charmed seas, thro' faëry lands,
Under a dearer dawn!
We entered our new world of love
With blessings in our wake,
While prospering Heavens smiled above
For Christie's sake.

We gazed with proud eyes luminous
On such a gift of grace —
All heaven narrowed down to us
In one dear little face!
And many a pang we felt, dear Wife,
With hurt of heart and ache,
All shut within like clasping knife,
For Christie's sake.

I would no tears might e'er run down
Her patient face, beside
Such happy pearls of heart as crown
Young Mother — new-made Bride!
For 't is a face that, looking up
To passing Heaven, might make
An Angel stop, a blessing drop,
For Christie's sake.

If Love in that child's heart of hers
  Should breathe and break its calm,
With trouble sweet as that which stirs
  The brooding buds of balm, —
Listening at ear of peeping pearl
  Glistening in eyes that shake
Their sweet dew down! God bless our Girl.
    For Christie's sake.

But Father! if our Babe must mourn,
  Be merciful and kind;
And if our gentle Lamb be shorn,
  Attemper thou the wind!
Across the Deluge guide our Dove,
  And to thy bosom take
With arm of love, and shield above,
    For Christie's sake.

We have had sorrows many and strange.
  Poor Christie! when I'm gone,
Some of my words will weirdly change
  If she read sadly on!
Lightnings, from what was dark of old,
  With meanings strange will break
Of sorrows hid or dimly told
    For Christie's sake.

Wife! we should still try hard to win
  The best for our dear Child;
And keep a resting-place within,
  When all without grows wild.
As on the winter graves the snow
  Falls softly flake by flake
Our love should whitely clothe our woe,
    For Christie's sake.

For one will wake at midnight drear
  From out a dream of death,
And find no dear head pillowed near;

No sound of peaceful breath!
May no weak wailing words arise,
No bitter thoughts awake
To see the tears in Memory's eyes:
For Christie's sake.

And *There!* where many crownless kings
Of earth a crown shall wear,—
The Martyrs who have borne the pangs
Their palm at last shall bear:
When, with our lily pure of sin
Our heavenward way we take;—
There, may we walk with welcome in;
For Christie's sake.

HUNT THE SQUIRREL.

It was Atle of Vermeland
In winter used to go
A-hunting up in the pine forest,
With snow-shoes, sledge, and bow.

Soon his sledge with the soft fine furs
Was heapt up heavily,
Enough to warm old Winter with,
And a wealthy man was he.

When just as he was going back home,
He lookt up into a Tree;
There sat a merry brown Squirrel that seemed
To say—"You can't shoot me."

And he twinkled all over temptingly,
To the tip of his tail a-curl!
His humour was arch as the look may be
Of a would-be-wooed, sweet Girl

That makes the Lover follow her, follow her,
All his life up-caught
A-floating on with sleeping wings,
High in the heaven of thought.

Atle he left his sledge and furs;
All day his arrows rung, —
The Squirrel went leaping from bough to bough, —
Only himself they stung.

He hunted far in the dark forest,
Till died the last day-gleams;
Then wearily laid him down to rest
And hunted it thro' his dreams.

All night long the snow fell fast
And covered his snug fur-store;
Long, long did he strain his eyes,
But never found it more.

Home came Atle of Vermeland,
No Squirrel! no Furs for the mart!
Empty head brought empty hand;
Both a very full heart.

Ah, many a one hunts the Squirrel,
In merry or mournful truth;
Until the gathering snows of age
Cover the treasures of Youth.

Deeper into the forest dark,
The Squirrel will dance all day;
Till eyes grow blind and miss their mark,
And hearts will lose their way.

My Darling! should you ever espy
This Squirrel up in the tree,
With a dancing devil in its eye,
Just let the Squirrel be.

CHRISTIE'S POOR OLD GRAN.

No green age, beautiful to see,
Hath Poor Old Gran:
No ripe life mellowed goldenly
Hath Poor Old Gran.
One by one we have left her fold,
Her lonely hearth is growing cold,
Faint is her smile as the primrose gold,
Our Poor Old Gran.

Ah! whitened face, and withered form,
Of Poor Old Gran!
Beaten and blancht in many a storm:
Poor Old Gran!
She hath wept the bitter tears that sow
The dark grave-violets in the snow
Where once the red young rose did glow,
Poor Old Gran!

There's few have lived a harder lot,
Poor Old Gran!
But she toiled on and murmured not;
Poor Old Gran!
For us she toiled on starvingly,
And fought the wolf of poverty;
Upon her heart's blood suckled me,
Our Poor Old Gran!

Her river of life hath roughly rolled;
Poor Old Gran!
A Wreck lies dark, its tale untold,
Poor Old Gran!
Yet shall her old heart laugh with ye,
My Birdsnest in the mouldering tree!
And soft in heaven her bed shall be!
Poor Old Gran!

The grip of Poverty is grim;
        Poor Old Gran!
Lustres of lip and eye soon dim;
        Poor Old Gran!
But thro' the frailty of her face
There gleams a light of tender grace,
Or else I see thro' a tearful haze
        Poor Old Gran!

You came in all our sorrowings,
        Poor Old Gran!
How your weakness hurried on wings,
        Poor Old Gran!
You stood at Bridal, Birth, and Bier:
Our darlings dead and gone seem near
When you are near, and make more dear
        Our Poor Old Gran!

So come to our Cottage up the lane,
        Poor Old Gran!
Follow our fortune's harvest wain,
        Poor Old Gran!
We 'll shelter you from wind and rain,
Hunger you shall not know again,
Plenty shall smile away your pain,
        Poor Old Gran!

And little laughing Stars shall rise
        On Poor Old Gran!
In the clear heaven of Childhood's eyes,
        For Poor Old Gran!
Wee fingers, stroking her grey hair,
Shall almost melt the hoarfrost there,
Wee lips shall kiss away the care
        From Poor Old Gran!

So come and sit beside our hearth,
        Poor Old Gran!
Come from the darkness and the dearth,

Poor Old Gran!
And you shall be our fireside guest,
And weary heart and head shall rest;
And may your last days be your best,
Our Poor Old Gran.

NEWS OF CHRISTIE.

We read your Letters! no word lost;
All, all is rememberéd;
And often when there comes no Post,
Once more are the old ones read.

Of all she did we love to hear,
And how the days have sped;
But to our listening hearts most dear
Is something "Christie said."

LITTLE WILLIE.

Poor little Willie,
With his many pretty wiles;
Worlds of wisdom in his looks,
And quaint, quiet smiles;
Hair of amber, toucht with
Gold of heaven so brave;
All lying darkly hid
In a Workhouse Grave.

You remember little Willie;
Fair and funny fellow! he
Sprang like a lily
From the dirt of poverty.

Poor little Willie!
  Not a friend was nigh,
When, from the cold world,
  He croucht down to die.

In the day we wandered foodless,
  Little Willie cried for bread;
In the night we wandered homeless,
  Little Willie cried for bed.
Parted at the Workhouse door,
  Not a word we said:
Ah, so tired was poor Willie,
  And so sweetly sleep the dead.

'T was in the dead of winter
  We laid him in the earth;
The world brought in the New Year,
  On a tide of mirth.
But, for lost little Willie,
  Not a tear we crave;
Cold and Hunger cannot wake him,
  In his Workhouse Grave.

We thought him beautiful,
  Felt it hard to part;
We loved him dutiful;
  Down, down, poor heart!
The storms they may beat;
  The winter winds may rave;
Little Willie feels not,
  In his Workhouse Grave.

No room for little Willie;
  In the world he had no part;
On him stared the Gorgon-eye,
  Thro' which looks no heart.
Come to me, said Heaven;
  And, if Heaven will save,
Little matters though the door
  Be a Workhouse Grave.

CHRISTIE'S PORTRAIT.

I.

YOUR tiny picture makes me yearn;
  We are so far apart!
My Darling, I can only turn
  And kiss you in my heart.
A thousand tender thoughts a-wing
  Swarm in a summer clime,
And hover round it murmuring
  Like bees at honey-time

II.

Upon a little girl I look
  Whose pureness makes me sad;
I read as in a holy book,
  I grow in secret glad!
It seems my darling comes to me
  With something I have lost
Over life's tossed and troubled sea,
  On some celestial coast.

III.

I think of her when spirit-bowed;
  A glory fills the place!
Like sudden light on swords, the proud
  Smile flashes in my face:
And others see, in passing by,
  But cannot understand
The vision shining in mine eye,
  My strength of heart and hand.

IV.

That grave content and touching grace,
  Bring tears into mine eyes;
She makes my heart a holy place
  Where hymns and incense rise!

Such calm her gentle spirit brings
As — smiling overhead —
White statued saints with peaceful wings
Shadow the sleeping dead.

V.

Our Christie is no rosy Grace
With beauty all may see
But I have never felt a face
Grow half so dear to me.
No curling hair about her brows,
Like many merry girls;
Well, straighter to my heart it goes
And round it curls and curls.

VI.

Meek as the wood anemone glints
To see if heaven be blue,
Is my pale flower with her sweet tints
Of heaven shining thro'!
She will be poor and never fret,
Sleep sound and lowly lie;
Will live her quiet life, and let
The great world-storm go by.

VII.

Dear love! God keep Her in His grasp,
Meek maiden, or brave Wife!
Till His good Angels softly clasp
Her closéd book of life;
And this fair picture of the Sun,
With birthday blessings given,
Shall fade before a glorious one
Taken of her in heaven.

MY MAID MARIAN.

I.

SPRING comes with violet eyes unveiled,
  Her fragrant lips apart!
And Earth smiles up as tho' she held
  Most honeyed thoughts at heart.
But nevermore will Spring arise
Dancing in sparkles of *her* eyes.

II.

A gracious wind low-breathing comes
  As from the fields of God;
The old lost Eden newly blooms
  From out the sunny sod.
My buried joy stirs with the earth,
And tries to sun *its* sweetness forth.

III.

The trees move in their slumbering,
  Dreaming of one that's near!
Put out their feelers for the Spring,
  To wake, and find her here!
My spirit on the threshold stands,
And stretches out its waiting hands;

IV.

Then goeth from me in a stream
  Of yearning; wave on wave
Slides thro' the stillness of a dream,
  To little Marian's grave:
For all the miracle of Spring
My long lost child will never bring.

V.

Where blooms the golden crocus-burst,
  And Winter's tenderling,

There lies our little Snowdrop! first
  Of Flowers in our love's spring!
How all the year's young beauties blow
About her there, I know, I know.

VI.

The Blackbird with his warble wet,
  The Thrush with reedy thrill,
Open their hearts to Spring, and let
  The influence have its will!
Tho' all around the Spring hath smiled,
She seems to have kissed where lies my child.

VII.

In purple shadow and golden shine
  Old Arthur's Seat is crowned;
Like shapes of Silence crystalline
  The great white clouds sail round!
The Dead at rest the long day thro'
Lie calm against the pictured blue.

VIII.

Thro' shutting Eve the stars may peep,
  But still there comes no night;
Only the Day hath fallen asleep,
  And smiles in dreams of light:
As tho' she felt the heart of Love
Beating in silent stars above.

IX.

O Marian, my maid Marian,
  So strange it seems to me!
That you, the Household's darling one
  So soon should cease to be.
Ah, was it that our praying breath
Might kindle heavenward fires of faith?

X.

So much forgiven for your sake
  When bitter words were said,

And little arms about the neck
  With blessings bowed the head!
So happy as we might have been,
Our hearts more close with you between.

XI.

Dear early Dew-drop! such a gleam
  Of sun from heaven you drew,
We little thought that smiling beam
  Would drink our precious dew!
But back to heaven our dew was kissed,
We saw it pass in mournful mist.

XII.

Our lowly home was lofty-crowned
  With three sweet budding girls!
Our sacred marriage-ring set round
  With darling wee love-pearls!
One jewel from the ring is gone,
One fills a grave in Warriston.

XIII.

We bore her beauty in our breast,
  As heaven bears the Dawn,
We brooded over her dear nest,
  Still close and closer drawn.
Hearts thrilled and listened, watched and throbbed,
And strayed not, — yet the nest was robbed!

XIV.

"Stay yet a little while, Beloved!"
  In vain our prayerful breath!
Across heaven's lighted window moved
  The shadow of black Death.
In vain our hands were stretched to save,
There closed the gateways of the Grave!

XV.

Could my death-vision have darkened up
  In her sweet face, my child;

I scarce should see the bitter cup
  I could have drank and smiled:
Blessing her with my last-wrung breath,
Dear Angel in my dream of death.

XVI.

Her memory is like music we
  Have heard some singers sing,
That thrills life thro', and echoingly
  Our hearts forever ring;
We try it o'er and o'er again,
But ne'er recall that wondrous strain.

XVII.

My proud heart like a river runs,
  Lying awake o' nights;
I see her with the shining Ones
  Upon the shining heights.
And a wee Angel-face will peep
Down starlike thro' the veil of sleep.

XVIII.

My yearnings try to get them wings
  And float me up afar,
As in the Dawn the sky-lark springs
  To reach some distant Star
That all night long swam down to him
In brightness, but at morn grew dim.

XIX.

She is a spirit of light that leavens
  The darkness where we wait;
And starlike opens in the heavens
  A little golden gate!
O may we wake and find her near
When work and sleep are over here!

XX.

No sweetness to this world of ours
  Is without purpose given,

The fragrance that goes up from flowers
  May be their seed in Heaven.
We saw Heaven in her face, may we
Her future face in Heaven see.

XXI.

In some far spring of brighter bloom,
  More life, and ampler breath,
My bud hath burst the folding gloom,
  A-flower from dusty death!
We wonder will she be much grown?
And how will her new name be known?

XXII.

I saw her ribboned robe this morn,
  Mine own lost little child;
Wee shoes her tiny feet had worn,
  And then my heart grew wild.
We only trust our hearts to peep
In on them when we want to weep.

XXIII.

But hearts will break or eyes must weep,
  And so we bend above
These treasures of old days that keep
  The fragrance of young love.
The harvest-field tho' reapt and bare
Will find a patient gleaner there.

XXIV.

I never think of her sweet eyes
  In dusky death now dim,
But waters of my heart will rise,
  And there they smile and swim,
Forget-me-nots so blue, so dear,
Swim in the waters of a tear.

XXV.

How often in the days gone by
  She lifted her dear head,

And stretcht wee arms for me to lie
  Down in her little bed.
And cradled in my happy breast
Was softly carried into rest.

XXVI.

And now when life is sore oppressed
  And runs with weary wave,
I long to lay me down and rest
  In little Marian's grave.
To smile as peaceful as she smiled—
For I am now the nestling child.

XXVII.

Immortal Love, a spirit of bliss
  And brightness, moves above,
While here forever Sorrow is
  The shadow cast by Love.
But love for her no sorrow will bring
And no more tearful leaves-taking.

XXVIII.

No passing sorrows on their march
  Will leave sad foot-prints now,
No troubles strain the tender arch
  Of that white baby brow.
No cares to cloud, no tears that come
To rob the cheek of pearly bloom.

XXIX.

All sweetest shapes that Beauty wears
  Are round about her drawn;
Auroral bloom, and vernal airs,
  And blessings of the dawn;
All loveliness that ne'er grows less;
Time cannot touch her tenderness.

XXX.

One sparkle of immortal light
  Our love for her shall shine

In that dew-drop that nestles white
  At heart with gleam divine,
But vanishes from Death's cold clasp,
When he the flower of life doth grasp.

XXXI.

The patient calm that comes with years,
  Hath made us cease to fret,
Tho' sometimes in the sudden tears
  Dumb hearts will quiver yet.
And each one turns the face, and tries
To hide WHO looks thro' parent eyes.

ROBIN'S SONG.

SING, Robin Redbreast,
  Tho' you fill our hearts with pain;
Sing, bonny Robin,
  Tho' our tears fall like the rain
For a Lamb far from the fold,
In the wet and wintry mould!
For a Bird out in the cold,
    Bird alane! Bird alane!

Sing, Robin Redbreast!
  You are welcome to our door;
Sing, darling Robin,
  Merry Larks no longer soar.
Autumn comes with feel of rain,
Mournful odours, wail of pain!
There's a Bird will come again
    Nevermore! Nevermore!

Sing, Robin Redbreast!
  For we love your song so brave,

Tho' you mind us of a Robin
 Where the willows weep and wave
To *her* little grave it clings,
Shakes the rain from its wet wings,
And for all the sadness sings
  By Her grave, by Her grave.

THE MAIDEN MARRIAGE.

SHE sat in her virgin bower
 Half sad with fancies sweet,
And wist not Love drew softly nigh,
 Till she nestled at his feet.
"Arise, arise, thou fair Maiden!
 And adieu, adieu, thou dear!
But meet me, meet me at the Kirk,
 In the May-time of the year."

Up in her face of holy grace
 The startled splendour broke;
Her smile was as a dream of Heaven
 Fulfilled whene'er she spoke.
She felt such bliss in her beauty
 And pleasure in her power
To richly clothe her perfect love
 For a peerless marriage dower.

"Now kiss me, kiss me, Mother dear;
 He calls me, I must go!"
She went to the Kirk at tryste-time,
 In raiment like the snow.
But he who claspt her there was Death;
 And he hath led her where
No voice is heard, there is no breath,
 Upon the frosty air.

NOT LOST, BUT GONE BEFORE.

ONE of God's own Darlings was my bosom's nestling Dove,
With her looks of love and sunshine, and her voice so rich and low:
How it trembled thro' my life, like an Immortal's kiss of love!
How its music yearns thro' all my memory now!

O! her beauty rainbows round me, and her sweet smile, silverly
As a song, fills all the silence of the Midnight's charmèd hours;
And I know from out her grave she'll send her love in death to me,
By the Spring in smiling utterance of Flowers.

O! my Love, too good for Earth, has gone into the land of light;
'T was hard, she said, to leave me, but the Lord had need of her;
And she walks the heavens in glory like a Star i' the crown of Night,
With the Beautiful and Blessed mingling there.

Gone before me, to be clothed on with bridal robe of white,
Where Love's blossom flowers to fruit, and suffering 's glorified!
And my love shall make me meet and worthy of her presence bright,
That in heaven I may claim her as my Bride.

THE POET.

A VAGRANT Wild Flower sown by God,
  Out in the waste was born;
It sprang up as a Corn-flower
  In the golden fields of Corn:
The Corn all strong and stately
  In its bearded bravery grew —
Gathered the gold for harvest —
  Grew ripe, in sun and dew;
And when it bowed the head, — as Wind
  And Shadow ran their race,
Like influences from Heaven
  Come to Earth, for playing place, —
It seemed to look down on the Flower
  As in a smiling scorn,
Poor thing! you grow no grain for food,
  Or garner, said the Corn.
The bonny Flower felt lonely,
  Its look grew tearful sad,
Till came a smile of sunshine
  And its beauty grew so glad!
Ah, bonny Flower! it bloomed its best
  Contented with its place,
God's blessing fell upon it
  As it lookt up in His face;
And there they grew together
  Till the Reapers white-wing'd came —
All their Sickles shining!
  All their faces were a-flame; —
The Corn they reapt for earthly use,
  But an Angel fell in love
With that Wild Flower and wore it
  At the Harvest-home above.

LITTLE LILYBELL.

WHEN unseen fingers part the leaves,
To show us Beauty's face;
And Earth her breast of glory heaves,
And glows from Spring's embrace:
Flowers Fairy-like on coloured wings
Float up, — Life's sea doth swell
And flush a world of vernal things,
Came little Lilybell.

And like a blessed Bird of calm
Our love's sweet wants she stilled,
Made Passion's fiery wine run balm, —
Life's glory half fulfilled!
From dappled dawn to twinkling dark,
Our witching Ariel
Moves thro' our heaven! O, like a lark
Sings little Lilybell!

And she is fair — ay, very fair!
With eyes so like the dove;
And lightly leans her world of care
Upon our arms of love!
It cannot be that ye will break
The promise-tale ye tell;
Ye will not make such fond hearts ache,
Our little Lilybell!

As on Life's stream her leaflets spread,
And tremble in its flow,
We shudder lest the awful Dead
Pluck at her from below!
Breathe faint and low, ye winds that start;
O stream, but softly swell;
Your every motion smites the heart
For little Lilybell!

We tremble lest the Angel Death,
  Who comes to gather flowers
For Paradise, at her sweet breath
  Should fall in love with ours!
O, many a year may come and go,
  Ere from Life's mystic well
Such stream shall flow, such flower shall blow,
  As little Lilybell!

Ah, when her dear heart fills with fears,
  And aches with Love's sweet pain,
And pale cheeks burn thro' happy tears,
  Like red rose in the rain!
I marvel, Sweet, if we shall see
  The sight, and say 't is well,
When the Beloved calls for thee,
  Our dainty Lilybell!

How rich Love made the lowly sod,
  Where such a flower hath blown!
O Love, we love, and think that God
  Is such a love full-grown!
Dear God! that gave the blessed trust,
  Be near, that all be well;
And morn and eve bedew our dust,
  For love of Lilybell!

OUR WHITE DOVE.

A WHITE DOVE out of heaven flew,
  White as the whitest shape of Grace
  That nestles in the soft embrace
Of heaven when skies are summer blue;

It came with dew-drop purity,
  On glad wings of the morning light,
  And sank into our life, so white
A VISION! sweetly, secretly!

Silently nestled our WHITE DOVE:
  Balmily made our bosoms swim
  With still delight, and overbrim;
The air it breathed was breath of love:

Our Dove had eyes of Baby blue,
  Soft as the speedwell's by the way,
  That looketh up as it would say,
"Who kissed me while I slept, did you?"

God love it! but we took our Bird,
  And loved it well, and merry made;
  We sang and danced around, or prayed
In silence, wherein hearts are heard.

It seemed to come from far green fields
  To meet us over life's rough sea,
  With leaf of promise from the tree
In which a dearer nest it builds.

As fondling Mother birds will pull
  The softest feathers from their breast,
  We gave our best to line the nest
And make it warm and beautiful!

We held it as the leaves of life
  In hidden silent service fold
  About a Rose's heart of gold,
So jealous of all outer strife!

When holy sleep in soothing palms
  Pillowed the darling little head,
  How lightly moved we round the bed,
And felt the silence fall in balms!

But all we did or tried to do,
  Our flood of joy it never felt;
  Only into our hearts would melt
Still deeper those dove-eyes of blue.

Quick with the spirit of field and wood,
  All other Birds would sing and sing
  Till hearts did ripple and homes did ring:
Our white Dove only cooed and cooed —

With every day some sweetness new,
  And night and day and day and night
  It was the voice of our delight,
That gentle, low, endearing coo!

God! if we were to lose our child!
  O, we must die, poor hearts would cry:
  She lookt on us so hushingly;
So mournfully to herself she smiled.

One day she pined up in our face
  With a low cry we could not still,
  A moaning we could never heal,
For sleep in some more quiet place.

We could not help and yet must see
  The little head droop wearily,
  The little eyes shine eerily,
My Dove! what have they done to thee?

The look grew pleading in her eyes,
  And mournful as the lonesome light
  That in a window burns all night,
Asking for stillness, while one dies.

The hand of Death so coldly clings,
  So strongly draws the weak life-wave
  Into his dark, vast, silent cave;
Our little Dove must use its wings!

And so it sought the dearer nest;
  A little way across the sea
  It kept us wingèd company,
Then sank into its leafier rest.

And left us long ago to feel
  A sadness in the sweetest words,
  A broken heartstring mid the chords
A tone more tremulous when we kneel.

But, dear my Christie, do not cry,
  Our White Dove left for you and me
  Such blessed promise as must be
Perfected in the heavens high.

The stars that shone in her dear eyes
  May be a little while withdrawn
  To rise and lead the eternal dawn
For us, up heaven in other skies.

Our Bird of God but soars and sings:
  Oft when life's heaving wave 's at rest,
  She makes her mirror in my breast,
I feel a winnowing of wings.

And meekly doth she minister
  Glad thoughts of comfort, thrills of pride;
  She makes me feel that if I died
This moment I should go to her.

Be good! and you shall find her where
  No wind can shake the wee bird's nest;
  No dreams can break the wee bird's rest;
No night, no pain, no parting there!

No echoes of old storms gone by!
  Earth's sorrows slumber peacefully;
  The weary are at rest, and He
Shall wipe the tears from every eye.

OUR LITTLE CHILD WITH RADIANT EYES.

WITH seeking hearts we still grope on,
 Where dropt our jewel in the dust:
The looking crowd have long since gone,
 And still we seek with lonely trust:
 O little Child with radiant eyes!

In all our heart-ache we are drawn,
 Unweeting, to your little grave;
There, on your heavenly shores of dawn,
 Breaks gentlier Sorrow's sobbing wave:
 O little Child with radiant eyes!

Dark underneath the brightening sod,
 The sweetest life of all our years
Is crowded in ae gift to God.
 Outside the gate we stand in tears!
 O little Child with radiant eyes!

Heart-empty as the acorn-cup
 That only fills with wintry showers,
The breaking cloud but brimmeth up
 With tears this pleading life of ours.
 O little Child with radiant eyes!

We think of you, our Angel kith,
 Till life grows light with starry leaven:
We never forget you, Darling with
 The gold hair waving high in heaven!
 Our little Child with radiant eyes!

Your white wings grown you will conquer Death!
 You are coming through our dreams even now,
With azure peep of heaven beneath

The arching glory of your brow,
Our little Child with radiant eyes!

We cannot pierce the dark, but oft
You see us with looks of pitying balm;
A hint of heaven — a touch more soft
Than kisses — all the trouble is calm.
Our little Child with radiant eyes!

Think of us wearied in the strife,
And when we sit by Sorrow's streams,
Shake down upon our drooping life
The dew that brings immortal dreams.
Our little Child with radiant eyes!

THE SUNBEAM AND THE ROSE.

"PRETTY Rosebud, are thy emerald
Curtains still undrawn?
Odalisque of Flowers, —
Tender soul o' the fervid South!
I am dainty of thy beauty,
All this dewy dawn;
I am fainting for the ruddy
Kisses of thy mouth."

Sweetly sang the Sunbeam,
With a voice made low to win;
Round the Rose-heart playing,
Till it toucht the tenderest strings;
"Pretty Rosebud, ope thy lattice,
Let thy true love in."
And for Heaven down-wavering warm,
She waved her leafy wings!
LISTEN, CHRISTIE, TO MY SONG O' THE SUNBEAM AND THE ROSE.

Out she sprang, kiss-coloured,
  In her eyes the dews of bliss;
All her beauty glowing
  With a blush of bridal light!
Gave her balm and bloom for banquet
  To the golden kiss;
Proudly oped each chamber
  For a princelier delight.

Soon the Serpent of Sweetness,
  Sated, could no longer stay;
And away he went, a-wooing
  Every flower that blows!
'T was the reign of Roses
  When that Sunbeam passed to-day:
Lonely in her rifled ruin
  Droopt the dying Rose.
LISTEN, CHRISTIE, TO MY SONG O' THE SUNBEAM AND THE ROSE.

CRAIGCROOK ROSES.

CRAIGCROOK Roses! red and golden,
  All a-glowing; faint with passion;
To the sweet flower-soul unfolden:
  Wreathe me in the old Greek fashion.
Queen of sweetness, crowned with splendour,
  Every rich round bud uncloses;
Yet so meek and womanly tender
  Are you royal Craigcrook Roses,
  Warm and winy Craigcrook Roses.

Leaning with some unknown yearning,
  You would make a lover sin, you
Pretty wooers, archly turning
  As you climb to make us win you.

Ripe perfection of fair fulness
  In your gracious bloom reposes;
And an emerald bower for coolness,
  Summer builds my Craigcrook Roses,
  Amorous-dreaming Craigcrook Roses.

When the year is old and hoary,
  And the day is dark with dolours;
Still you come, my guests of glory,
  In voluptuous dance of colours.
And — tho' Earth like Age is toiling
  In the snow-drifts — perfumed posies
Kiss me, crown my spirit smiling
  Down a dream of Craigcrook Roses,
  Dear, delicious Craigcrook Roses.

Fairest of Light's daughters seven,
  With your dainty dreamy graces;
You might light with loving leaven
  Smiles of spring in wintriest faces
At the solemn shut of daylight
  When the fair life-vision closes;
May my spirit float away light
  On a cloud of Craigcrook Roses,
  Cooled and crowned with Craigcrook Roses

THE SINGER.

Up out of the Corn the Lark caroll'd in light,
Like a new splendour sprung from the dark husk
    of Night,
Green light shimmer'd laughing o'er forest and sod;
The rich sky was full of the presence of God,
And with brave careless rapture he lavisht around
Rare violet fancies and rose-leaves of sound:
All thro' the Morn's sun city sea-like his psalm

With melodious waves dasht the bright world of calm:
BUT HEAVILY HUNG THE DROOPT EARS OF THE CORN:
THEY WERE GATHERING GOLD IN THE DEWY MORN.

And he sang, as on heaven's fire-grains he had fed,
Till his heart's merry wine had made drunken his head.
How he sang! as his honey in Life's cells ne'er dwindled,
And bon-fires of Joy on all Life's hills were kindled:
O! he sang, as he felt that to singing was given
The magic to build rainbow-stairways to heaven!
And he could not have sung with more lusty cheer,
Had all the world listened a-tiptoe to hear!
ALL THE WHILE HEAVILY HUNG THE CORN,
AND ITS DROWSY EARS HEARD NOT THE SWEETHEART OF MORN.

A MAIDEN'S SONG.

I LOVE! and Love hath given me
Sweet thoughts to God akin,
And oped a living Paradise
My heart of hearts within:
O from this Eden of my life
God keep the Serpent Sin!

I love! and into Angel-land
With starry glimpses peer!
I drink in beauty like heaven-wine,
When One is smiling near!

And there's a Rainbow round my soul
For every falling tear.

Dear God in heaven! keep without stain
My bosom's brooding Dove:
O clothe it meet for angel-arms,
And give it place above!
For there is nothing from the world
I yearn to take, but Love.

POOR BIDDY.

Poor Biddy was peculiarly proud,
And often passed along the public road
Riding a Stick: She would have been a witch
In the old days, and weirdily filled her niche.

The mocking Bairns would cry, as she would stalk,
"Biddy, you might as well on two legs walk;"
And she would say, says she, the poor daftling!
"I might! but for the grandeur of the thing."

Alas, how many pitiful tricks we play
Like Biddy, in less Natural kind o' way:
And ride our stick, and have our foolish fling,
God help us! for the grandeur of the thing.

WHEN CHRISTIE COMES AGAIN.

WHEN the merry spring-tide
  Floods all the land;
Nature hath a Mother's heart,
  Gives with open hand;
Flowers running up the lane
  Tell us May is near.
Christie will be coming then!
  Christie will be here!
O the merry spring-tide!
  We 'll be glad in sun or rain,
In the merry, merry days
  When Christie comes again.

Pure is her meek nature,
  Clear as morning dew,
We can see the Angel
  Almost shining through;
To Earth's sweetest blessing
  She the best from Heaven did bring;
Good Genius of our Love-lamp!
  Fine Spirit of the Ring!
O the merry spring-tide!
  We 'll be glad in sun or rain,
In the merry, merry days
  When Christie comes again.

All our joys we 'll tell her,
  But for her dear sake,
Not a word of Sorrow,
  Lest her little heart would ache.
She shall dance and swing and sing,
  Do as she likes best;
Only I must have her hand
  In ramble or in rest.

O the merry spring-tide!
  We 'll be glad in sun or rain,
In the merry, merry days
  When Christie comes again.

We 'll romp in jewelled meadows,
  Hunt in dingles cool with leaves,
Where all night the Nightingale
  Melodiously grieves.
In her cheek so tender
  The shy and dainty rose,
Shall gaily come for kisses,
  To every wind that blows.
O the merry spring-tide!
  We 'll be glad in sun or rain,
In the merry, merry days
  When Christie comes again.

Hope will lay so many eggs
  In her little nest;
Don't your heart run over,
  Christie, in your breast?
Thinking how we 'll greet you
  Safe once more at home,
Ours will run to meet you,
  Often ere you come.
O the merry spring-tide!
  We 'll be glad in sun or rain,
In the merry, merry days
  When Christie comes again.

O the joy in our house,
  Hearts dancing wild!
Christie will be coming soon,
  She 's our darling child.
Holy dew of heaven
  In each eyelid starts,
Feeling all her dearness,
  Darling of all hearts.

O the merry spring-tide!
  We'll be glad in sun or rain,
In the merry, merry days
  When Christie comes again.

Dreary was our winter;
  Come! and all the place
Shall breath a summer sweetness,
  And wear a happy face;
There will be a sun-smile
  On stern, old Calaby,
Tender as the spring-gold
  On our old Oak-Tree!
O the merry spring-tide!
  We'll be glad in sun or rain,
In the merry, merry days
  When Christie comes again.

Jack, the Dog, will run before,
  First to reach the Rail;
Jack, the Pony, whisk you home,
  With long trotting tail!
We have had our struggles, dear,
  But could n't part with Jack;
We shall all be waiting there,
  To welcome Christie back!
O the merry spring-tide!
  We'll be glad in sun or rain,
In the merry, merry days
  When Christie comes again.

Then blow you Winds, and shake up
  The sleeping flower-beds!
Make the Violets wake up,
  The Daisies lift their heads;
The Lilacs float in fragrance,
  Dim-purple, saintly-white!
And bring the bonny bairn to us,
  The flower of our delight.

O the merry spring-tide!
  We'll be glad in sun or rain,
In the merry, merry days
  When Christie comes again.

ONLY A DREAM.

ONLY A DREAM.

The silvery veil of Sleep came trembling down
Like sweet snow white and warm in a silent world,
And softly covered up the face of life.
The nurse-like Spirit laid my body to rest,
And went to meet her Bridegroom in the night,
Who comes like music o'er the star-shored sea,
And clasps her at the portal with a kiss.
When lo, a hand reacht thro' the dark, and drew
Her gliding wraith-like on, and looking up
The unfeatured gloom grew into Charmian's face.
I read her look, and we two wandered forth
In the cool glory of the glimmering night:
The Earth lay faint with love at the feet of Heaven:
Her breath of incense went up thro' the leaves
In a lown sough of bliss. Warm winds on tiptoe
Walkt over the tall tree-tops. Above us burned
The golden legends on Night's prophet-brow;
The Moon rose o'er the city, a glory of gold;
Around us Life rehearst Death's mystery.
And Charmian wore her June-like loveliness
As in a stole of sorrow; by day she moved
In some serene elysium; queenly sweet,
And gracious; breathing beauty; a heaven of dreams
In her large lotus eyes, darkly divine:
Warm-wingéd Ardours plumed her parted lips.
But now her blooming Life's luxuriant flower
Seemed withered into ashen spirit-fruit,
And like a spirit flasht her white, lit face!
Portentous things which hid themselves by day,
Sweet-shadowed 'neath her sunning beauty-bloom,
Came peering thro' the dim and sorrowy night.

Her lips, red-ripe to crush their fire-strong wine,
Pouting persuasive in perpetual kiss,
Were thin with anguish, bitter with pale pain.
And from the windows whence young Beauty laught
As Age went by, a life of suffering lookt,
And perisht visions flasht their phantom light.
White waves of sea-like soul had climbed, and dasht
The red light from its heaven of her cheek.
Her bounteous breast that breathed magnificence,
And billowed with proud blood, sighed meekly now.
The flowers her Spartan spirit crowned her with
For the life-battle, dropt about her dead.
Diaphanous in the moonlight grew her life
With all its written agony visible;
Down the dark deep of her great grief I stared,
And saw the Wreck with all its dead around.
And my heart melted in its mournfulness;
She moaned, as hers were breaking in its pain;
And then her voice vibrated piteous as
A Spirit wailing in a world of tears,
But stifled half its pathos not to hurt.

"Earth sleepeth in the moonlight's mystic grace,
The breath of blessings round her; and all heaven
Is passing thro' her dream; it trembles near;
She feels the Seraph-kisses on her face;
But she will wake at morn in tears to find
The glory gone — all was a dream o' the night.
And thus my young Life slumbered, dreamed, and
woke!

"It ran in shadow like the woodland brook,
Feeling its way, with yearnings for the light,
Until it surges flashing in the sun,
And takes a crown of radiance on its head.
Even so I found him whom my soul had sought,
And fled into his breast with a cry of triumph,
Who lit up all things beautiful for me.
And thro' my happy tears there lookt in mine

A face as sweet as morning violets,
A face alight with love ineffable,
The starry heart-hid wonder trembling through:
And o'er me leaned, — as Spring-heaven over earth,
Dropping her love down in a rain of flowers, —
To feed me with all flowers of delight,
And crown me as his queen of all delight.
Light hung a garland grace about his brow ;
His voice, like footprints in the yielding snow,
Sank deepest with its softest fall of words.
He gave the casket of his happiness
Rich with Love's jewel for my hands to keep.
Around his stalwart beauty twined my life,
In golden oneness, and in proud repose ;
And like a God he claspt me with his strength!
And like a God he held me in his heaven;
And all the air was golden with my God.

"Alas, that Woman's life divorced from Man's,
And seeking to be one again in love,
So often flies back thro' the grim wide wound!
Alas, that Time should crown with fruit of pain,
That seed from Eden whose fair flower is love!
They tore me from my Love! they thrust him forth,
Spurned his rich love, and scorned his poverty;
Rent all the twining tendrils of my life
To shrink back bleeding in their desolate home.
My heart was shivered like the charmèd cup
That, breaking, brings the Hall in ruins round;
And every fragment mirrored the great wrong!

"And while my mind yet wandered dark and dumb,
They sold me to a Worldling wrinkled, rich
And rotten, who bought Love's sweet name for gold.
They drest me in bride-flowers who should have worn
The white and wimpled weeds of widowhood,
And led me forth, a jewelled mockery!

'Twas like a wedding with the sheeted dead,
In silent hurry, and white ghastliness.
No bosoms beat Love's cymbals music-matcht;
No blisses blusht, no bridal-kisses burned.
The ring was on my hand, few saw the chain
By which my Husband drew me to his home,
And many envied me my happiness.
That night as we sat alone I felt his eyes
Burningly brand me to the core, his Slave.

"I dwelt amid a wildering world of wealth,
Which flamed a glistering glory, bloomed a warmth
Without, within was cold as a fireless hearth.
The Image of Nuptial Love to which they led me
A maiden sacrifice i' the Sanctuary,
That should have raised me, smiled my tears away,
And into quickness all my coldness kist,
And fed with precious oil the lamp of love
That in my heart, as in a tomb, burned on,
Was a gaunt Skeleton whose grave-like arms
Claspt me for ever to a loveless breast.

"He was a cruel Tyrant, just too mean
To murder, altho' pitiless as the grave;
A human ink-fish spreading clouds around
When eyes of tender ruth would come too near.
He had a thin-lipt lust of power which lookt
On torture in no rage of fiery blood,
But with infernal light of gloating eyes.
And yet I strove to love him. O my God!
While reaching from the heights of blessedness,
To pluck the rainbow-fruit Heaven held to me,
How had I fallen into a chasm that closed
Its dark inevitable arms, and crusht
Me, bruised and blind! I struck, and struck, and beat
With bleeding strength, in vain. A hundred hands
Fought in the gloom with mine as water weak.
At every step there stirred some hissing snake.

I felt as one that's bound, and buried alive;
The black, dank death-mould stampt down overhead,
And cried, and cried, and cried, but no help came.

"I heard the sounds above me far away;
The feet of hurrying Life, and loitering Love;
Rich bursts of music, hum of low, sweet talk;
The dance of Pleasure dancing in her heaven,
And rustling rain of a thousand dear delights.
I knew the pictured world was lighted up,
And bloomed, like bridal-chamber, soft and warm:
How sang the merry, merry birds of bliss;
How Beauty's flower-guests stood crowned and drank
The health of Heaven in its own brave wine.
But not a crumb of all the glad life-feast,
Nor drop of all the wanton wealth for me,
And if I stretcht weak arms to clasp my world,
A wormy mouth to my wild warmth was prest,
And if I turned to lift a prayer to God,
Above me burned two eyes like bottomless pits
In which a nest of devils lurk and leer.
And down my night there stoopt no smiling heaven,
With golden chances of a starry throne,
And beckoning looks that bid us come be crowned.

"Around me rose the phantoms of the dark,
The Grave's Somnambules troubled in their dream
Who walk and wander in the sleep of Death,
And cannot rest, they were so wronged in life.
The crownless Martyrs of the marriage-ring!
Meek sufferers who walkt in living hell,
And died a life of spiritual suttee.
They came to claim their kin in misery,
And show me, as they passed in shadowy train,
Their symbols of unutterable woe,—
Scarred loves that bore the rack and told no tale;
Tear-drownéd hearts and stifled agonies;

The bleeding lips struck dumb by brutal hands;
Slow murders of the curtained bridal-bed;
The silent tortures and the shrouded deaths.

"I wandered with them in the pitiless night
Who seek the jewel fallen from Life's crown;
Oft stumbling, bled upon the cruel thorns,
But rose, and struggled on. I strained mine eyes
Upon the dark, and raised mine empty cup;
Surely with one gold drop of honey-dew,
Somewhere the heavens ran o'er t' enrich my life?

"Then came to me a thing most sweet and strange,
As tho' an angel kist me in the night,
Or Magic Rose flusht sudden in the gloom.
A loosening charm wrought in my brain; the weight
That ached to be dasht out in utter death,
Was melting like a wintry clod in flowers.
In love's dead ashes burst a spark. I cried,
'O sweet light-bringer, in a bloom of dawn
Rise, let me see what treasure I have found!
My rich, warm jewel, crimson with sweet life,
Come shine where now I cross but empty palms,
And clasp the new love-raiment radiant round.
My little Bird shall hurry out the night,
Till all my world is toucht with rosy gold:
My little Bird of God shall sit and sing
The dear day long, the dearer for the dark!

"'If thou rise beautiful from Sorrow's sea,
As Venice, Sorrow's Child, is Beauty's Queen,
Perchance thy little smiles, my Babe, may bring
Some human softness in his face, and I
Shall press the hand that hurts, for thy dear sake.
And I shall walk with thee, my Child, with thee,
Beneath new heavens, on an enchanted earth.
When I enfold thee in my arms, sweet Babe,
My heart will scarcely breathe lest it should wake

The sleeping wings of its new-nestling bliss.
When thou art born, my Child, all will be well;
For surely Love but vanisht in the dark
To come back in the morning with my Babe;
And all the sweetness liveth on when all
The bitterness is past; and eyes that yearn
Wet thro' the gloom are glorified at last.
Soft baby-fingers feeling round my heart
Shall melt its frost; and baby-lips shall draw
My tears in milk, and suck my sorrows dry.
All hell may wrestle in one human heart;
All heaven will nestle in my drop of dew.'

"It came, my dazzling dawn's re-orient hope!
My tiny babe, with its sweet mournful eyes!
And the pale innocent but fanned his hate
To frenzy; for, in many a desolate day,
And midnight, lying with my heart awake,
I had turned tearfully to look upon
A precious picture worn by Memory,
And in its beauteous image grew my Babe:
Its luminous look had gathered all the light
That lost beloved Presence left with me.

"He poured his poison in the brimming glass
My babe-joy-bearer lifted to my lips,
And dasht the new love-vintage in the dust.
I ran the gauntlet of his hell for years,
And fell down on the threshold mad. My Child!
They took my Babe from me, my pleading Babe;
And when the pretty one pined for me, and cried.
Straining his dim eyes for me till he died;
They called the Mother in to see her child
That lay there in the little shroud with all
Its beauty folded up for God in heaven:
Dead! dead! its dear eyes closed by stranger hands.

"Much misery hath not made my spirit meek:
Mine agony rends the bridal-veil: I cry,

Come see what ghastly wounds bleed hidden here
Behold where all the Tortures of the Past
Are stored by Law, and sanctified for use.
I drag my burthen to a nation's throne,
And pray deliverance from this Tyrant's power.
Pity me, all good people, as ye sit
Within the happy circle of sweet marriage,
Loving and loved, glorying and glorified;
Whose love makes life so dear, that when ye die
And sit on heavenlier heights, your eyes will search
To find the garden where Love's fruitage grew;
The nest from whence your pretty nurslings flew
Our old World smiling thro' its cloudy fold,
And love it for the marriage love of old."

She ceased, and from afar methought there came
Across the night an echo sad and low,
Love answering love, heart crying unto heart.

"In the merry spring-tide when green buds start,
Wings break from the husk of care,
And the dead beauty blossoms again in my heart,
As I dream of the things that were;
The buried Past lifteth a radiant brow;
A phantom-bark toucheth life's shore;
And it floateth me far from the sorrowful Now,
Into Love's happy Nevermore.

"She rises before me, that Darling of mine,
Whom I lost in the world so wide;
O come to me, come to me, let thine arms twine
About me, my life! my Bride!
Ah me! I am breaking my heart to see
But the Image enshrined at its core;
Yet Memory's sighs bring a balm to me,
Out of Love's happy Nevermore.

"How I poured all my life in a beaker of bliss
For her! how I held the cup,

As the leaves, though the wanton winds will kiss,
  Their tremulous dews hold up!
And my mind it walkt in a raiment white,
  Where starry thoughts reared a dome;
And the feast was spread, and the chamber alight
  For the guest that never came home.

"Lovely she was as the lily is white,
  When the beauty of morn it wears:
Pure she was as the perfect light
  That haloeth happy tears.
Hearts straightway rose from the shadow and cloud,
  Where the light of her presence kist;
Yet over the might of the proudest she rode,
  Like Music, as she list.

"Love, rosy clear, in her cheek's faint dyes,
  Its first sweet bloom just took;
Love came trembling up in her eyes,
  As the stars in a happy brook:
Dear eyes! they were dreams of heaven, with a dance
  Of light in their deep rich gloom;
Whence the smiling heart lookt like the golden glance
  From the pansy's purple bloom.

"O Darling of mine! does she ever think
  Of the old-time thoughts and things?
O Darling of mine! does she come to drink
  At these wormwood spirit-springs?
For I sometimes dream as I bend above,
  That the touch of her lip clings there,
And the fading balm of her breath of love
  Is eloquent in the air.

"If we met unaware, just to ease her heart's pain,
  Would she fall on my bosom and sob?
Or would old memories glide thro' her brain
  With never an added throb?
Is her pillow e'er wet in the dead night-hours?
  When the heat of the day is o'er,
Does she turn, like me, for a handful of flowers,
  Into Love's happy Nevermore?

"O there is no heart that loves on earth
  But may live to be loved again:
Some other heart hath the same dear birth,
  And aches with the same sweet pain.

And Love may yet come with a golden ray
  Shall lighten my life's despair:
But Love hath no second shaft can slay
  The first love nestling there.

"In the merry spring-tide when green buds start,
  Wings break from the husk of care,
And the dead beauty blossoms again in my heart,
  As I dream of the things that were:
The buried Past lifteth a radiant brow,
  A phantom-bark toucheth life's shore:
And I am borne far from the sorrowful Now,
  Into Love's happy Nevermore."

All this was but the imagery of dream;
For when the Morn in restless radiance rose,
Her breath of beauty palpitating light,
With clouds of colour smiling from the ground;
A sparkling ecstasy in the blue air;
And I with marvelling eyes had broke the seal
Of slumber, read the letter of my Dream,
Lo, Charmian in her summer-sumptuous beauty
And oft the dimple gleamed upon her cheek,
To vanish like a dew-drop in a rose;
And oft her laugh with reckless richness rung,
And shook a shower of music-pearls around.
I peered into the luminous dark of her eyes,
As one might come by light of day to look
Adown the glade where he had seen the dance
Of weird Elves in the night, but finds no trace.
An aspect of the Graces! who could know
The wreathen face that writhéd in my dream?

But still, as in my Dream, I see her stand,
Too living for a picture in romance,
Telling the wild stern story of her wrongs,
Holding the great Curse up to heaven for ever,

To call God's lightning down, altho' it kill
Her with her wedded Curse. And in my Dream
The kings and queens of prospering love go by,
And little heed this Martyr by the way;
This poor weak woman trembling 'neath her load;
This life fast fettered to a festering corse;
This love that bleeds to death at many wounds:
This passing Tragedy of Soul within
Our five acts of the Sense, that breaks its way
Thro' human hearts i' the Theatre of a world.

ENGLAND AND LOUIS NAPOLEON.

ENGLAND AND LOUIS NAPOLEON.

1855.

There was a poor old Woman once, a daughter of our nation,
Before the Devil's portrait stood in ignorant adoration.
"You're bowing down to Satan, Ma'am," said some Spectator civil:
"Ah, Sir, it's best to be polite, for we may go to the Devil."
Bow, bow, bow:
We may go to the Devil, so it's just as well to bow.

So England hails the Saviour of Society, and will tarry at
His feet, nor see her Christ is he who sold him, curst Iscariot.
By grace of God, or sleight of hand, he wears the royal vesture,
And at thy throne, Divine Success! we kneel with reverent gesture,
And bow, bow, bow:
We may go to the Devil, so it's just as well to bow.

O when the Sun is over us, we venerate the sunlight;
But when Eclipse is over it, we venerate the dunlight.
No matter what is uppermost, upon all-fours we revel,

And when Hell triumphs over heaven—conciliate the Devil,
And bow, bow, bow:
We may go to the Devil, so it's just as well to bow.

Ah, Louis, had you come to us despisèd and rejected,
You might have gone to—Coventry, unnoticed and neglected:
But as you've done one Nation so, and left another undone,
We kiss you Sire at Windsor—crown you more than king in London,
And bow, bow, bow:
We may go to the Devil, so it's just as well to bow.

Our Idol's hands are red with blood, with blood his eyes are sodden,
But we know 't is only guilty blood which he has spilt and trodden!
He wears the imperial purple now, that plotting prince of evil;
He lets us share his glory if we bow down to the Devil;
And we bow, bow, bow:
We may go to the Devil, so it's just as well to bow.

With hand to hilt, and ear to earth, waits Revolution, breathless,
To catch the resurrection sound of Liberty the deathless!
We see no Danger hug us round—no Sword hang o'er us gory,
While to this mocking Mirage in the sunset of our glory
We bow, bow, bow:
We may go to the Devil, so it's just as well to bow.

Back, back, you foolish Peoples, slink into your weeping places,
Quench Freedom's torch in tears, and put her light out in your faces:
The heart of England beats no more to the old heroic level;
The poor old Woman bows before her Portrait of the Devil.
Bow, bow, bow:
She may go to the Devil, so it's just as well to bow.

THE OLD FLAG.

An Emperor babbled in his dreams, —
Ne'er sleeps the secret in his soul, —
"The Lion is old, and ready he seems
To draw my Chariot to its goal."
With awful light the Lion's eye
Began to flame — sublime he stands!
With looks that make the Tyrant try
To hide his bloody hands.
Thank God, the advancing tide is met!
Thank God, the Old Flag's flying yet.

We love our native land and laws,
And He would rather we did not!
We are Conspirators because
We are in our little green grass plot!
But let him follow up his frown,
Marshal his myriads for the blow;
Those who are doomed to drown must drown,
The rest we'll take in tow!
In Cherbourg's sight their gallows set
Beside the Old Flag flying yet.

Our Ghost of Greatness hath not fled
At crowing of the Gallic Cock;

A foreign Despot's heel shall tread
  No print upon our English rock.
Here Freedom by the Lion grand
  Sits safe, and Una-like doth hold
Him gently with her gentle hand;
  And long as seas enfold,
High on our topmost height firm-set,
We'll keep her Old Flag flying yet.

To Freedom we must aye be true;
  Our England must be Freedom's home;
For sake of our dead Darlings who
  Went heavenward crowned with martyrdom.
'Twas she who made us what we are,
  Throned on our sea-cliffs grey and grand;
Great image of majestic care!
  Fair Bride of Fatherland!
We do but pay the filial debt
To keep her Old Flag flying yet.

This little Isle is Freedom's Bark
  That rideth in a perilous path:
Around us one wide sea of dark
  That beats and breaks in stormy wrath.
The Despots drove poor Freedom forth,
  By bloody footprints trackt her road;—
And homeless, homeless, else on earth
  She takes to her sea-abode!
She turns on us her eyes tear-wet;
Ah, keep the Old Flag flying yet.

Statesmen have drawn back meek and mute,
  Or pardon begged from bullying foes,
Whene'er a Military boot
  Was stampt upon retreating toes.
They shrink to hear Him at our gates,
  This ominous thing of gloom and gore,
Tho' Revolution for him waits
  At Danger's every door.

But little do we heed his threat!
We keep the Old Flag flying yet.

Over the praying peoples rolled
  The dark tide, and we helpt them not.
Yet on our lifted hands, behold,
  We cry, behold no bloody spot!
This famous people's heart is sound,
  It fights for all that bleed and smart;
We — banned above — meet underground,
  Meet in a touch of heart.
We cannot our old fame forget;
We keep the Old Flag flying yet.

We have a true and tender clasp
  For Freedom's friends where'er their home,
And for her foes as grim a grasp,
  No matter when or whence they come.
We like that gay light-hearted France
  That into stormy splendour breaks,
When its brave music for the dance
  Of Death the battle makes;
And foot to foot would proudly set
To keep the Old Flag flying yet.

But what is France? this cruel Power
  That builds upon her martyred dead,
Whose spirits thicken hour by hour
  The air about its doomèd head?
This Death-in-Life throned on the grave,
  That in the darkness waits its prey?
Like Coral-workers neath the wave,
  It dies on reaching day.
The Sun of France hath not thus set,
But, keep the Old Flag flying yet.

France, who hath stood erect and first,
  Will not lie latest in the dust:

Ere long her breath of scorn will burst
  This bubble blown of bloody lust.
Quietly, quietly turns the tide,
  And when this shore lies black and bare,
There shall be no more sea to hide
  The Wrecker's secrets there.
Our lot is cast, our task is set,
To keep the Old Flag flying yet.

Save him? this Burglar of the night
  Broke into Freedom's sacred shrines!
This Lie uncrowned whene'er the light
  Of merciless next morning shines!
This terror of a land struck dumb,
  Who fed the Furies with brave blood!
We cannot save him when they come
  For his. Not if we would.
So slippery is the hand blood-wet!
Ah, keep the Old Flag flying yet.

The Tyrant sometimes waxeth strong
  To drag a fate more fearful down:
He veileth Justice who ere long
  Shall see Eternal Justice frown.
The Kings of Crime from near and far
  Shall come to crown him with their crown;
Under the shadow of doom his Star
  Will redden, and go down.
And day shall dawn when it hath set,
But, keep the Old Flag flying yet.

Leaves fall, but lo! the young buds peep!
  Flowers die and still their seed shall bloom;
From death the quick young life will leap
  When Spring goes by the wintry tomb.
And tho' their graves are husht, in stern
  Heroic dream the dead men lie!
To God their still white faces turn:
  The murdered do not die.

Will God the Martyrs' seed forget?
No. Keep the Old Flag flying yet.

This triumph of the spoken word
  Is well, my England, but give heed!
The world leans on thee as a Sword
  For Freedom in her battle-need.
Star of a thousand battles red,
  Be thou the Beacon of the Free!
Turn round thy luminous side, and shed
  God's light o'er land and sea.
Thro' floods, or flames, or bloody sweat,
Keep thou the Old Flag flying yet.

The splendid shiver of brave blood
  Is thrilling through our England now!
She who so often hath withstood
  The Tyrants, lifts her brightened brow.
God's precious charge we proudly keep
  In circling arms of victory!
With Freedom we shall live, or sleep
  With our dear dead who are free.
God forget us when we forget
To keep the Old Flag flying yet.

ENGLAND AND LOUIS NAPOLEON.

MAY, 1859.

MAJESTIC Mother! Thine was not a brow
To bend, and blindly take a tinsel Crown
From hands like His. Thy glorious Sons have won
More crowns than thou canst wear, tho' all the year
A fresh one glistened daily. These are crowns

Untarnishable by the breath of scorn!
And crowns that never can be melted down
And minted for the market. Thine was not
A soul to wear the fetters that made fast
His stolen throne to him, and gracefully
To drape the imperial purple round, and hide
The blood that splasht there, red till Judgment
Day.
He stole on France, deflowered her in the night,
Then tore her tongue out lest she told the tale;
And Statesmen called him friend, and proudly held
Our Banner over him, while moneyed worldlings,
So pleased they knew not on which leg to stand,
Went on their knees, and worshipt his success,
So prostrate in their souls, so prone in dust,
They saw not how the feet were only clay,
For all the golden Image; they forgot
How meanest reptiles crawl up tallest towers.

Our England is long-suffering, and slow
Of judgment, lulled by seeming to the last.
And they are busy dreaming their dark dreams,
While she is sleeping sound in trustful peace.
'Tis well for thee, my Country, when the day
Breaks, thou canst never match them in the dark!
Thine eyes are blind where Birds of night see best.
But instinct, that Veiled Prophet of the Soul,
Flashes up, startled from its seeing trance,
As tho' God's hand had toucht it while we slept.
There's some invisible danger drawing near,
That hath not taken shape yet, but it comes.
The still small voice cries wake, my Country, wake,
And sleep no more while that Man's in the world.
The treacherous dealer will deal treacherously;
The lawless Power is still above all Law!
The Foe that cometh at the dead of night
May find the Goodman slumbering with the arms
Too rusted on the walls. Make the Sword sharp!
Watch warily, you lookers from the hill!

Arm every rampart, rock, and tower of Right,
And arm the people; thus, securely armed,
We may sit safe and hold the hands of War
In ours, he cannot strike us for the time.

Once more the war-wave surges gaily out
From Paris with its gallant armaments,
In music's pomp, and bannered pride, and dance
Of life light-hearted, and light-headed crests.
The Ghost of Buonaparte hath broken loose
From hell this time! ripe Scholar in its lore!
With Ruin's lighted torch half hidden in
The Devil's own dark lanthorn. We shall see
The night-side of Napoleon, as he tracks
His old earth foot-prints black with rusted blood.
Alas, poor Italy! the Storm of War
From its fire-mountain throne sweeps burning down,
Its purple lava-mantle trails behind,
Embracing all and blasting all it folds.
A sea of soldiery breaks over her;
Her fair face darkens in the shadow of Swords;
Destruction drives his ploughshare thro' her soil,
But will he turn her old lost Jewel to light?
Another crop of young heroic life
Is ready for the Reaper; it springs fast
In such a land, so watered, with such blood.

Poor fools! this Despot turned Deliverer is
A sneaking Cutpurse, not a Cutthroat grand,
Like him that lifted up a Sword of fire,
Whose flashes frightened nations, and went forth,
A prairie-flame consuming men as grass:
How dazzlingly his beacon-star that danced
From crown to crown did shine above the lands
He covered with his purple and his pall!
He stormed the dizziest heights, and there he stood
In sanguine glory! Like a Battle God
Ruling the strife with face of marble calm!
The eyes of Heaven that look down on us with

The earnestness of all eternity,
Saw our old world turn blood-red mirroring Him!
Napoleon dilated till he filled
The vision of France instead of Liberty.
And such the glamour of his grandeur, She
Knew not which Image crowned the Column lifted
A heaven above her, in her love and worship.
But this Man leads her eyeless, blind in blood.
He bears a Burglar's Bludgeon, not a Sword:
Great Oath-breaker, and not World-Victor He.

How far the tide may flood, how quick return
With wreck and ruin for its freightage home,
We know not, nor how soon the nether pit
May open and stern Nemesis rise up
For vengeance infinitely terrible!
As in the grim Norse dream Loke lyeth bound
Down at the heart o' the world, so Tyranny keeps
A potent spirit fettered underground,
And o'er it hangs a Serpent horrible,
With eyes thro' which all hell crowds up to see
The poison-fire spit in that Spirit's face;
In straining waves it writhes along to squeeze
Its soul of venom into every drop:
And there sits Wife-like Patience at the side,
Catching the poison till her cup will hold
No more, and she must empty it. Ah then
The poison burns! and with one great heart-heave
That Spirit's bonds are burst! an Earthquake's
born.

These Despots do but throw with loaded dice;
They lose or win by other will than theirs!
A Goddess blind leads worshippers as blind.
Henceforth we have no part in this man's lot,
No faith in him; he goes his way, we ours:
If we were true to him we must be false
To all our dearest deeds and noblest dreams!
We are no close-chained Mob for one to walk

Over our heads, and kiss the feet that tread!
Our welding oneness binds up all our wounds,
And one heart and one breath make healing life.
We trust in God, and mean to hold our own.
We are not stainless; there are wrongs on wrongs
Crying for Right! the patient heavens have lookt
On many a failing sadly! England's Star
Hath winkt on many a crime, and thro' the gloom
Suffering still doggeth Sin, to strike at last.
May God forgive us, we are apt to grow
Unmindful of our blessings, and forget
That this is England, and forget how He
Hath wrought for England; that the sacred Ark
Rests on this Ararat; we dare not face
The world with that same faith we dare profess
Kneeling to God. And so at times we need
A hint from Heaven, and these are often stern.
May God forsake not England, but in need
Look smilingly upon her!
We at least
Will never run beside this Tyrant's car
Of triumph, glorying in the dust we raise!
Our voice at least shall cry aloud his fall,
Tho' but a lonely trumpet in the night,
And spare not him who plots against our land.

O statesmen, ye who lead this noble land,
May you prove wise and worthy! Great good
Men,
With hearts that beat to high heroic measures,
And strength still equal to the sternest time;
With faith to fight and patience to work on,
Still knowing these live longer than a Lie!
The pyramid of our power is not complete
Until it touches heaven for its crown!
And if the Bloody Star should turn this way
Its red eye of destruction, fierce to see
The pride and prowess of our might go down
With England for funereal pyre; then give

No quarter to the foes that strike at us!
Thro' fire and foam flash on them, and strike home
Like Lightnings of the Lord! fuel the flames
Of Battle with the Revolution's wrecks
That drift upon our shores. In Tyrant-land
A young Deliverer lies a-dream, and sees
Such splendours in his visions only eyes
When veiled can look on! tell him the time's
come!
He will arise and stretch his hand and snatch
The Sword. It will be resurrection day!
The Tyrant's fortresses and palaces
Built with the Headsman's scaffold will dissolve;
The piles of ghastly, gory heads shall turn
To flaming-sworded Spirits! the dry bones
Will stir and rise up in a dance of life.

You lovers of our England, do but look
On this dear country over whose fair face
God droopt a bridal veil of tender mist,
That she might keep her beauty virginal,
And He might see her thro' a softer glory;
So very meek and reverent doth she stand
Within this shadow soft of Love Divine,
More lovable, and not as brighter lands
Whose bolder beauty stares up in heaven's face.
Look on her now, this jewel of the world,
Set in that marriage-ring of circling sea!
She smiles upon her Image in its calm,
Like some proud Ship that floateth in its shadow.
And as a happy lover clasps his Bride,
The fond Sea folds her round, and his brimmed life
Runs rippling to her inmost heart of hearts,
Until it swims a-flood with happiness;
And all the waters of her love leap back
To him exultant from a thousand hills.
From his salt virtue comes her northern sweetness.
How his rough kisses make her roses bloom!
Once in his rousèd wrath he lifted up

A mighty Armada in his arms, and dasht
It into sea-drift at his Mistress' feet.
And still he threatens with his voice of storms
The plots of all Invaders; still he keeps
Eternal watch around. How proud in peace,
The wild white horses rear and foam along
And bring to her the harvests of the world!
How grand in war they bear her battle line
In strength half-smiling, perfect Power crowned
With careless grace, which seemeth to all eyes
The plume of Triumph nodding as it goes;
For visible victory sits upon her brow,
And shines upon her sails.
See where she sits
Holding at heart her noble dead, and nursing
Her living Children on the old brave virtue;
Wearing the rainy radiance of the morning,
With silver sweetness swimming in her tears,
Feeling the glory rippling down from heaven
With smiles from all her wild flowers, her green leaves,
And nooks where old times live their shepherd ways.
We cannot count her heroes who lay down
In quiet graveyards when their work was done;
But mound on mound they rise all over the land
To bar a Tyrant's path, and make his feet
To stumble like the blind man among tombs.
Her brave dead make our earth heroic dust;
Their spirit glitters in our England's face
And makes her shine, a Star in blackest night,
Calm at her heart, and glory round her head.
We think of all who fought, and who are now
Immortals in the heaven of her love;
The Martyrs who have made of burning wrongs
Their fiery chariot, and gone up to God;
The saintly Sorrows that now walk in white
Till faces bloom like battle Banners flusht
All over with most glorious memories.

We are a chosen People ; Freedom wears
Our English Rose for her peculiar crest,
Whoso dares touch it bleeds upon the thorn :
It may be that the time will come again
For one more desperate struggle to the death.
The Devil's eye upon our England looks
With snaky sparkle still. It may be they
Will rouse the tamed Berserkir rage, and make
The vein of wrath throb livid on her brow,
And wake the old Norse War-dog in her blood,
Until she springs afloat upon the sea
Like an Immortal white-winged on the air,
The joy of swiftness lightning thro' her veins.

Thrice hath our England swept the seas, and cleared
Her ocean path, the highways of the world,
And shall again if Robbers lie in wait.
She hath stood fast when towering Nations poured
In one wild wave their culminating power!
Thro' all that harvest-day of bloody death,
They charged in vain, and dasht upon the edge
Of her red sword, and fell, at Waterloo!
We kept the shamble slopes of Inkermann!
Thro' blood and fire and gloom of Indian War
We swam the Red Sea, and rode out the storm!
So shall we hold our own dear land with all
The old unvanquisht soul, and we shall see
Their changing Empires shift like sand around
The Island Rock, the footstool of the Lord,
Where Freedom also lays her head, and rest
In calm or storm the best hopes of a world.

Ah, let the Peacemen preach, but let our Peace
Be Right victorious, not triumphant Wrong!
These pallid Peacemen are to true men what
Our world might be without its iron ore ;
But never may the grand old bravery die.
No, no! we must not let the death-fires dance
Along our heights with their funereal flames,

As Hell had thrust up many red-hot tongues
To get its lap of blood when earth is drencht.
Our green fields must not blush in blood for us!
We must not let them pluck the old land down
To throne them in her seat; they must not wear
The Crown she raced for round the world and
won.
Our Country has a name and fame might fill
The eyes of Hate and Envy with tame tears;
And they shall never lay her low while we
Are true to her in heart and head and hand.
And all who come in peace will find a home,
And all who come in war a mouthful of
Our dust in death, and Sea-beach for a grave.

Great starry thoughts grow luminous in the dark!
The Bird of Hope goes singing overhead!
We cannot fear for England, we can die
To do her bidding, but we cannot fear:
We who have heard her thunder-roll of deeds
Reverberating thro' the centuries;
By battle fire-light had the stories told;
We who have seen how proudly she prepares
For sacrifice, how radiantly her face
Flasht when the Bugle blew its bloody sounds,
And bloody weather fluttered her old Flag;
We who have seen her with the red heaps round;
We who have known the mightiest powers dashed
back
Broken from her impregnable sea-walls;
We who have learned how in the darkest hour
The greatest light breaks out, and in the time
Of trial she reveals her noblest strength;
For we have felt her big heart beat in ours.

Hail to thee, Mother of Nations! mighty yet
To strive, and suffer, and give overthrow!
For all the powers of nature fight for thee.
Spirits that sleep in glory shall awake,

Come down and drive thy Car of victory
Over thine enemies' necks.
Long will they wait
Who privily lurk to stab thee when the night
Shall cover all in darkness.
Dear old Land,
Thy shining glories are no Sunset gleams,
But clouds that kindle round some great new
Dawn.

THE BROAD-BOTTOMED MINISTRY.

Now tell me you who wink, or blink, or think,
What good is a *Broad* bottom if we sink?
Not Whigs! not Tories! we want English souls
Where-thro' there yet reverberates and rolls
Some echo of old greatness; good stout hands
Must bear our Banner over seas and lands!
Our forms of freedom must not choke the breath,
The outer mail be forged for inner death!
There is a wild hour coming for us when
We must all weather it as Englishmen.

We cannot leave the land for watch and ward
To those who know not what a gem they guard;
Who bind us helpless for the Bird of Blood
To swoop on; who would have this famous flood
Of English Freedom stagnate till it stink,
While reptiles wriggle in their slimy drink,
And frogs shall reign in darkness; croak all night.
And call the Stars false Prophets of the light.

Our good ship may be driving on the rocks;
We want a Compass, and not Weather-Cocks!
We have had leaders who strode forward all

On fire to serve her at their Country's call;
They did not stoop, till blind, for place and pelf,
Their whole life burned a sacrifice of self!
They faced the Spirit of the Storm and Strife,
And with an upward smile laid down their life.

But now our leaders are the coward and cold;
The Gnomes whose daylight is a gleam of gold;
The Dwarfs who sun them in a Tyrant's smile;
The Peacemen who would set our dear green Isle
Spinning their Cotton till the judgment hour,
With Ocean turning round for water-power.
These pander to this Plunderer of the night;
Confused their little sense of Wrong and Right!
And they would bow our England's dear head down
Trustfully in his lap to leave her crown!
See her sit weeping where her brave lie dead;
Blood on her raiment, ashes on her head.

A Palmerston now crawls where Cromwell stood;
A Tyrant's Parasite, that licks the blood
From his red hand, an old eternal stain!
And takes, for Glory's sign, that brand of Cain!
He is an Eve in innocence we know,
But leans and listens to the Serpent so,
We are no safer although well we weet
The fruit of knowledge He will never eat.

In Milton's patriot seat sits little John,
Who to the muzzle loads his monster gun,
And fires in air if it goes off at all,
To find his own lead on his own head fall,
If he have any, for, since he who bled
Upon a Tyrant's block *once* lost his head,
To keep up the tradition Lord John is
Determined to be *always* losing his.

And Gladstone aims at nothing, sure to hit,
Or splits fine hairs till he have none to split.

Who rides out from the ranks for challenge, He
May toss the Sword and catch it gracefully,
But *must* be able, when the onsets come,
To drive with slaying hand his hilt heart-home.
He is a *Seer*, but, so many-eyed,
He sees so many ways from many a side!
His eyes like horses in old punishment,
Whereby all ways at once the doomed was rent,
Draw to divide him, follow if he dare,
He is to pieces pulled by either pair.

These be our Leaders now! Napoleon's Pal
Is head of England's power, and crowning all,
To cool the blood, and soothe all sin to rest,
The great castrated Quaker Interest
Stands Eunuch at the Privy chamber.
Wake
My England! *these* thy Sword and Shield? they make
A Ministry *broad* bottomed without doubt
For better Target when you kick them out.

OLD HARLEQUIN PAM.

Our Greatest of Men is Harlequin Pam,
The "Times" says so, and the "Times" cannot bam!
But I'll prove it true. In an Age of Sham,
Our greatest of Humbugs is Harlequin Pam.
Humbug in riches it reeks and it rolls,
Humbug in luxury lazily lolls,
Humbug in Senate and Humbug in Shop,
Humbug makes sweet the Assassin's last drop;
And Pam, Pam is the King of all Sham,
So our greatest of Men must be Harlequin Pam.

England, this is the Man for you,
The "Times" says so, and it must be true.

Did the Vessel of State hurry down to the Fall,
No stay from the current, no help for the call!
To the uttermost edge of destruction trackt,
On the crumbling brink of the Cataract,
Pam would go thro' the leap like a Clown
In the Ring, and with grace and applause go down!
Tho' the whirl sank the Ship it could scarce keep a straw in!
And all one to Pam come éclat or a clawin'!
Pam, Pam, you're a wonderful sham!
And we can't do without you, old Harlequin Pam!
England, this is the Man for you,
The "Times" says so, and it must be true.

That he pulls with the People at first sight is seen;
Look again! they are chained with a post between!
He bullies the weak, to the strong he's a slave,
Best card in the pack when the Despots play knave!
How he jauntily trips up the Palace back stair,
To quiet the mob in the Public Square!
Look up, what a firework of words red hot!
But lo! in the enemy's camp not a shot!
Pam, Pam, you're a wonderful sham!
And we can't do without you, old Harlequin Pam!
England, this is the Man for you!
The "Times" says so, and it must be true.

To oblige his Emperor friend who, one day,
Won Imperial stakes as he played foul play,
He put the old Lion in blinkers, and held him,

And tried, per French pattern, to carve him and
gild him.
And ere long another high wind will blow,
Then ho, ho! but the Crowns will go!
And what will they do if this Judas of Freedom
then
Can't help the Despots who terribly need him
then?
Pam, Pam, you're a wonderful sham,
And we can't do without you, old Harlequin
Pam!
England, this is the Man for you!
The "Times" says so, and it must be true.

This dazzling shallow will shimmer so,
The blind don't see there's no depth below!
This sparkling Sham for a jewel will pass,
If set in a Crown, tho' 't is only cut glass!
This political firefly tho' faded no matter,
'T will gleam out again when it gets in hot water!
This bubble as long as you puff it will float,
And so my song ends with its Cuckoo note.
Pam, Pam, you're a wonderful sham,
But we can't do without you, old Harlequin
Pam!
England, this is the Man for you,
The "Times" says so, and it must be true.

THE SEA KINGS.

I.

THE Spaniard thought to wear our crown,
Three hundred years ago;
And bend the head of England down
To kiss the Pope's great toe!

And next the Dutchman swept the Sea
  With besom topmast high,
Gone is their Ocean sovereignty!
  To-day, how low they lie!

II.

And now the Frenchman's old wounds burn
  Like devils in their pain,
And bode the weather of war will turn
  To a bath of bloody rain.
Tingle and ring the ears of France
  With sound of battle hymns;
As on Ambition's dark, mad trance
  The bloody vision swims.

III.

Sons of the old Norse sailors brave,
  We fill their place to-day, —
No wreath of foam upon the wave,
  To flash and pass away.
Our perilous prize we guard and keep
  Till last relief God brings,
Then lie in calm majestic sleep
  Along with the old Sea Kings.

IV.

Well may your proud eyes sparkle, ye
  Rough Sea Kings, young and old;
The salt sea-spirit laughs to see
  The Frenchman grown so bold.
Sword-bayonets, rifled cannon, may
  The poor of heart alarm,
But pluck at last will win the day
  With naked strength of arm.

V.

We are not beaten at a dash,
  Nor swiftly overthrown, —
Let ship with ship together lash,
  We know who must go down.

No man in Gallic land will live
  To see us dispossest;
When our sun sets at sea we give
  Our glory to the West.

VI.

Those old unconquerable waves,
  They mock at Tyranny;
And never can a land of slaves
  Be Ruler of the Sea.
But would you see their Empress, now
  Behold her! here she smiles,
This diadem on Ocean's brow,
  This Glory of the Isles.

VII.

We 've fed the Sea with English souls,
  And every mounded wave
To Heaven bears witness, for it rolls
  Some English seaman's grave!
Our rivers bear heroic dust
  For burial in that sea,
Which helps to keep our noble trust,
  And battles for the Free.

VIII.

Not always down the primrose path
  Of dalliance can we tread,
Ofttimes the Chosen People hath
  To climb with foot-prints red:
Our highest life with cross, and scorn,
  And tears, may yet be trod,
And England wear a crown of thorn,
  Whose Roses bloom in blood.

IX.

We have immortal quarrel with
  The men who war with Right;
We will not own him kin or kith,
  Who fails us in this fight.

No room for him on English ground,
 No bed in Ocean's breast,
Who draws her purple curtains round
 Unfathomable rest.

X.

If those old Greeks for Beauty wrought
 Their ten-years' daring deed,
Shall it be said that less we fought
 For Freedom in her need?
No. Fight till all the Brave lie dead,
 And grass grows on the mart;
But Freedom here shall rest her head
 Upon Old England's heart.

XI.

Like some old Eagle on her nest,
 Up in her pride of place,
Our England sits with brooding breast,
 And looks with sharpened face!
She feels the Shadow of a Hand,
 But ere it touch her brood,
The Sea that narrows round our land
 Shall run a moat of blood.

XII.

Wave out, Old Bird! or still brood on!
 They shall not bring you low;
A thousand years have come and gone,
 A thousand more shall go!
Our True Hearts still shall tread the deck,
 Our Ships sail every sea,
And ride like those who rein the neck
 Of rearing Tyranny.

XIII.

We 've mounted many a windy wave,
 We 've weathered many storms;

Unshaken still we hear them rave,
  Safe in the eternal arms.
For if the worst comes — every man —
  We 'll perish in our place,
And then the Frenchman, if he can,
  May lead the new Sea-Race!

THE MOTHER'S IDOL BROKEN.

Tenderly did he usher us within
The holy of holies of a Father's heart,
Where gloomed the first great sorrow still and stern —
The dark, unfeatured Guest — now fading slow
In hallowed, healing light.
Ah, few there be
But miss some sweetest thing Earth lifted up
In her old arms to take Heaven's blessing — pure
As white foam-spirit flashing to the Moon,
And gone as quickly from our mortal night.

THE MOTHER'S IDOL BROKEN.

I.

Twice the Mother had divéd down
  Into her sea of sorrow;
O my love! O my life! my own sweet Wife!
  God send you a merry good-morrow.
Betide her weal, or betide her woe,
  Her smile it was calm and fearless;
And proud were her eyes as she rose with the prize,
  A pearl in her palms! my peerless!

O found you a little sea-syren,
  In some perilous palace left?
Or is it a little child-angel,
  Of her high-born kin bereft?
Or came she out of the Elfin-land,
  By earthly love beguiled?
Or hath the sweet Spirit of Beauty
  Taken shape as our starry Child?

Dear, do but look in her love-nest of sweets,
  Where she lies in a smiling calm:
Wee armful of fruitage; a sheaf of ripe bliss;
  On a bosom breathing balm.
Fresh as the drop of dew cradled at morn,
  On leaves of a lily in blossom;
Sweet as the fragrance newly born
  In a violet's virgin bosom.

II.

God's Butterfly on our love's flower alight!
  It seemeth the beautiful thing,

At the first surmise of the heaven she hath left,
For the winterless world will wing.
So we fold her about with our love as 't were heaven,
Around her weave many a wile;
And our hearts up-leap, living fountains of joy,
In the golden dream of her smile.

III.

On my ripely rounding Rose-tree,
Dreaming of life are three flowers:
One pusheth up her ruby-rose-cup,
For the rain of God's quickening showers.
With a magical burst of beauty, one glows
Dewily-dear in the sheen of love;
And one pretty Softling, our baby-bud-rose,
Lies tenderly shut in the green of love.

IV.

O fair befall my dainty flowers,
Summering on their stem;
Smiling up to the crowning Rose,
As she smileth down upon them.
Smiling up to their Queen in her beauty,
That smiles on each bonny breast-gem:
Blossoming, brimming with love for her
Who leans ruddy with love over them!
O fair befall my dainty flowers,
Summering on their stem!
And O the armful of rich love,
My fragrant human Roses!
Smile on them all, sweet Heaven,
And kiss my darling Roses.

V.

THERE be three little maidens; three loving maidens;
Three bonny maidens mine;
Three precious jewels are set in Life's crown,
On prayer-lifted brows to shine.
Six starry eyes, all love-luminous,
Look out of our heaven so tender;
Since the honey-moon, glowing and glorious,
Arose in its ripening splendour.

There 's Lilybell, duchess of wonderland,
With dance of life, dimples and curls;
Whose bud of a mouth into red kisses bursts
A-smile with the wanton white pearls:
And Sweetcheek, our rosily-goldening peach
On the sunniest side o' the wall
But Marian 's Mother's darling,
Marian 's idol of all.

VI.

LIKE the merry voice-bird that sings on the bough,
I sing, O my woman Dove,
To a nest I know in the leaves below,
Full of eyes alive with love.
Two of our little Birds wander on wings,
One can but flutter and fall;
Sing, Marian Mother's wee darling,
Marian 's Idol of all.

VII.

ALL in our marriage garden
Grew, smiling up to God,

A bonnier flower than ever
  Suckt the green warmth of the sod.
O beautiful unfathomably
  Its little life unfurled;
Love's crowning sweetness was our wee
  White Rose of all the world.

From out a balmy bosom,
  Our bud of beauty grew;
It fed on smiles for sunshine,
  And tears for daintier dew.
Aye nestling warm and tenderly,
  Our leaves of love were curled
So close and close about our wee
  White Rose of all the world.

Two flowers of glorious crimson
  Grew with our Rose of light;
Still kept the sweet heaven-grafted slip
  Her whiteness saintly white.
I' the wind of life they danced with glee,
  And reddened as it whirled;
White, white and wondrous grew our wee
  White Rose of all the world.

With mystical faint fragrance,
  Our house of life she filled—
Revealed each hour some fairy tower,
  Where wingéd Hopes might build.
We saw—though none like us might see—
  Such precious promise pearled
Upon the petals of our wee
  White Rose of all the world.

But evermore the halo
  Of Angel-light increased;
Like the mystery of Moonlight,
  That folds some fairy feast.

Snow-white, snow-soft, snow-silently,
  Our darling bud up-curled,
And dropt i' the Grave — God's lap — our wee
  White Rose of all the world.

Our Rose was but in blossom;
  Our life was but in spring;
When down the solemn midnight
  We heard the Spirits sing:
"Another bud of infancy,
  With holy dews impearled;"
And in their hands they bore our wee
  White Rose of all the world.

You scarce could think so small a thing
  Could leave a loss so large;
Her little light such shadow fling,
  From dawn to sunset's marge.
In other springs our life may be
  In bannered bloom unfurled;
But never, never match our wee
  White Rose of all the world.

VIII.

THIS is a curl of our poor "Splendid's" hair!
A sunny burst of rare and ripe young gold—
A ring of sinless gold that weds two worlds!
Our one thing left with her dear life in it.
Poor Misers! o'er it secretly we sum
Our little savings hoarded up in heaven,—
Our rich love-thoughts heart-hid to doat upon,—
And glimpse our lost heaven in a flood of tears.
A magic ring, through which fond Sorrow reads
Of strange heart-histories, and conjures up
A vanisht face, with its sweet spirit-smiles,
Babe-wonderings, and little tender ways.

At birth her hair was dark as it were dipt
In the death-shadow; but it rarefied
In radiance as her head rose nigher heaven,
Till she—white Glory!—lookt from a golden
midst.
This is her still face as she lay in death!
Spirit-like face! set in a silver cloud,
It comes to us in silent glooms of night;
The wee wan face that gradually withdrew
And darkened into the great cloud of death.

O ye who say, "We have a Child in heaven;"
And know how far away that heaven may seem;
Who have felt that desolate isolation sharp
Defined in Death's own face; who have stood beside
The Silent River, and stretcht out pleading hands
For some sweet Babe upon the other bank,
That went forth where no human hand might lead,
And left the shut house with no light, no sound,
No answer, when the mourners wail without!
What we have known, ye know, and only know.

She came like April, who with tender grace
Smiles in Earth's face, and sets upon her breast
The bud of all her glory yet to come,
Then bursts in tears, and takes her sorrowful leave.
She brought us Eden just within the space
Of the dear depths of her large, dream-like eyes,
Then o'er the vista fell the death-veil dark.
She only caught three words of human speech:
One for her Mother, one for me, and one
She crowed with, for the fields, and open heaven.
That last she sighed with a sweet farewell pathos
A minute ere she left the house of life,
To come for kisses never any more.

Pale Blossom! how she leaned in love to us!
And how we feared a hand might reach from
heaven

To pluck our sweetest flower, our loftiest flower
Of life, that sprang from lowliest root of love!
Some tender trouble in her eyes complained
Of Life's rude stream, as meek Forget-me-nots
Make sweet appeal when winds and waters fret.
And oft she lookt beyond Us with sad eyes,
As for the coming of the Unseen Hand.
We saw, but feared to speak of, her strange beauty,
As some husht Bird that dares not sing i' the night,
Lest lurking foe should find its secret place,
And seize it through the dark. With twin-love's
strength
All crowded in the softest nestling-touch,
We fenced her round — exchanging silent looks.
We went about the house with listening hearts,
That kept the watch for Danger's stealthiest step.
Our spirits felt the Shadow ere it fell.

Then the Physician left our door ajar
A moment, and the grim thief Death stole in.
Some Angel passing o'er life's troubled sea,
Had seen our jewel shine celestial pure,
And Death must win it for her bosom pearl.
We stood at Midnight in the Presence dread.
At midnight, when Men die, we strove with Death,
To wrench our jewel from his grasping hand.
Ere the soul loosed from its last ledge of life,
Her little face peered round with anxious eyes,
Then, seeing all the old faces, dropt content.

The mystery dilated in her look,
Which, on the darkening death-ground, faintly
caught
The likeness of the Angel shining near.
Her passing soul flasht back a glimpse of bliss.
She was a Child no more, but strong and stern
As a mailed Knight that had been grappling Death.
A crown of conquest bound her baby-brow;
Her little hands could take the heirdom large;

And all her Childhood's vagrant royalty
Sat staid and calm in some eternal throne.
Love's kiss is sweet, but Death's doth make immortal.

The Mornings came, with glory-garland on,
To deck heaven's azure tent with hangings brave;
Birds, brooks, and bees were singing in the sun,
Earth's blithe heart breathing bloom into her face,
The flowers all crowding up like Memories
Of lovelier life in some forgotten world,
Or dreams of peace and beauty yet to come.

The soft south-breezes rockt the baby-buds
In fondling arms upon a balmy breast;
And all was gay as universal life
Swam down the stream that glads the City of God.
But we lay dark where Death had struck us down
With that stern blow which made us bleed within,
And bow while the Inevitable went by.

And there our Darling lay in coffined calm;
Beyond the breakers and the moaning now!
And o'er her flowed the white, eternal peace:
The breathing miracle into silence passed:
Never to stretch wee hands, with her dear smile
As soft as light-fall on unfolding flowers;
Never to wake us crying in the night:
Our little hindering thing for ever gone,
In tearful quiet now we might toil on.
All dim the living lustres motion makes!
No life-dew in the sweet cups of her eyes!
Nought there of our poor "Splendid" but her brow

A young Immortal came to us disguised,
And in the joy-dance dropt her mask, and fled.

The world went lightly by and heeded not
Our death-white windows blinded to the sun;

The hearts that ached within; the measureless
loss;
The Idol broken; our first tryst with Death.
O Life, how strange thy face behind the veil!
And stranger yet will thy strange mystery seem,
When we awake in death and tell our Dream.
'T is hard to solve the secret of the Sphinx!
We had a little gold Love garnered up,
To bravely robe our Babe: the Mother's half
Was turned to mourning-raiment for her dead:
Mine bought the first land we called ours — Her
grave.
We were as treasure-seekers in the earth,
When lo, a death's-head on a sudden stares.

Clad all in spirit-beauty forth she went;
Her budding spring of life in tiny leaf;
Her gracious gold of babe-virginity
Unminted in the image of our world;
Her faint dawn whitened in the perfect day.
Our early wede away went back to God,
Bearing her life-scroll folded, without stain,
And only three words written on it — two
Our names! Ah, may they plead for us in heaven!

IX.

VERY softly hold the Rose,
On thy happy breast that blows!
Thus from out my heart there sprang a flower of
tender pride.
All too wild my passion burned:
For the cooling dews it yearned:
In my hot hands droopt my gentle flower and died.

Be thy glory meekly worn:
Fairest fruit is lowliest borne:

Mine grew high as Life could climb, and arms could
reach above.
O, so proudly heaved my breast;
All the world should see how blest;
And the seeing Heavens took my lifted love.

X.

THERE is her nest where balmily smiled
Our Babe, as we leaned above;
Or her pleading face asked for the tenderest place
In all our world of love.
Very silent and empty now! yet we feel
It rock; and a tiny footfall
Comes over the floor in the thrilling night-hush,
And our hearts leap up for the call
Of our puir wee lammie dead and gone;
Our bonnie wee lammie dead and gone.

Last night, with hands to cracking claspt
In the furnace-fire of my heart,
Sitting, I saw the dead world
All into spirit-life start
At the mystic touch of the white Moonlight.
My spirit arose likewise,
And wandered away to the Graveyard,
Where, a jewel in Death's hand, lies
Our puir wee lammie dead and gone;
Our bonnie wee lammie dead and gone.

Slowly, slowly rose the dead,
All in their robes of white!
Weirdly, weirdly rose the dead,
Up in the silent night!
Like lilies for God, from the dark grave-bed,
They grew in a glory-rain;
And the crownéd Darling of Heaven, at the head
Of all that glorified train,

Was our puir wee lammie dead and gone;
Our bonnie wee lammie dead and gone.

In my dream I stood at the death-door dark,
  Alone and tremblingly,
Till a Shining One came in a crescent bark,
  Moonlike, o'er a purple sea.
She smiled as to say that she knew the way,
  And at some secret sign,
A memory of the old life stirred,
  And I knew that Angel mine!
Our puir wee lammie dead and gone;
Our bonnie wee lammie dead and gone.

XI.

WITHIN a mile of Edinburgh Town
We laid our little darling down;
Our first seed in God's acre sown!

So sweet a place! Death looks beguiled
Of half his gloom; or sure he smiled
To win our wondrous, spirit child.

God giveth His Beloved sleep
So calm, within its silence deep,
As Angel-guards the watch did keep.

The City looketh solemn and sweet;
It bares a gentle brow, to greet
The mourners mourning at its feet.

The sea of human life breaks round
This shore o' the dead, with softened sound:
Wild-flowers climb each mossy mound

To place in resting hands their palm,
And breathe their beauty, bloom, and balm;
Folding the dead in fragrant calm.

A softer shadow Grief might wear;
And old Heartache come gather there
The peace that falleth after prayer.

Poor heart, that danced among the vines
All reeling-ripe with sweet love-wines,
Thou walk'st with Death among the pines!

Lorn Mother, at the dark grave-door,
She kneeleth, pleading o'er and o'er,
But it is shut for evermore.

Blind, blind! She feels, but cannot read
Aright; then leans as she would feed
The dear dead lips that never heed.

The spirit of life may leap above,
But in that grave her prisoned dove
Lies, cold to th' warm embrace of love,

And dark, tho' all the world is bright;
And lonely, with a City in sight;
And desolate in the rainy night.

Ah, God! when in the glad life-cup
The face of Death swims darkly up;
The crowning flower is sure to droop.

And so we laid our darling down,
When Summer's cheek grew ripely brown,
And still, tho' grief hath milder grown,

Unto the Stranger's land we cleave,
Like some poor Birds that grieve and grieve,
Round the robbed nest, and cannot leave.

XII.

Ah, the sweet Dream, the singing Dream, that sang
We knew not what, so sweet the melody!
Made dim woe glimmer golden while we slept;
And when we woke the lulling Dream was gone.

We who had glowed like Angels in the sun,
With life so lighted by her loveliness:
We let her down into the drowning Dark,
Sailing the awful Sea in our World-bark.

God's messenger of death seems blindly stern:
And 't is so hard to leave a little babe
Within the Grave's cold arms, alone! while Sorrow
Comes Home and chills the nest her sweet life warmed.

So little to the world! but what a world
Of difference in our little world of home!
This stillness where the sweet Bird chirpt to us;
This good-night-parting-and-morn-greeting loss.

And yet perchance the kind dark-Angel drew
Her in the secret shadow of his cloud,
Out of our warm and golden air, to hide
Her from some fearful Fate far-hurrying up.

XIII.

To-day, when winds of winter blow,
And Nature sits in dream of snow,
With Ugolino-look of woe:

Wife from the window came to me,
Now leaves were fallen she could see
That wee grave in the Cemet'ry.

With wintriness all life did ache
For that dead darling's sainted sake;
And lips might kiss, but hearts would quake.

Ho, ye who pass her narrow house,
By which the dark Leith sea-ward flows;
O clasp your pretty darlings close;

And if some tender bud of light
Is drooping, as the snowdrop white,
With looks that weird wild heartstrings smite,

Think of our babe will never wake,
And fold your own till fond hearts ache,
Sweet souls, for little Marian's sake.

XIV.

O HAPPY tree;
Green and fragrant tree;
Spring with budding jewels deckt it like a Bride!
All so fair it bloomed,
And the summer air perfumed;
Golden autumn fruitage smiled in crowns of pride

O human tree;
Waesome wailing tree;
In the winter wind how it rocks! how it grieves!
On a little low grave-mound,
All its bravery lies discrowned:
O'er its fallen fruit it heaps the withered leaves.

XV.

"PRETTY flowers on Baby's head;
Who'll cry flowers when Baby's dead?"

Singing hearts oft questionéd,
In the sweetest summer fled.
Marian, Marian.

Tearful words, how lightly said!
Mournfully rememberéd,
Now the sweet new year hath spread
Blossom-life on Baby's bed.
Marian, Marian.

Tender emerald, white and red,
Flowers of her beauty bred:
Breathing all of her that's dead,
Cry, "We crown her Baby-head!"
Marian, Marian

"Who'll cry flowers when Baby's dead?"
Praying looks to heaven are led,
And it smiles as tho' it said,
"Early her sweet fame hither sped."
Marian, Marian.

"Faith, look up and firmly tread:
Poor Bereaved, be comforted;
I will nurse the Child instead;
My Flowers garland Baby's head."
Marian, Marian.

God's unguessed reply is read:
Tears that came not, tears that pled
Crying darkly, here are shed:
Soft rest you, Darling! dead
Marian, Marian.

XVI.

Our leaves are shaken from the tree,
Our hopes laid low,

That after our Spring-nurslings, we
 May long to go.

The warm love-nest our little Doves leave
 With helpless moan,
As they for us at heart would grieve
 In heaven—alone!

The tender Shepherd beckoningly
 Our Lambs doth hold,
That we may take our own when He
 Makes up the fold.

ROBERT BURNS.

A CENTENARY SONG.

A HUNDRED years ago this morn,
He came to walk our human way;
And we would change the Crown of Thorn
For healing leaves to-day.

But we can only hang our wreath
Upon the cold white Marble's brow!
Tho' loud we speak, or low we breathe,
We cannot reach him now.

He loved us all! He loved so much!
His heart of love the world could hold;
And now the whole wide world with such
A love would round him fold.

'T is long and late before it wakes,
So kindly, yet a true world still;
It hath a heart so large, it takes
A century to fill.

AY, tell the wondrous tale to-day,
While songs are sung, and warm words said
Tell how he wore the hodden grey,
And won sweat-sweetened bread,

With wintry welcome at the door
Did Nature greet him to his lot;
Our royal Minstrel of the Poor,
Hid in an old clay Cot.

There, in the bonny Bairntime dawn,
He nestled at his Mother's knee,
With such a face as might have drawn
The Angels down to see

That rosy Innocent at prayer,
So pure and ready for the hand
Of Her who is Guardian Angel where
Babes sleep in Silent Land.

There, young Love slyly came, to bring
Rare balms that will bewitch the blood,
To dance while happy Spirits sing,
With life in hey-day flood.

And there she found her darling Child,
The robust Muse of sun-browned health,
Who nurst him up into the wild
Young heir of all her wealth:

And there she rockt his infant thought,
Asleep with visions glorious
That hallow now the Poor Man's Cot
For evermore to us:

Disguised Angelic Playmates were
Those still ideal dreams of Youth,
That drew it on to Greatness, there
We find them shaped in truth!

And there he learned the touch that thrills
Right to the natural heart of things;
Struck rootage down to where Life heals
At the eternal Springs:

Before the lords of earth there stood
  A Man by Nature born and bred,
To show us on what simple food
    A Hero may be fed.

No gifts of gold for him, no crown
  Of Fortune ready for his brow;
But wrestling strength to earn his own;
    It shines in glory now!

He rose up in a dawn of light
  That burst upon the olden day;
Many weird voices of the night
    In his music passed away.

He caught them, Witch and Warlock! ere
  They vanisht; all the revelry
Of wizard wonder we must wear
    The Mask of sleep to see.

Droll Humours came for him to paint
  Their pictures! straight his merry eye
Had taken them, so queer and quaint,
    We laugh until we cry.

Wild music on lone shingly shores;
  Wild winds that break in seas of sound;
Sad twilights eerie on the moors;
    The murdered Martyr's mound;

Dark awful shadows trailing like
  The great skirts of the hurrying Storm;
Wan purple thunder-lights that strike
    The woodlands wet and warm;

12

Meek glimpses of peculiar grace
  Where Beauty lieth in undress
Asleep in secret hiding place,
    Out in the wilderness;

Those sunsets where-thro' God's good-night
  To our fair world is smiled, and felt;
All, all enrich his ear and sight—
    Thro' all his being melt.

He knew the sorrows of poor folk,
  He felt for all their patient pain;
And from his clouded soul he shook
    A music soft as rain.

For them his eyes would brim with balm,
  Dark eyes, and flashing as the levin—
Grew at a touch as sweet and calm
    As are the eyes of heaven.

So rich in sadness is his breast
  That tenderness, heaven-mirroring, fills,
As lies the soft blue lake at rest
    Among the rugged hills.

And quick as Mother's milk will rise,
  At thrill of her babe's touch, and strong
It heaves his heart, and floods his eyes,
    And overflows his song;

In Life's low ways, and starless night,
  The Poor so often have to creep
Where Manhood may not walk full height,
    And this made Robin weep.

But none dare sneer, who see the tear
  In Robin Burns's honest eye,
With all the weakness, it comes clear
    From where the Thunders lie.

Such Ardours flash from out that dew,
  And quiver in that pearl of pain,
The Spirit of Lightning thrilling thro'
    Its drop of tempest rain!

Of all the Birds the Robin he
  Is darling of the gentle Poor;
His nest is sacred, he goes free
    By window or by door:

His lot is lowly, and his wings
  Are only of the homely brown,
But in the rainy day he sings
    When gayer friends have flown,

And hoarded up for us he brings,
  In that brave breast of bonny red,
A gathered glory of the Springs
    And Summers long, long fled.

Even so all Birds of Song above,
  To which the poor man smiling turns,
The darling of his listening love
    Is gentle Robin Burns:

His summer soul our winter warms,
  He makes a glory in our gloom;
His nest is safe from all the storms,
    For ever in our home.

Yes, there is such a human glow
  Of life and love in Robin's breast,
Its warmth can melt the winter snow
    In Poverty's cold nest.

Auld Scotland's Music wandered long,
  And wailed and wailed about the land,
Divinely yearning in her wrong,
    And sorrowfully grand;

And many toucht responsive chords,
  But could not tell what she would say;
Till Robin wed her with his words,
    And they were One for aye.

His Ministers of Music win
  Their way where night is all so mirk,
You scarce can see the Devil in
    That darkness at his work,

Or feel the face of friends from foes;
  But these Song-Spirits softly come,
And lo! a light of heaven glows
    Within the poorest home.

On either side the hearth they glide,
  And take the empty seat of Care,
Immortal Presences that bide
    In blessed beauty there.

They set us singing at our work,
  Or where no ringing voice is found;
Out smiles the music that may lurk
    In thoughts too fine for sound.

They weave some pictured tints that shine
  Luminous in life's cold grey woof;
They make the vine of Patience twine
    About the barest roof.

More sweet his songs, to him who plods
  Shut up in smoky city prison,
Than to the cagéd Lark cool sods
    Cut ere the sun be risen.

The Soldier feels them as a spring
  Of healing mid the Indian sand;
They gush within him, and they bring
    Such news of the old land!

With them the Sailor warms his heart,
  Out on the bitter wintry sea;
With them our serfs ennobled start
    I' the knighthood of the Free!

Ah, how some old sweet Cradle-song
  The wayward wandering heart still brings
Home! home again, with ties as strong
    As Love's own leading-strings.

We hug the Homestead, and more near
  The fresh and fonder tendrils twine
To make our clasp more close for fear
    Our dear ones we may tine.

When Hesper thro' some shady nook
  Sparkles on Lovers face to face,
Where droopt lids shade a burning look,
    With beauty's shyer grace —

And holy is the hour for love,
  And all so silent comes the Night,
Lest even a breath of faërie move
    That poise so feather light —

Where two hearts weigh, to blight or bless,
  Till swarming like a summer hive,
The inner world of happiness
    With music grows alive —

There as Life aches so, heart in heart,
  And hand in hand so fondly yearns,
Love shakes his wings, and soars and sings
    Some song of Robin Burns.

THINK how those Heroes, true till death,
  In Lucknow listened thro' the strife,
And held what seemed their latest breath
    They had to draw in life,

To hear the old Scots' Music dear
  Ask, down the battle pauses brief,
As Havelock's men, with fire and cheer,
    Swept in to their relief —

"*Should auld acquaintance be forgot?*"
  Thro' flaming hell we come! we come!
To keep that pledge, not given for nought,
    Around the hearth at home;

"*We'll take a cup o' kindness*" here,
  For Scotland yet, and Auld Lang Syne;
Ay, tho' that cup be filled with dear
    Heart's blood instead of wine;

"*And here's a hand, my trusty friend,*"
  And then it seemed the dear old Land
Did burst their tomb, the death-shroud rend,
    And clasp them with her hand.

How dearly Robin lo'ed the land
  That gave such gallant heroes birth;
Its wee blue bit of heaven, and
    Its dear green nook of earth.

And dearer is the purple heath,
  The bonny broom of beamless gold;
And sweeter is the mellow breath
    Of Autumn on the wold!

Where he once lookt with glorious gaze,
  In all our way-side wanderings,
Shy Beauty lifts her veil of haze,
    And smiles in common things.

The Daisy opes its eye at dawn,
  And straight from Nature's heart so true,
The tear of Burns peeps sparkling! one
    Immortal drop of dew!

With eyes a thought more tender, we
  Look on all dumb and helpless things;
In his large love they stand, as He
    Had sheltered them with wings.

Down by the singing burn we greet
  His voice of love and liberty;
High on the bleak hill-side we meet
    His Spirit blythe and free!

And on this land should Foe e'er tread,
He will fight for it at our side,
Flame on our Banners overhead,
In songs of victory ride.

A HUNDRED years ago To-day,
The great and glorious Stranger came;
Men wondered as he went his way
A wild and wandering flame.

The fiercer fire of life confined,
With higher wave 't will heave and break,
And higher should the mountain mind
Thrust up its starward peak:

But often is the kindling clay
With its red lightnings rent and riven,
And Earth holds up a wreck to pray
For healing hand of Heaven.

Around his soul more sternly warred
The powers that smite for Wrong and Right
And thunder-scathed and battle-scarred,
Death bore him from the fight.

But now we recognise in him,
One of the high and shining race;
All gone the mortal mists that dim
The fair immortal face.

The splendour of a thousand Suns
Is shining! and the tearful rain
No more with passionate pathos runs,
And there is no more pain.

The sorrow and suffering, soil and shame
  All gone! all far away have passed;
He sitteth in the heavens of fame,
    Quietly crowned at last.

The prowling Ghoul hath left his grave,
  Husht is the praying Pharisee;
His frailties fade, his Virtues brave
    Shall work immortally.

The Spots on this side of our Star,
  We saw because it burned so bright;
But on the other side they are
    All lost in greater light.

Weep, weep exulting tears that he,
  The lowly born, the Peasant's son,
Hath wrought for us imperishably;
    A peerless place hath won!

And such a Crown to bind thy brow,
  Thy glorious Child hath gained for thee,
Thou grey old nurse of Heroes! thou
    Proud Mother, Poverty!

Look up! and let the big tears be
  Triumphant toucht with sparks of pride;
Look up! in his great glory we
    Are also glorified.

Or weep the tear that Pity wrings
  To think his brightness he should dim;
Then 'tis the tear of sorrow brings
    Us nearer unto him:

'T is here we touch his garment, here
The poorest or the frailest earns
The right to call him kinsman dear,
Our Brother, Robin Burns.

In fires of suffering far more fair
We forge the precious bond of love
Ah, Robin, if God hear our prayer
'T is all made well above.

And you who comforted His Poor
In this world, have eternal home
With those He comforteth, His Poor!
In all the world to come.

Dear Highland Mary went before
To plead for you in saintly sooth,
Whom she remembered when you wore
The purity of Youth.

With those high Bards who live for aye,
Your faults and failings all forgiven —
May there be festival to-day,
And a great joy in Heaven!

The truth afar off found at last;
The triumph rung impetuously
Thro' all that Crystal Palace vast
Of white Eternity.

Ah, Robin, could you but return
Once more, how changed it all would be
The heart of this wide world doth yearn
To take you welcomingly

Warm eyes would shine at windows; quick
  Warm hands would greet you at the door,
Where oft they let you pass heart sick,
    So heedlessly of yore!

And they would have you wear the Crown
  Who bade you bear the crushing cross;
Their glorious gain was all unknown,
    Without the bitter loss:

The cup you carried was so filled,
  The pressing crowd so eager round,
Dragged down your lifted arm, and spilled
    Such dear drops on the ground!

How we would comfort your distress,
  Would see you smile as once you smiled,
And hold your hands in silentness,
    Strong man and little child!

Your poor heart heaving like the waves
  Of seas that moan for evermore,
And try to creep into the caves
    Of Rest, but find no shore —

Poor heart! come rest thee from the strife;
  Come, rest thee, rest thee in the calm,
We'd cry: come bathe thy weary life
    In Love's immortal balm!

We cannot see your face, Robin!
  Your flashing lip! your fearless brow;
We cannot hear your voice, Robin!
    But you are with us now:

Altho' the mortal face is dark
  Behind the veil of spirit-wings,
You draw us up as Heaven the Lark
    When its music in him sings.

With tender awe we feel you near,
  You make our lifted faces shine;
You brim our cup with kindness here,
    For sake of Auld Lang Syne.

We are one at heart as Britain's sons,
  Because you join our clasping hands,
While one electric feeling runs
    Thro' all the English lands.

And near or far where Britons band,
  To-day the leal and true heart turns
More fondly to the fatherland
    For love of Robin Burns.

TO A BEREAVED FRIEND.

God comfort you, my Friend, God comfort you
How mighty, how immeasurable your loss
I can but dimly know; yet I have learned
That only the most precious die so soon.
I can but stand without, and dare not thrust
My hand betwixt the curtains of your grief;
I cannot reach you sitting in the dark
Of that lone desert where the silence stuns,
And sound of sobbing would be kind relief.
But might I speak some word that with a touch
Should make your cup of sorrow overbrim
In tears that suck the sting from out the soul!
I too have felt the gloom that brings heaven near,
The love whose kissings are all unreturned,

And longed to lie down with the quiet dead
And share their long sweet rest. I too have known
This strain and crack of heart-strings, this wild whirl
And wallow of sense in which the soul seems drowned.
You are the husband of an angel, I
Have two sweet Babes in bliss. We are very poor
On earth, my Friend, but very rich in Heaven.
Two years ago you comforted my loss;
One year ago I sang your wedding song,
And now She is not! She who had only lookt
On life thro' coloured windows of her dreams!
All in the softest, sweetest breath of God
The bud of her dear beauty seemed to have blown,
Your one-year darling who but sprang, and died,
And left the fragrance of her memory,
A blessed memory and a blessed hope!
She had the shy grace of a woodland flower;
In her Love veiled his look with timid wings;
And her eyes deepened with a sadness rich,
As tho' the mountain-tops of heaven-toucht thought
Made mirrored shadows in their lakes of light.
Only a brief while did she wear the mask
Of flesh that kept the fond immortal face
Without a stain of earth or soil of time,
And now her Nun-like spirit takes the veil
In Heaven's cloistral calm. Look up, my friend,
And bravely bear the mantle of her pain,
Which fell from her for you to wear for her!
Look up, my friend, and may one blessed glimpse
Of all her glory touch your tears with light!
Only in heaven can the dark grow starry,
Only in heaven comes the wished-for dawn.
She liveth in the sight of Him that sees
You also; Ye are one still in God's eye
That from his picture of the Universe
Turns on us in whatever worlds we move.

LONG EXPECTED.

O MANY and many a day before we met,
I knew some spirit walkt the world alone,
Awaiting the Beloved from afar;
And I was the anointed chosen one
Of all the world to crown her queenly brows
With the imperial crown of human love,
And light its glory in her happy look.
I saw not with mine eyes so full of tears,
But heard Faith's low sweet singing in the night,
And, groping thro' the darkness, toucht God's hand.
I knew my sunshine somewhere warm'd the world,
Tho' I trode darkling in a perilous way;
And I should reach it in His own good time
Who sendeth sun, and dew, and love for all:
My heart might toil on blindly, but, like earth,
It kept sure footing thro' the thickest gloom.
Earth, with her many voices, talkt of thee!—
Low winds, and whispering leaves, and piping birds;
The amorous sunlight, and the virgin dews;
Eve's crimson air and light of twinkling gold;
Spring's kindled greenery, and her breath of balm;
The dance of happiness in summer woods,
To silver dulcimer of sunny rain.
Thine eyes oped with their rainy lights, and laughters,
In April's tearful heaven of tender blue,
With all the changeful beauty melting thro' them,
And Dawn and Sunset ended in thy face.
And standing as in God's own presence-chamber,
When silence lay like sleep upon the world,
And it seem'd rich to die, alone with Night,
Like Moses 'neath the kisses of God's lips!
The Stars have trembled thro' the holy hush,
And smiled down tenderly, and read to me

The love hid for me in a budding breast,
Like incense folded in a young flower's heart.
Strong as a sea-swell came the wave of wings,
Strange trouble trembled thro' my inner depths,
And answering wings have sprung within my soul:
And from the dumb waste places of the dark,
A voice has breathed, "She comes!" and ebb'd again;
While all my life stood listening for thy coming.
O, I have guess'd thy weird invisible presence,
And felt it in the beating of my heart.
When all was dark within, sweet thoughts would come,
As starry guests come golden down the gloom,
And thro' Night's lattice smile a rare delight:
While, lifted for the dear and distant Dawn,
The face of all things wore a happy light,
Like those dream-smiles which are the speech of Sleep.
Thus Love lived on, and strengthen'd with the days,
Lit by its own true light within my heart,
Like a live diamond burning in the dark.
Then came there One, a mirage of the Dawn:
She swam on towards me sumptuous in her triumph,
Voluptuously upborne, like Aphrodite
Upon a meadowy swell of emerald sea.
A ripe, serene, smile-affluent graciousness
Hung like a shifting radiance on her motion,
As feathered flames upon the Dove's neck burn.
Her lip might flush a wrinkled life in bloom!
Her eyes were an omnipotence of love!
"O eyes!" I said, "if such your glories be,
Sure 't is a warm heart feedeth ye with light!"
The silver throbbing of her laughter pulst
The air with music rich and resonant, —
As, from the deep heart of a summer night,
Some bird with sudden sparklings of fine sound
Strikes all the startled stillness into song.
And from her sumptuous wealth of golden hair

Down to the delicate, pearly finger-tip,
Fresh beauty trembled from its thousand springs:
And standing in the outer porch of life,
All eager for the templed mysteries,
With a rich heart as full of fragrant love
As May's musk-roses are of morning's wine,
What marvel if I question'd not her brow,
For the flame-signet of the Hand divine,
Or gauged it for the crown of my large love?
I plunged to clutch the pearl of her babbling beauty,
Like some swift diver in a shallow stream,
That smites his life out on its heart of stone.
Ah! how my life did run with fire and tears!
With what a Titan-pulse my love did beat!
But she, rose-warm without,—God pity her!—
Was cold at heart as snow in last year's nest,
And struck like death into my burning brain.
My tears, that rain'd out life, she froze in falling,
And wore them, jewel-like, to deck her triumph!
But love is never lost, tho' hearts run waste;
Its tides may gush 'mid swirling, swathing deserts,
Where no green leaf drinks up the precious life:
Yet love doth evermore enrich itself,—
Its bitterest waters run some golden sands!
No star goes down but climbs in other skies;
The flower of Sunset folds its glory up,
To burst again from out the heart of Dawn;
And love is never lost, tho' hearts run waste,
And sorrow makes the chasten'd heart a seer;
The deepest dark reveals the starriest hope,
And Faith can trust her heaven behind the veil.

WOOED AND WON.

THE plough of Time breaks up our Eden-land,
And tramples down its flowery virgin prime.
Yet thro' the dust of ages living shoots
O' the old immortal seed start in the furrows;
And, where Love looketh on with glorious eye,
These quicken'd germs of everlastingness
Flower lusty, as of old in Paradise!
And blessings on the starry chance of love!—
And blessings on the morn of merry May!
That led my footsteps to your beechen bower.
Thus hangs the picture in my mind, sweet Wife!
Clear as a Millais in its tint and tone.
Nature went by me with her glorious shows.
The birds were singing on the blossoming sprays,
With Love's sweet mystery stirring at their hearts,
Like first spring-motions in the veins o' the flowers.
A light of green laught up the shining hills,
That rounded through the mellowing, gloating air,
As their big hearts heaved to some heart beyond,
Or strove with inner yearnings for the crown
Of purple rondure smiling there in heaven!
The Flowers were forth in all their conquering beauty,
And, winking in their Mother Earth's old face,
Said, all her children should have happy hearts.
Deeper and deeper in the wood's green gloom
I nestled for the fever at life's core:
And thirstily my heart was drinking in
Rich overflowings of some Cushat's love;
When lo! the air instinct with glory grew,
As if the world, while on her starry journey,
Found sudden harbour in the clime of heaven.
Upon a primrose bank you sat,—a sight
To couch the old blind sorrow of my soul!
A sweet, new blossom of Humanity,

Fresh fallen from God's own home to flower on
earth.
A golden burst of sunbeams glinted through
The verdurous roof's lush-leavy greenery,
And on you dropt its crown of wavering light.
Your eyes—half-shut, while through their silken
eaves
Trembled the secret sweetness hid at heart—
Oped sudden at full, and wide with wonderment!
The sweetest eyes that ever drank sun for soul:
As subtly tender as a summer heaven,
Brimm'd with the beauty of a starry night!
Your face, so dewy fresh and wondrous fair,
Kindled as Love transfiguringly rose
Like heavenward martyr thro' a birth of fire!
The fleetest swallow-dip of a tender smile
Ran round your mouth in thrillings; while your
cheek
Dimpled, as from the arch God's finger-print,
Out flew his signal, fluttering in a blush!
And when your voice broke up the air for music,
It smote upon my startled heart as smites
The new-born babe's first cry a mother's ear,
Yet strangely toucht some mystic memory,
And dimly seem'd an old familiar sound.
That day, with an immortalizing kiss,
You crown'd me monarch of your rich heart-world,
Which heaved a boundless sea of love, whose tides
Ran radiant pulsings thro' your rosy limbs.
How the love-lights did float up in your eyes,
Star after star from violet depths of night!
Dear eyes! all craving with Love's ache and hun-
ger!
And all the spirit stood in your face athirst!
And from the rose-cup of your murmuring mouth
Sweetness o'erflow'd, as from a fragrant fount.
O kiss of life! that oped our Eden-world!
The harvest of an age's wealth of bliss
In that first kiss was reapt in one rich minute!

The wanton airs came breathing like the touch
Of fragrant lips that feed the blood with flame!
The very earth heaved bosom-like, and heaven
Clung round and claspt us as in glowing arms,
To crush the wine of all your ripen'd beauty,
Which were a fitting sacrament for death—
Into a costly cup of life for me.

THE BRIDAL.

SHE comes! the blushing Bridal Dawn,
With her Auroral splendours on!
And green Earth never lovelier shone:

She floateth on her azure way,
In dainty dalliance with the May,
Jubilant o'er the happy day!

Earth weareth heaven for bridal-ring,
And the best garland of glory, Spring
From out old Winter's world can bring.

All in white are the hawthorn boughs,
The green blood reddens in the Rose!
And every May-bud gleams or glows.

The Apple-tree on its green bough
Hath caught a cloud of rosy snow;
Up in the blue the Chestnuts blow.

Cloud-shadow-ships swim faërily
Over the greenery's sunny sea,
That runs and ripples down the lea.

The Birds, a-brooding, strive to sing,
Feeling the life warm under the wing:
Their love, too, blossoms with the Spring!

The winds that make the flowers blow,
Heavy with balm, breathe soft and low,
A budding warmth, an amorous glow!

More sweet than the Sabean South,
They kiss like some endearing mouth,
And balm the splendour's drooping drouth:

Such a delicious feel doth flood
The eyes, as laves the burning bud
When cool rains feed ambrosial blood.

O, merrily Life doth revel and reign!
Light in heart, and blithe in brain;
Running like wine in every vein.

Alive with eyes, the Village sees
The Bridal dawning from the trees,
And Housewives swarm i' the sun like Bees.

Silence sits i' the Belfry-Choir!
Up in the twinkling air the spire
Throbs, golden in the bickering fire.

The winking windows burn and blush
With colours rare as flow and flush
Thro' summer sunsets bloom'd and hush.

But, enter: rarer splendours brim,
Such mists of gold and purple swim,
And the light falls so rich and dim.

Even so doth Love Life's doors unbar,
Where all the hidden glories are,
That from the windows shine afar.

Love's lovely to the passers-by,
But they who love are region'd high
On hills of Bliss, with heaven nigh.

Sumptuous as Iris, when she swims
With rainbow robe on dainty limbs,
The Bride's rare beauty overbrims!

The gazers drink rich overflows,
Her cheek a livelier damask glows,
And on his arm she leans more close.

A drunken joy reels in his blood,
He wanders an enchanted wood;
She ranges realms of perfect good.

Dear God! that he alone hath grace
To light such splendour in her face,
And win the blessing of embrace!

She wears her maiden modesty
With tearful grace toucht tenderly,
Yet with a ripe Expectancy!

Her virgin veil reveals a form,
Flowering from the bud so warm,
It needs must break the Cestus-charm.

Last night, with her white wedding arms,
And thoughts that throng'd with quaint alarms,
She trembled o'er her mirror'd charms,

Like Eve first-glassing her new life;
And the Maid startled at the Wife,
Heart-painéd with a sweet, warm strife.

The unknown sea moans on her shore
Of life: she hears the breakers roar;
But, trusting Him, she fears no more;

For, o'er the deep seas there is calm,
Full as the hush of all-heaven's psalm:
The golden goal, — the Victor's palm!

And at her heart Love sits and sings,
And broodeth warmth, begetting wings
Shall lift her life to higher things.

The Blessing given, the ring is on;
And at God's Altar radiant run
The currents of two lives in one!

Husht with happiness, every sense
Is crowded at the heart intense;
And silence hath such eloquence!

Down to his feet her meek eyes stoop,
As *there* her love should pour its cup;
But, like a King, he lifts them up.

Her flashing face to heaven up-turns,
As for God's gracious kiss it yearns:
Through all her life Hope's sunrise burns!

And now she trembles to his breast,
To proudly crown his loving quest;
And make it aye her happy nest:

His arms her hyacinth head caress,
And fold her fragrant slenderness,
With all its touching tenderness.

Now, on heaven's coast of crystal, crown'd
Hesper lights life's outward-bound:
And Evening folds her purple round.

A palace rich with glorious shows
She maketh his life's narrow house
To-night: but there he keeps no rouse!

Alone they hold their marriage-feast:
Fresh from the Chrism of the Priest,
He would not have the happiest jest

To storm her brows with a crimson fine;
And, sooth, they need no wings of wine
To waft them into Love's divine.

So Strength and Beauty, hand-in-hand,
Go forth into the honey'd land,
Lit by the love-moon golden-grand,

Where God hath built their Bridal-bower;
And on the top of life they tower,
And taste of Eden's perfect hour.

No lewd eyes o'er my shoulder look!
They do but ope the blessed book
Of Marriage, in their hallowed nook.

O, flowery be the paths they press,
And ruddiest human fruitage bless
Them, with a lavish loveliness!

Melodious move their wedded life
Thro' shocks of time, and storms of strife,—
Husband true, and perfect wife!

WEDDED LOVE.

The summer Night comes brooding down on Earth,
As Love comes brooding down on human hearts,
With bliss that hath no utterance save rich tears.
She floats in fragrance down the smiling dark,
Foldeth a kiss upon the lips of Life,
Curtaineth into rest the weary world,
And shuts us in with all our hid delights.
The stars come sparkling thro' the tender gloom,
Like dew-drops in the fields of heaven; or tears
That hang rich jewels on the face of Night.

A spirit-feel comes down the calm, and soft
The Flowers fold their cups like praying hands,
And with droopt head await the blessing, Night
Gives with her Motherly magnanimity.
'T is evening with the world; but in my soul
The light of wedded love is still at dawn!
And skies my world, an everlasting Dawn.
My heart rings out in music, like a Lark
Hung in the charmèd palace of the Morn,
That circles singing to its mate i' the nest,
With luminous being running o'er with song:
So my life flutters round its mate at home!
There, with her eyes turn'd on her heart, she reads
The golden secrets written in its heaven,
And broodeth o'er its hidden wealth of love,
As Night i' the hush and halo of her beauty
Bares throbbing heaven to its most tremulous depths,
And broods in silence o'er her starry wealth.
And, fingering in her bosom's soft, white nest,
A fair babe, beautiful as Dawn in heaven,
Made of a Mother's richest thoughts of love, —
Lies like a smile of sunshine among lilies,
That giveth glory — drinketh fragrant life.
Sweet bud upon a Rose! our plot of spring,
And burst of bloom amid a wintry world!
How dear it is to mark the look of life
Deepen, and darken, in her large, round eyes, —
To watch the little rose put forth its leaves,
And guess the perfumed secret of its heart;
To catch the silver words that come to break
The golden silence hung like heaven around!
But lo, my hush of thought is thrilling, as
A wood at night is filled with sudden song:
Dear Wife! with sweet, low voice, she syllables
Some precious music hoarded in her heart,
And I am flooded with melodious rain,
Like Nature standing crown'd with sunlit showers.

"As the surging heart o' the Sea yearneth everlastingly
For the Moon, heaven-charmèd by her influence:
And as Star to Star with love palpitateth like a dove,
So my heart yearns up to his bright eminence.

"O my Love, he seems to stand where Heaven leans so near at hand,
That from other world his lineaments take light:
And he fills my cup of wonder, flooding all my life with splendour,
As a glorious, golden Moon fills all the night.

"At his violet-sweet words my heart carols like a bird's,
And rich instincts burst from out it like heaven-flowers;
Wings bud in me at his kiss, all my being brims with bliss,
As a valley brims with life in spring-tide hours.

"O my life was dark and cold as the night-dews on the wold,
Waiting to be made alive with fire of dawn;
Till his presence on me lighten'd, and his blessing on me brighten'd,
And my life like dews lit up for heaven shone."

NAY, Sweet Heart! that should be my song, who search
Love's lore in vain for meet similitudes
To symbol what thy love hath been to me.
The God lies prison'd in the mountain stone,

The muffled Music slumbers in the strings,
Awaiting the Deliverer's magic touch!
So, thou belovèd! did I wait for Thee,
To waken at thy touch. My Tree of being
But made blind gropings in the dark, cold earth,
And moan'd and trembled in the wintry air,
Stretching out naked hands to pluck at life:
Until you came, with all your light, and warmth,
Encircling round it like a summer heaven,
And fed, and clad it with your fragrant beauty,
Till budding branches burst on fire with bloom,
And into ripe fruits mellow'd goldenly.
My life lay barren as a desolate moor
That breaks, and burns, in twinkling green and gold,
When Spring doth greet it with her kiss of life.
As weary earth goes darkling thro' the night,
So my heart toil'd on, tearful with its burthen:
No beacon burn'd thro' all the gloom, to break
The sea of dark, with shining piers of light:
Then on a sudden rose the blessed Morn,
Sun-crown'd my life, made all things beautiful,
And gave the world its Eden-robes again.
My spirit rose up orient with light;
Thy presence caught my heart up at the leap,
Wing'd like a young world from the hands of God!
Methought a thousand graves of buried hopes
Could crush it not from its proud eminence.
The Future's dim cloud-curtain rent in twain,
And lighten'd radiant revelation: All
Life's purpose dawn'd, as unto dying eyes
The dark of Death doth blossom into stars.
And since we met, thy life-long thought hath been
To be cup-bearer of the wine of joy
To one leal heart, and to make rich one life.
Pulse after pulse, thy life hath surged in mine,
Like sea-waves hurrying up the beach to crown
Their shore, and break in starry showers of light.
Thou hast brought radiant sunrise every morn,

Renewing all the glory past away.
Thy tender love hath twined about my life,
Like the fair Woodbine wedded to the Thorn;
Hiding its harshness with her wealth of flowers!
My heart drinks inspiration at thine eyes,
And lights my brain up as with fragrant flame:
Sweet eyes of starry tenderness, thro' which
The soul of some immortal sorrow looks!
Sorrow that addeth grace to loveliness,
As its sad bloom enricheth blushing fruit.
Dear Eyes! they have a radiant Alchemy,
And pierce my being with such quickening light
As makes my heart a jewel-mine of love;
Even as the Sun strikes thro' the dark cold Earth,
And fires her million veins with precious life.
My Life ran like a river in rocky ways,
And seaward dasht, a sounding cataract!
But thine was like a quiet lake of beauty,
Soft-shadow'd round by gracious influences,
That gathers silently its wealth of earth,
And woos heaven till it melts down into it.
They mingled: and the glory, and the calm,
Closed round me, brooding into perfect rest.
O blessings on thy true and tender heart!
How it hath gone forth like the Dove of old,
To bring some leaf of promise in Life's deluge!
Thou hast a strong up-soaring tendency,
That bears me God-ward, as the stalwart oak
Uplifts the clinging vine, and gives it growth.
Thy reverent heart familiarly doth take
Unconscious clasp of high and holy things,
Like little children playing of old with Christ;
And trusteth where it may not understand.
We have had sorrows, love! and wept the tears
That run the rose-hue from the cheek of Life;
But Grief hath jewels as Night hath her stars,
And she revealeth what we ne'er had known,
With Joy wreaths danced about o'er our blinded
eyes.

The heart is like an instrument whose strings
Steal nobler music from Life's many frets:
The golden threads are spun thro' Suffering's fire,
Wherewith the marriage-robes for heaven are woven:
And all the rarest hues of human life
Take radiance, and are rainbow'd out in tears.
Thou 'rt little changed, dear love! since first was wed
To mine, the blossom of thy crimson lips;
Thy beauty hath climaxt like a crescent Moon,
With glory great'ning to the golden full.
Thy flowers of spring are crown'd with summer fruits,
And thou hast put a queenlier presence on
With thy regality of Womanhood!
Yet Time but toucheth thee with mellowing shades
That set thy graces in a wealthier light.
Thy soul still looks with its rare smile of light,
From the Gate Beautiful of its palace-home,
Fair as the spirit of the evening Star,
That lights its glory as a radiant porch
To beacon earth with brighter glimpse of heaven.
We are poor in this world's wealth, but rich in love;
And they who love feel rich in every thing.
The heart of Ocean — thick with gems, as earth
With blooms — is jewell'd like a Bride o' the East:
The heart of Heaven swarms with golden worlds:
A subtle heart of wealth hath our old world,
And darks of diamonds, grand as nights of stars:
But richer is the human heart that shrines
God's peerless wealth — th' immortal jewel Love!
So let us live our life: and let our love,
Our large twin-love, bend o'er our little Babe,
As the calm grand old heavens bend over earth,
Revealing God's own starry thoughts and things!
So shall the image of our hearts' Ideal —
The angel nestling in her bud of life —

Smile upward in the mirror of her face
A daily beauty in our darken'd ways,
And a perpetual feast of holy things.
O let us walk the world, so that our love
Burn like a blessed beacon, beautiful
Upon the walls of Life's surrounding dark.
Ah! what a world 't would be if love like ours
Made heaven in human hearts, and clothed with smiles
The sweet sad face of our Humanity!
What lives should quicken into sudden spring!
What flowers of glory burst their frozen soil!
Like the red pulse of Dawn thro' cold grey skies,
New life should flush up in the darken'd face
That readeth as a written epitaph
Above the grave of beauty and of soul!
Love-light should glimmer on the Helot's brow,
As mellow moonlight silvers thro' a cloud;
And God should come into the mirkest being,
As Stars new-kindled, light up nights of space.

LYRICS OF LOVE.

MY BONNY LADY.

EVE gave us her fair Daughters to restore
The Eden that their Mother lost of yore;
They lead us thro' the Angel-guarded door,
And where they smile it blooms for evermore.
Dearest of all Eve's Daughters dear is she
Who makes an Eden in my Home for me;
My Bonny Lady.

No seeming beauty perilous to know,
Like dream of ripeness on the sour sloe,
But sweet to the true heart as summer fruit,
And sound and strong to love's most secret root;
A soul made human by its kindling life!
A woman ripened to the perfect Wife!
My Bonny Lady.

She grows in graces as the flowers bloom;
Her robe of beauty woven in Heaven's loom!
She wears her jewels in her lips and eyes:
Diamond sparks! warm rubies! pearls of price!
And see what shapely sweetness may be shown,
Bright budding from a simple morning gown!
My Bonny Lady.

Upon her dear brow is no band of care
That binds the heavy burden souls must bear;
The dew of childhood's Heaven yet lingering lies
Cool in the shadows of her morning eyes;
So may some spirit in its brightness wait
With welcome at the beautiful heaven gate.
My Bonny Lady.

Eyelids once lifted with the kiss of Love,
Droop tender after as the brooding dove!
Lips, when the soul of joy is tasted, will
Hush its loud sound of laughter, and be still.
Yet is she happy as the lark that sings,
Winnowing out the music with his wings;
My Bonny Lady.

Lo, how she bows with soft and settled bliss,
Over her babe in breathless tenderness!
Her image that my Lily bends above,
To mingle One in my heart's sea of Love!
Thus hath she doubled love and Love's caress,
With doubled blessing,.doubled power to bless.
My Bonny Lady.

Her smile the sum of sweetness infinite!
Her neck a throne where many graces sit!
Like music of the soul her motion is,
But none can know the inner sanctities;
Outside they stand in wonder, I alone,
Pass in to worship at the spirit-throne.
My Bonny Lady.

Behold her in religious lustre stand,
Clothed all in white and fit for spirit land!
Her thankful eyes uplift fo · angel food;
And you might worship her, so pure, so good;
For all shy beauty, all sweet shadowy grace,
Breaks into brightness through my Lady's face;
My Bonny Lady.

I think of her and mine eyes softly close
While all my heart with sweetness overflows;
Each breath it breathes in blessing sets astir
Some gracious balm, and sweet as hidden myrrh.
My Rest while toiling up the hill of life!
A Halfway House to Heaven! my noble Wife!
My Bonny Lady.

TO A BELOVED ONE.

HEAVEN hath its crown of Stars, the Earth
Her glory-robe of flowers —
The Sea its gems — the grand old Woods
Their songs and greening showers:
The Birds have homes, where leaves and blooms
In beauty wreathe above;
High yearning hearts, their rainbow-dream —
And we, Sweet! we have love.

We walk not with the jewell'd Great,
Where Love's dear name is sold;
Yet have we wealth we would not give
For all their world of gold!
We revel not in Corn and Wine,
Yet have we from above
Manna divine, and we 'll not pine,
While we may live and love.

There 's sorrow for the toiling poor,
On Misery's bosom nursed:
Rich robes for ragged souls, and Crowns
For branded brows Cain-curst!
But Cherubim, with clasping wings,
Ever about us be,
And, happiest of God's happy things!
There 's love for you and me.

Thy lips, that kiss till death, have turn'd
Life's water into wine;
The sweet life melting thro' thy looks,
Hath made my life divine.
All Love's dear promise hath been kept,
Since thou to me wert given;
A ladder for my soul to climb,
And summer high in heaven.

I know, dear heart! that in our lot
May mingle tears and sorrow;
But, Love's rich Rainbow 's built from tears
To-day, with smiles To-morrow.
The sunshine from our sky may die,
The greenness from Life's tree,
But ever, 'mid the warring storm,
Thy nest shall shelter'd be.

I see thee! Ararat of my life,
Smiling the waves above!
Thou hail'st me Victor in the strife,
And beacon'st me with love.
The world may never know, dear heart!
What I have found in thee;
But, tho' nought to the world, dear heart!
Thou 'rt all the world to me.

WHEN I COME HOME.

Around me Life's hell of fierce Ardours burns,
When I come home, when I come home;
Over me Heaven with its starry heart yearns,
When I come home, when I come home.
For a feast of Gods garnisht, the palace of Night
At a thousand star-windows is throbbing with light.
London makes mirth! but I know God hears
The sobs i' the dark, and the dropping of tears;
For I feel that he listens down Night's great dome
When I come home, when I come home;
Home, home, when I come home,
Far i' the night when I come home.

I walk under Night's triumphal arch,
When I come home, when I come home;

Exulting with life like a Conqueror's march,
    When I come home, when I come home.
I pass by the rich-chamber'd mansions that shine,
O'erflowing with splendour like goblets with wine:
I have fought, I have vanquisht the dragon of Toil,
And before me my golden Hesperides smile!
And O but Love's flowers make rich the gloam,
When I come home, when I come home!
    Home, home, when I come home,
    Far i' the night when I come home.

O the sweet, merry mouths up-turn'd to be kist,
    When I come home, when I come home!
How the younglings yearn from the hungry nest,
    When I come home, when I come home!
My weary, worn heart into sweetness is stirr'd,
And it dances and sings like a singing Bird,
On the branch nighest heaven,—a-top of my life:
As I clasp my winsome, wooing Wife!
And her pale cheek with rich, tender passion doth bloom,
When I come home, when I come home;
    Home, home, when I come home,
    Far i' the night when I come home.

Clouds furl off the shining face of my life,
    When I come home, when I come home,
And leave heaven bare on her bosom, sweet Wife,
    When I come home, when I come home.
With her brave smiling Energies,—Faith warm and bright,—
With love glorified and serenely alight,—
With her womanly beauty and queenly calm,
She steals to my heart with a blessing of balm;
And O but the wine of Love sparkles with foam,
When I come home, when I come home!
    Home, home, when I come home,
    Far i' the night when I come home.

ICHABOD.

SEVEN Summers' Suns have set! and earth is once
more sweetly flooded
With fragrance, for the virgin-leaves and violet-
banks have budded:
Heaven claspeth Earth, as round the heart first
broodeth Love's rich glow;
A blush of Flowers is mantling where the lush
green grasses grow!
All things feel summering sunward, golden tides
flood down the air,
Which burns, as Angel-visitants had left a glory
there!
But darkness on my aching spirit shrouds the merry
shine, —
I long to feel a gush of Spring in this poor heart of
mine.

Morn opes Heaven's secret portal, back the golden
gates are drawn,
And all the fields of glory blossom with the crimson
Dawn:
But never comes thy clasping hand, or carol of thy
lips,
That made my heart soar like a God, when burst-
ing Death's eclipse.
Sweet voice! it came like saintly music, quiring
angels make,
When pain sat heavy on my brow, and heart was
like to break:
Methought such love gave wings to climb some
starry throne to win;
Thou didst so lift my life's horizon — letting heaven
in.

I'm thinking, darling, of the days when life was all divine,
And love was aye the silver chord that bound my heart to thine;
When life bloom'd at thy coming, as the green earth greets the sun,
And, like two dew-drops in a kiss, our twin souls wed in one.
Ah! still I feel ye at my heart! and 'mid the stir and strife,
Ye sometimes lead my feet to walk the angel-side of Life!
The magic music yearns within, as unto thee I turn,
And those brave eyes, a-blaze with soul, thro' all my being burn.

Come back,—come back; I long to clasp thee in these arms, mine own;
Lavish my heart upon thy lips, and make my love the Crown
And Arc of Triumph to thy life. Why tarry? Time hath cast
Strange shadows on my spirit since we met and mingled last!
Yet there be joys to crown thee with; the sunshine and the sweet
Are hived, like honey, in my heart, to share them when we meet:
How I have hoarded up my life! how tenderly I strove
To make my heart fit home for thee, its nestling Bird of love!

God bless thee! once the radiant world thy beauty crownlike wore,
But life hath lost the strange sweet feel that cometh never more!

The flowers will bud again in spring, and happy birds make love,
With melting hearts, a-brooding o'er their passion in the grove.
But thou wilt never more come back, to clothe my heart with spring;
Dear God! Love's sweetest chord is turn'd to Pain's most jarring string!
The Glory hath departed! and my spirit pants to go
Where 'mid Life's troubled waters, 't will not see the wreck below.

HUSBAND AND WIFE.

O, PROUDLY I stood in the rare Sunrise,
  As the dawn of your beauty brake;
But I fear'd for the storm, as I lookt at the skies,
  And trembled for your sweet sake!
And O, may the evil days come not, I said,
  As I yearn'd o'er my tender blossom!
Strong arm of love! shelter the dear one's head;
  And I nestled you in my bosom.
May the tears never dim the love-light of her eye,—
  May her Life be all Spring-weather!—
Was the prayer of my heart, ere you, Love, and I,
  Were Husband and Wife together.

But the suns will shine, and the rains will fall,
  On the loftiest, lowliest spot!
And there 's mourning and merriment mingled for all
  That inherit the human lot.
So we 've suffer'd and sorrow'd and grown more strong,
  Heart-to-heart, side-to-side, we have striven,

With the love that makes summer-tide all the year
long,
And the heart that is its own heaven!
We clung the more close as the storm swept by,
And kept the nest warm in cold weather;
And seldom we 've falter'd since you, Love, and I,
Have been Husband and Wife together!

Like the sweet happy flowers of the wilderness,
You have dwelt life to life with Nature;
And caught the wild beauty and grace of her ways,
And grown to her heavenlier stature!
In prospering calm, and in quickening strife,
Hath your womanly worth unfolden;
And sunshine and show'r have enricht your life,
And ripen'd its harvest golden.
There is good in the grimmest cloud o' the sky,
There are blessings in wintry weather:
Even Grief hath its glory, since you, Love, and I,
Have been Husband and Wife together.

O, Life is not perfect with Love's first kiss:
Who would win the blessing must wrestle;
And the deeper the sorrow, the dearer the bliss,
That in its rich core may nestle!
Our Angels oft greet us in tearful guise,
And our saviours come in sorrow:
While the murkiest midnight that frowns from the
skies,
Is at heart a radiant Morrow!
We laugh and we cry, we sing and we sigh,
And Life will have wintry weather!
So we 'll hope, and love on, since you, Love, and I,
Are Husband and Wife together.

LOVE ME.

"All dear as the feeling when first-flowers start,
Thou cam'st in thy musical lightness:
And the cloud wept itself in rich rain on my heart,
That had hidden thy beauty and brightness.
'T was as Life's topmost window oped suddenly, bright
With the glittering face of an Angel,
The sweet secret out-flasht on thy forehead of light,
And I knew thee, my own love-Evangel!
O how shall I crown thee, Love, on my heart's throne,
Thou art so far, far above me?"
And aye, as her dear eyes lookt love in my own,
The Maiden answered, "Love me."

"My Belovéd is fair as some beautiful star
That walks in an air of glory;
And her large-hearted looks and her lineaments are
As some Queen's of the old Greek story!
There 's never night now, since those dear eyes of thine
Smiled on me their soft sweet splendour,
And I drank of the wine of thy kisses divine:
O what for such love shall I render?"
And aye, as I knelt at my true Love's shrine,
She bent in her beauty above me:
And aye, as her sweet eyes lookt love into mine,
The Maiden answered, "Love me."

"O could my heart, mountain-region'd in bliss,
Thy life with Love's affluence dower,
Thou shouldst have heaven in a world e'en like this,
And the joy of a life in each hour!

Thou shouldst go forth like a conquering Queen,
    Reaping rich heartfuls of treasure,
Nor strive where the worn of heart wearily glean
    But handfuls, in harvesting pleasure."
And aye, as I knelt at my true Love's shrine,
    She bent in her beauty above me:
And aye, as her sweet eyes lookt love into mine,
    The Maiden answered, "Love me."

LOVE-IN-IDLENESS.

We sit serenely 'neath the night,
As still as stars with swift delight;
In tears, that show how in Life's deep
The hidden pearls of beauty sleep!
And quiet, as of sleeping trees,
And silence, as of sleeping seas.
The channels of our bliss run fill'd,
Their faintest happy murmur still'd.

Upon my forehead rests thy palm,
And on my spirit rests thy calm.
I cannot see thy cheek, but know
Its sea of rose-bloom hath a glow
Like ruby light, and richly lies
The dew i' the shadow of thine eyes:
Deep eyes! like wells of tenderness,
That ask how they may soothliest bless.

Warm fragrance like the soul o' the South,
Is round us, and thy damask mouth
With the sweet spirit of its breath,
Dissolves me in delicious death.
Musk-roses blowing in the gloom,
Drop fragrance fainting in the room,
Such sensuous sadness fills the air,
Ripe life a bloom of dew doth wear

The harping hand hath dull'd the lyre
Of thrilling heartstrings — by their fire
That droops, the dreamy Passions doze
In large luxuriance of repose.
While we our fields of pleasure reap,
Our Babes lie in the wood of Sleep:
One, first love's dream of beauty wrought!
One, the more perfect afterthought.

We sit with silent glory crown'd,
And Love's arms wound like heaven round:
Or on rich clouds of fragrance swim
The summer dusk so cool and dim.
I only see — that thou art near;
I only feel — I have thee dear!
I only hear thy beating heart,
And know that we can never part.

SONG.

O SHY and simple Village Girl,
  With daisy-drooping eyes;
Like light asleep within the pearl,
  Love in your young life lies.
A hundred times in meadow and lane
  With careless hearts we walkt;
But we shall never meet again,
  And talk as we have talkt.
All in a moment life was crost,
  In a fairy spell I 'm bound;
Yet fear to tell you what I 've lost,
  Or know what I have found.

When last I met you, tearful meek
  The emerald gloaming came;
Some veil fell from you, in your cheek
  The live rose was aflame!

So distant and so dear you grew,
  More near, yet more estranged,
And at your parting touch I knew
  How all the world was changed.
All in a moment life was crost,
  In a fairy spell I 'm bound;
Yet fear to tell you what I 've lost,
  Or know what I have found.

Your fairness haunts me all night long,
  I walk in a dream by day;
My silent heart breaks into song,
  And the prayerless kneels to pray.
Ten times a day the hot tears start,
  For very pride of you:
Would God you were safe at home in my heart,
  To rest the rough world through.
All in a moment life was crost,
  In a fairy spell I 'm bound;
Yet fear to tell you what I 've lost,
  Or know what I have found.

My heart! She comes by lane and style,
  With glances shy and sweet;
Making the sunlight with her smile,
  And music with her feet.
Ah! could I clasp her in mine arm
  Until she named the hour
When life should move from charm to charm,
  And love from flower to flower!
All in a moment life was crost,
  In a fairy spell I 'm bound;
Yet fear to tell her what I 've lost,
  Or know what I have found.

A BALLAD OF THE OLD TIME.

SWEET Night, drop down from thy starry bower
  Thy influence dewy mild;
Softly bend over my love's tender flower,
  As a Mother bends over her child.
Hush the hills in a deep, dark dream;
  To slumber stretch valley and lea;
Fold over all thy purple and pall,
  And bring my Love to me.

You white witching Moon, with your beautiful smile;
  You flowers that fondle his feet;
You weird wee Women of fairyland, wile
  Not my Love with your kisses sweet.
For him my bower in the old gray tower
  Is dighted daintilie:
All gentle Powers that walk the night-hours,
  Hasten my Love to me.

I count my love's rosary over again,
  With its feelings and fancies and fears;
Till it breaks in my brain with the tension of pain,
  And my pearls are but trembling tears!
I sorrow and sing with the thorn at my breast,
  But mine eyes watch unweariedly:
Come crown them, and calm them, and kiss them to rest;
  Dear my Love, hurry to me.

The ripe swelling buds that are quick with spring,
  Will peep from their silken fold;
And my broidered belt is too short to cling
  Round my waist with its girdling gold.
But my Love he will bring the gay gold ring;
  Base-born his Babe shall not be!

Leal is his love as the heaven above:
  He never will lightly me.

My Love he hath little of silver or gold;
  Of land he hath never a sod;
But my Love is a gay gallant gentleman—
  He 's a king by the grace of God.
He has borne up the battle-tide broad-sword in
      hand!
  He is comely as any ladye!
O and were I a King's daughter,
  None other should marry me.

My Love shall not wait at the Castle-gate,
  My Love shall not tirl at the pin;
My Love he shall climb to my bower-window;
  Sing O, but I 'll let my Love in.
The dragon below lieth weary and old,
  Sleeping all under the tree;
While I feast my Love upon apples of gold—
  But soft! He is coming to me.

IN THE NIGHT.

EARTH like a Lover poor and low
Feasts on Night's queenly beauty now;
While I, with burning heart and brow,
    Awake to weep for thee, Love!
The spangled glories of the Night,
The Moon that walks in soft, white light,
These cannot win my charmèd sight,
    Or lure a thought from thee, Love!

I 'm thinking o'er the short, sweet hour,
Our fond hearts felt Love's growth of power,
And summer'd as in Eden's bower,

When I was blest with thee, Love!
There burn'd no beauty on the trees,
There woke no song of birds or bees,
But Love's cup for us held no lees,
And I was blest with thee, Love.

Then grand and golden fancies spring
From out my heart on splendid wing,
Like Chrysalis from Life's wintering,—
Burst bright and summeringly, Love!
And as a Chief of battle lost
Counts, and recounts his stricken host,
Stands tearful Memory making most
Of all that 's toucht with thee, Love.

Perchance in Pleasure's brilliant bower
Thy heart may half forget Love's power,
But at this still and starry hour
Does it not turn to me, Love?
O, by all pangs for thy sweet sake,
In my deep love thy heart-thirst slake,
Or, all-too-full, my heart must break:
Break! break! with loving thee, Love!

SWEET-AND-TWENTY.

Like a Lady from a far land,
Came my true Love brave to see!
As to heaven its rainbow garland,
Is her beauty rich to me.

Nearest to my heart I wear her;
As a bark the waves above—
O so proudly do I bear her
On the bosom of my love.

Or as some dim lake may mirror
  One fair star that shines above,
So my life — aye growing clearer —
  Holds this tremulous star of love.

Look you, how she cometh, trilling
  Out her gay heart's bird-like bliss!
Merry as a May-morn, thrilling
  With the dew and sunshine's kiss.

Ruddy gossips of her beauty
  Are her twin cheeks: and her mouth
In its ripe warmth smileth, fruity
  As a garden of the south.

Ha! my precious Sweet-and-Twenty,
  Husband up your virgin pride!
Just a month and this dear, dainty
  Thing shall be my wedded Bride.

A LYRIC OF LOVE.

The Bird that nestles nearest earth,
  To Heaven's gate nighest sings;
And loving thee, my lowly life
  Doth mount on Lark-like wings!
Thine eyes are starry promises:
  And affluent above
All measure in its blessing, is
  The largess of thy love.

Merry as laughter 'mong the hills,
  Spring dances at my heart!
And at my wooing, Nature's soul
  Into her face will start!
The Queen-moon, in her starry bower,

Looks happier for our love;
A dewier splendour fills the flower,
And mellower coos the Dove.

My heart may sometimes blind mine eyes
With utterance of tears,
But feels no pang for thee, Belov'd!
But all the more endears:
And if life comes with cross and care
Unknown in years of yore,
I know thou 'lt half the burthen bear,
And I am strong once more.

Ah! now I see my life was shorn,
That, like the forest-brook
When leaves are shed, my darkling soul
Up in heaven's face might look!
And blessings on the storm that gave
Me haven on thy breast,
Where life hath climaxt like a wave
That breaks in perfect rest.

KISSES.

One kiss more, Sweet!
Soft as voluptuous wind of the west,
Or silkenest surge of thy balmy breast,
Ripe lips all ruddily melting apart,
Drink up the honey and wine of my heart!
On all the bounds of my being let Bliss
Break with its dear drowning sea —
In a Kiss!

One kiss more, Sweet!
Warm as a morning sunbeam's dewy gold
Slips in a red Rose's fragrantest fold,

Sets its green blood all a-blush, burning up
At the fresh feel of life, in its crimson cup!
On all the bounds of my being let Bliss
Break with its dear drowning sea —
    In a Kiss.

NOT I, SWEET SOUL, NOT I.

All glorious as a Rainbow's birth,
  She came in Spring-tide's golden hours;
When Heaven went hand-in-hand with Earth,
  And May was crown'd with buds and flowers!
The mounting devil at my heart
  Clomb faintlier, as my life did win
The charméd heaven, she wrought apart,
  To wake its slumbering Angel in!
With radiant mien she trode serene,
  And past me smiling by!
O! who that lookt could chance but love?
  Not I, sweet soul, not I.

Her budding breasts, Love's fragrant fruit,
  Peer'd out, a-yearning to be prest:
Her voice shook all my heart's red root!
  Yet might not break a babe's soft rest!
Her being mingled into mine,
  As breath of flowers doth mix and melt,
And on her lips the honey-wine
  Was royal-rich as spikenard spilt;
With love a-gush, like water-brooks,
  Her heart smiled in her eye;
O! who that lookt could chance but love?
  Not I, sweet soul, not I.

The dewy eyelids of the Dawn
  Ne'er oped such heaven as hers can show:

O Love! such dear eyes might have shone
  As jewels in some starry brow!
Her brow flasht glory like a shrine,
  Or lily-bell with sunburst bright;
Where came and went love-thoughts divine,
  As low winds walk the leaves in light:
She wore her beauty with the grace
  Of Summer's star-clad sky;
O! who that lookt could chance but love?
  Not I, sweet soul, not I.

A POOR MAN'S WIFE.

HER dainty hand nestled in mine, rich and white,
  And timid as trembling dove;
And it twinkled about me, a jewel of light,
  As she garnisht our feast of love:
'T was the queenliest hand in all lady-land,
  And she was a poor Man's wife!
O! little ye 'd think how that wee, white hand
  Could dare in the battle of Life.

Her heart it was lowly as maiden's might be,
  But hath climb'd to heroic height,
And burn'd like a shield in defence of me,
  On the sorest field of fight!
And startling as fire, it hath often flasht up
  In her eyes, the good heart and rare!
As she drank down her half of our bitterest cup,
  And taught me how to bear.

Her sweet eyes that seem'd, with their smile sub-
    lime,
  Made to look me and light me to heaven,
They have triumph'd thro' bitter tears many a time,
  Since their love to my life was given:

And the maiden-meek voice of the womanly Wife
  Still bringeth the heavens nigher;
For it rings like the voice of God over my life,
  Aye bidding me climb up higher.

I hardly dared think it was human, when
  I first lookt in her yearning face;
For it shone as the heavens had open'd then,
  And clad it with glory and grace!
But dearer its light of healing grew
  In our dark and desolate day,
As the Rainbow, when heaven hath no break of blue,
  Smileth the storm away.

O! her shape was the lithest Loveliness, —
  Just an armful of heaven to enfold!
But the form that bends flower-like in love's caress,
  With the Victor's strength is soul'd!
In her worshipful presence transfigured I stand,
  And the poor Man's English home
She lights with the Beauty of Greece the grand,
  And the loveliest Raphael in Rome.

LOVE.

O Love! Love! Love!
  Its glory smites our gloom,
And, flower-like flusht with life, the heart
  Doth burgeon into bloom!
Sweet as the sunshine's golden kiss,
  That crowns the world anew:
Sweet as in Roses' hearts of bliss,
  Soft, summer-dark, drops dew.

O Love! Love! Love!
May make the brave heart ache;
Pulse out its lavish life, and leave
It, mournfully to break!
But O how exquisite it starts
The thoughts that bee-like cling,
To drain the honey from young hearts,
And leave a bleeding sting!

O Love! Love! Love!
Its very pain endears!
And every wail and weeping brings
Some blessing on our tears!
Love makes our darkest days, sweet dove!
In golden Suns go down,
And still we'll clothe our hearts with love,
And crown us with Love's crown.

I LOVE MY LOVE, AND MY LOVE LOVES ME.

THE life of life's when for another we're living,
Whose spirit responds to ours like a sweet Psalter;
When heart-smiles are burning, and flame-words out-giving
The fire we have lit on the heart's holy Altar!
O Love, God's religion! Love, fervid and starried!
The soul must be beautiful where thou art palaced;
I mark where thy kiss-seal is set on the forehead,
I know where thy dew of heaven's richliest chaliced.

That radiant brow breaketh thro' cloud and world-stain,
And strong is that soul in the battle of Duty;
Smiling May-sunshine thro' Life's Winter-rain,
All outer things clothing with inner world beauty!
'T is writ in the face, whose heart singeth for glee,
"I love my Love, and my Love loves me."

Once I was a-weary of life and the world,
And the voice of Delight on my heart fell accurst,
And my eyes oft with tear-drops unweetingly pearl'd,
I had no one to love, tho' with Love my heart burst:
Then on me a sweet dream of Paradise stole —
Turn'd to radiance the shadows that brooded around me:
And walking the gardens that Eden my soul,
One morning, my Love, like another Eve, found me;
He lookt, and a maëlstrom of joy whirled my bosom;
He smiled, and my being ran bliss to the brim:
He spake, and my eager heart flusht into blossom;
Dear Heaven! 't was the music set to my Life's hymn!
And up went my soul to God, shouting for glee —
"I love my Love, and my Love loves me."

I know, Love of mine! time may nevermore bring
Back the lost freshness that clad my young heart:
But, looking on thee, dear! sweet thoughts will upspring,
As from the cold tomb the green verdure will start!

I look in thine eyes, and, O joy to the weeper!
  Their love-light makes sunshine of all my dark fears;
And what made my heart faint, lifts it now, a strong leaper!
  The rivers of bliss flood its channels of tears.
I had deem'd its wealth flung on sands barren and burning,
  And sweet 't is to find my Life's current again,
Caught up in thy Love's precious chalice—returning
  Like dew that hath been to heaven, dropping in rain.
    And my heart's perpetual hymn shall be,
    "I love my Love, and my Love loves me."

UNDER THE MISLETOE.

'T WAS on a merry Christmas night,
  A many years ago,
I saw my Love, with dancing sight,
  As she came over the snow.
The Elvish Holly laught above;
  A sweeter red below!
When first I met with my true love,
  Under the Misletoe bough.

Bright-headed as the merry May Dawn
  She floated down the dance:
I thought some angel must have gone
  Our human way by chance.
I held my hands, and caught my bliss,
  Children, I'll show you how!
And Earth toucht Heaven in a kiss,
  Under the Misletoe Bough.

Ere leaves were green we built our nest,
  The March winds whistled wild;
But in our love we were so blest
  Old Poverty he smiled.
And Love the heart of Winter warmed,
  Love blossomed 'neath the snow;
All fairy-land in blessings swarmed
  Under the Misletoe bough.

The storms of years have beat our Bark,
  That rocks at anchor now;
But She was smiling thro' the dark,
  My Angel at the prow.
And brimming tides of love did bear
  Us over the rocks below!
To-night, all safe in harbour here,
  Under the Misletoe bough.

May you, Boys, win just such a Wife;
  Come drink the toast in wine!
And you, Girls, may you light a life
  As she hath brightened mine.
Dear was the bonny Bride, and yet
  I'm prouder of her now
Than on the merry, merry night we met,
  Under the Misletoe bough.

THE PATRIOT TO HIS BRIDE.

Will you leave the fond bosom of Home, where
  Joy hath been from your earliest waking?
Can you give its endearments to come, where
  Life hath many a hot heart-aching?
Have you counted the cost to stand by me,
  In the battle I fight for Man?

Shall your womanly love deify me,
Who stand in the world's dark ban ?
O, a daring high soul you will need, dear love,
To brave the life-battle with me :
For your true heart may oftentimes bleed, dear love,
And your sweet eyes dim tearfully.

Sweet ! know you of gallant hearts perishing, —
The fine spirits that dumbly bow ?
For a little of Fortune's cherishing,
They are breaking in agony now !
And without the sunshine that life needeth,
Alas ! Sweet ! for me and for you :
But little the careless world heedeth
For love like ours, tender and true !
O, a daring high soul you will need, dear love,
To brave the life-battle with me :
For your true heart may oftentimes bleed, dear love,
And your sweet eyes dim tearfully.

Well, you 've sworn, I have sworn, God hath bound us,
In a covenant the world shall not part :
I have flung my love's war-cloak around us,
And you live in each pulse of my heart !
It may be our name in Earth's story
Shall endure when we are no more ;
For love lives while the Stars burn in glory,
And the Flowers bud on Earth's green floor.
But a daring high soul you will need, dear love,
To brave the life-battle with me :
For your true heart may oftentimes bleed, dear love,
And your sweet eyes dim tearfully.

SWEET SPIRIT OF MY LOVE.

SWEET Spirit of my love!
Thro' all the world we walk apart:
Thou mayst not in my bosom lie:
I may not press thee to my heart,
Nor see love-thinkings light thine eye:
Yet art thou with me. All my life
Orbs out in thy warm beauty's sphere;
My bravest dreams of thee are rife,
And colour'd with thy presence dear.

Sweet Spirit of my love!
I know how beautiful thou art,
But never tell the starry thought:
I only whisper to my heart,
"She lights with heaven thy earthliest spot."
And birds that night and day rejoice,
And fragrant winds, give back to me
A music ringing of thy voice,
And surge my heart's love-tide to thee.

Sweet Spirit of my love!
The Spring and Summer bloom-bedight,
That garland Earth with rainbow-showers, —
Morn's kissing breath, and eyes of light,
That wake in smiles the winking flowers,
The air with honey'd fragrance fed,
The flashing waters, — soughing tree, —
Noon's golden glory, — sundown red,
Aye warble into songs of thee.

Sweet Spirit of my love!
When Night's soft silence clothes the earth,
And wakes the passionate bird of love;
And Stars laugh out in golden mirth,
And yearning souls divinelier move;

When God's breath hallows every spot,
And, lapp'd in feeling 's luxury,
The heart 's break-full of tender thought;
Then art thou with me, still with me.

Sweet Spirit of my love!
I listen for thy footfall, — feel
Thy look is burning on me, such
As reads my heart; 'twill sometimes reel
And throb, expectant for thy touch!
For by the voice of woods and brooks,
And flowers with virgin-fragrance wet,
And earnest stars with yearning looks,
I know that we shall mingle yet.

Sweet Spirit of my love!
Strange places on me smile, as thou
Hadst pass'd, and left thy beauty's tints:
The wild flowers even the secret know,
And light and shade flash mystic hints.
Meseems, like olden Gods, thou 'lt come
In cloud; but mine anointed eyes
Shall see the glory burn thro' gloom,
And clasp thee, Sweet! with large surprise.

MATRIMONY.

Two human Stars in passing are
Attracted as thro' Heaven they float,
Sometimes they form a double Star,
Sometimes they put each other out:
And sometimes one and one make three,
This world's most perfect trinity.

CHILDLESS.

DARK and still is our House of Life,
  The fire is burning low;
Our pretty ones all are gone, old Wife,
  'T is time for us to go.
Our pretty ones all are gone to sleep,
  And happed in for the night:
So to our bed we'll quietly creep,
  And rest till morning light.

DESERTED.

LOVE came to me in a rosy cloud,
  With a golden glory kist;
And caught me up, and in heaven we rode,
  Till it melted in mournful mist.
Gone! gone! is the light that shone,
  With the dream of my earlier day:
And the wild winds moan, and alone, alone,
  I wander my weary way.

The days come and go, and the seasons roll,—
  In their glory they pass me by;
And the lords of life and the happy in soul
  Walk under a smiling sky.
And the sweet springtide comes back to us o'er
  The soothéd winter sea;
But He will return no more, no more,
  Never come back to me.

It were better that I lay sleeping
  With his baby upon my breast,
Where the weary have done with their weeping,
  And the wretched are rockt to their rest.

The world is a desolate, dreary one,
  And full of sad tears at best:
God, take back thy wandering weary one,
  Like a wounded bird home to its nest.

DESOLATE.

The Day goes down red darkling,
  The moaning waves dash out the light,
And there is not a star of hope sparkling
  On the threshold of my night.

Wild winds of Autumn go wailing
  Up the valley and over the hill,
Like yearning Ghosts round the world sailing,
  In search of the old love still.

A fathomless sea is rolling
  O'er the wreck of the bravest bark;
And my pain-muffled heart is tolling
  Its dumb-peal down in the dark.

The waves of a mighty sorrow
  Have whelméd the pearl of my life:
And there cometh to me no morrow
  Shall solace this desolate strife.

Gone are the last faint flashes,
  Set is the sun of my years;
And over a few poor ashes
  I sit in my darkness and tears.

As the White Snow crowns the Hills, and the arms of Ether fills,
With the lustre of its loveliness — a presence as of light,
And it looks up in Heaven's face with all a Virgin's trusting grace:
So the Maiden walkt on Purity's white height.
But the Snow will blush for bliss, at the red Dawn's fervent kiss;
And fall from its high throne, and lose the brightness from its brow;
And be trodden on the highways, and be trampled in the byeways:
So the Maiden's life is stain'd and trampled now.

"IN THE DEAD UNHAPPY MIDNIGHT."

'Tis Midnight hour, and the Dead have power
Over the Wronger now!
He is tortured and torn by the crown of thorn
That fell from the Suicide's brow.

Wind him around in the toil of thy charms;
Nestle him close, young Bride!
At the Midnight hour he is drawn from thy arms;
Thro' the dark with the Dead he must ride.

The rose of her mouth is red-wet, red-warm:
She smiles in her heaven of calm.
Tost! hurried! and sered in a pitiless storm;
Slumber for him hath no balm.

He feels that ghostly groping along
  The Corridor of Dreams!
And a dark Desolation Lightning-lit
  Is his face by ghastly gleams!

Love's cup flushes up for his crowning kiss,
  With his lip at the burning brim!
Lo, the Dead uncurtain his bower of bliss,
  Stretching wild arms for him!

Wind him around in the toil of thy charms;
  Nestle him close, young Bride!
Yet, at Midnight hour he is drawn from thy arms;
  Thro' the dark with the Dead he must ride.

And the Dark hath a million burning Eyes,
  All of his secret tell!
And the whispering winds are damnéd fiends
  That hiss in his ears of Hell!

Warm in her bed the young Bride lies,
  Breathing her peaceful breath:
Dear Mother and Babe with their drownéd eyes
  Stare dim thro' the watery death.

'T is Midnight hour, and the Dead have power
  Over the Wronger now!
He is tortured and torn by the crown of thorn
  That fell from the Suicide's brow.

ON A WEDDING DAY.

Thus, hand in hand, and heart in heart,
  Face nestling unto face,
Forgotten things like Spirits start
  From many a hiding place!

There is no sound of Babe or Bird,
  And all the stillness seems
Sweet as the music only heard
  Adown the land of dreams.

And if, because it is so proud,
  My heart will find a voice,
And in its dear dream love aloud,
  And speak of sweet still joys,
It is no genuine gift of God,
  But only goblin gold,
That withers into dead leaves, should
  The secret tale be told.

Nine years ago you came to me,
  And nestled on my breast,
A soft and wingéd mystery
  That settled here to rest;
And my heart rockt its Babe of bliss,
  And soothed its child of air,
With something 'twixt a song and kiss,
  To keep it nestling there.

At first I thought the fairy form
  Too spirit-soft and good
To fill my poor, low nest with warm
  And wifely womanhood.
But such a cozy peep of home
  Did your dear eyes unfold;
And in their deep and dewy gloom
  What tales of love were told!

In dreamy curves your beauty droopt,
  As tendrils lean to twine,
And very graciously they stoopt
  To bear their fruit, my Vine!
To bear such blessed fruit of love
  As tenderly increased

Among the ripe vine-bunches of
  Your balmy-breathing breast.

We cannot boast to have bickered not
  Since you and I were wed;
We have not lived the smoothest lot,
  Nor found the downiest bed!
Time hath not passed o'er-head in Stars,
  And underfoot in flowers,
With wings that slept on fragrant airs
  Thro' all the happy hours.

It is our way, more fate than fault,
  Love's cloudy fire to clear;
To find some virtue in the salt
  That sparkles in a tear!
Pray God it all come right at last,
  Pray God it so befall,
That when our day of life is past
  The end may crown it all.

Ah, Dear! tho' lives may pull apart
  Down to the roots of love,
One thought will bend us heart to heart,
  Till lips re-wed above!
One thought the knees of pride will bow
  Down to the grave-yard sod;
You are the Mother of Angels now!
  We have two babes with God.

Cling closer, closer, for their loss,
  About our darlings left,
And let their memories grow like moss
  That healeth rent and rift; —
For his dear sake, our Soldier Boy,
  For whom we nightly plead
That he may live for God, and die
  For England in her need, —

For her, who like a dancing boat
  Leaps o'er life's solemn waves,
Our little Lightheart who can float
  And frolic over graves;
And Grace, who making music goes,
  As in some shady place
A Brooklet, prattling to the boughs,
  Looks up with its bright face.

Cling closer, closer, life to life,
  Cling closer, heart to heart;
The time will come, my own wed Wife,
  When you and I must part!
Let nothing break our band but Death,
  For in the worlds above
'T is the breaker Death that soldereth
  Our ring of Wedded Love.

SONG AT EVENTIDE.

I SIT beneath my shadowing Palm,
  All in the green o' the day at rest:
And pictured in a sea of calm,
  The Past arises in my breast.
The winter world takes leafy wing
  In that sweet April tide of ours;
And hidden Love lies listening,
  And nodding smile the bridal flowers.

I sing, and shut mine eyes and dream
  I see her singing, my young Bride!
Who on a-sudden from Life's stream
  Rose Swan-like swimming at my side.
God love her! she was very fair,
  And in her eyes, to light my way,

The Love-Star sprang and sparkled where
 The hidden Babe of Blessing lay.

With healing as of summer showers
 That only nestle down to bless;
And silent ministry of flowers,
 That only breathe their tenderness;
She, softly as a starry scheme,
 My charméd world hath circled round,
Till life doth seem a pleasant dream
 The victor dreameth sitting crowned.

Gone is the sunshine from her hair,
 That made her beauty needless bright,
To tint a many clouds of care,
 And make my tears to smile with light.
But so she lives that when the wind
 Of winter shreds the leaves, dear Wife!
Seed ripe for Heaven Death may find
 On the poor withered stem of life.

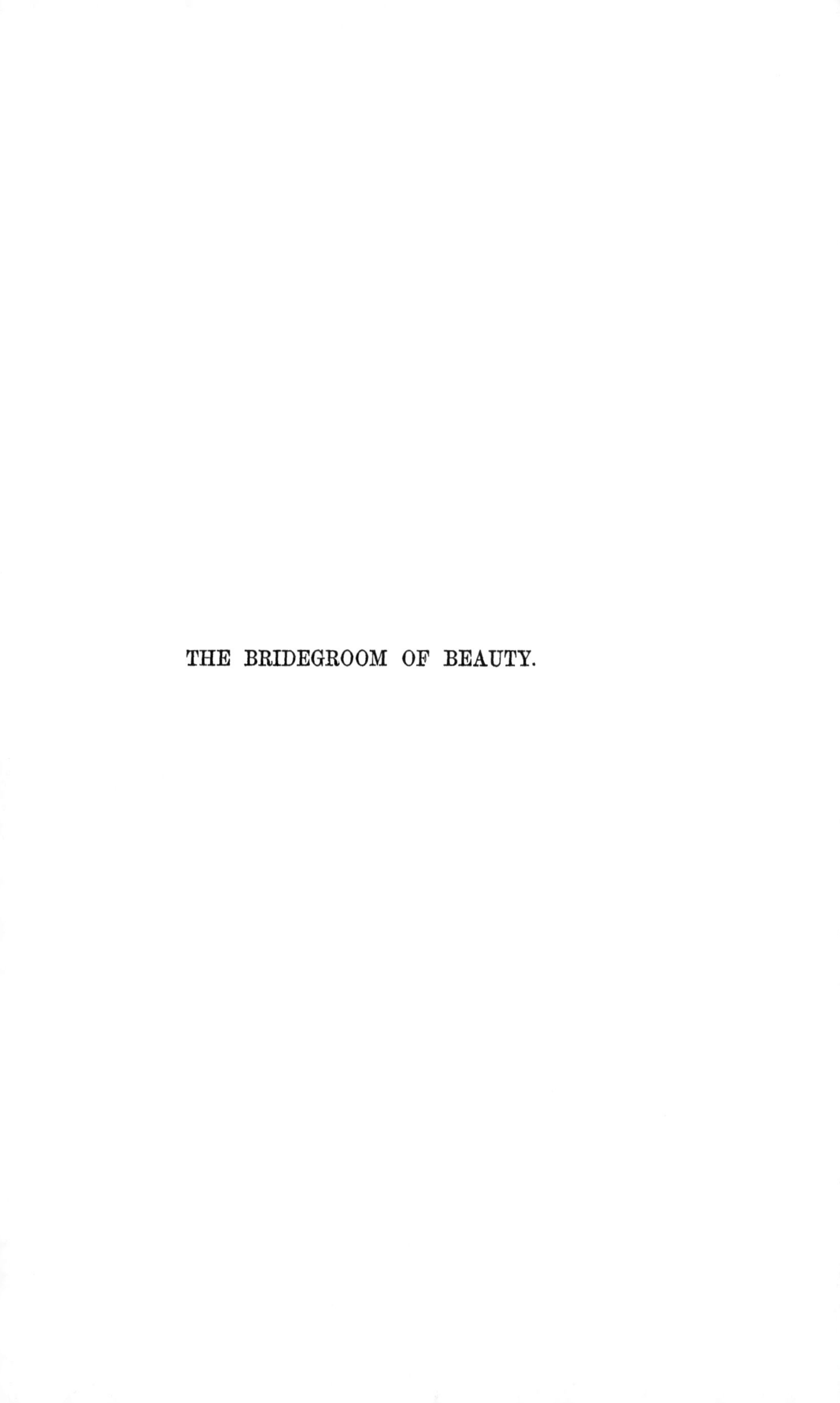

THE BRIDEGROOM OF BEAUTY.

THE BRIDEGROOM OF BEAUTY.

WHO wears a singing-robe is richly dight,
Said Mabel; he is greater than a King.
I would I were a Poet happy-mad;
Up like a Lark i' the morning of the times,
To sing above the human harvesters;
Drop fancies, dainty-sweet, to cheer their toil,
And hurry out a ripe luxuriance
Of life in song, as though my heart would break;
And sing them sweet and precious memories,
And golden promises, and throbbing hopes;
Hymn the great Future with its mystery,
That startles us from out the dark of time
With secrets numerous as a night of stars:
Those days hung round with loftier heavens, where
 move
The larger souls with grandly solemn pace:
Or send wronged Nations to the battle-field
With eyes that weep and burn — stir as with fire
The grand wild beast of Valour, till it leapt
The red Arena fiery for the fight:
Then bind with garlands brave the Patriot's brow.
Anon I would sing songs so sweetly pure,
That they might pillow a budding Maiden's cheek,
Like spirit-hands, and catch her tender tears;
Or nestle next her heart lapt up in love: —
Songs that in far lands, under alien skies,
Should spring from English hearts like flowers of
 home.
I 'd strive to bring down light from heaven to read
The records writ on Poverty's prison walls,
The signs of greatness limned in martyr blood,

And make worn faces glow with warmth of love
Into the lineaments of heavenly beauty.

Who wears a singing-robe is richly dight;
The Poet, he is greater than a King.
He plucks the veil from hidden loveliness:
His gusts of music stir the shadowing boughs,
To let in glory on the darkened soul.
Upon the hills of light he plants his feet
To lure the people up with harp and voice;
At humblest human hearths drops dew divine
To feed the violet virtues nestling there.
His hands adorn the poorest house of life
With rare abiding shapes of loveliness.
All things obey his soul's creative eye;
For him earth ripens fruit-like in the light;
Green April comes to him with smiling tears,
Like some sweet Maiden who transfigured stands
In dewy light of first love's rosy dawn,
And yields all secret preciousness, his Bride.
He reaps the Autumn without scythe or sickle;
And in the sweet low singing of the corn,
Hears coming Plenty hush the pining Poor.

The shows of things are but a robe o' the day,
His life down-deepens to the living heart,
And Sorrow shows him her wise mysteries.
He knoweth Life is but a longer year,
And it will blossom bright in other springs.
The soul of all things is invisible,
And nearest to that soul the Poet sings;
A sweet, shy Bird in darkling privacy.
He beckons not the Pleasures as they pass,
And lets the money-grubbing world go by.
He hath a towering life, but cannot climb
Out of the reach of sad calamity:
A many carking cares pluck at his skirts;
Wild, wandering words are hissing at his ear;
He runs the gauntlet of world-woes to reach

The inner sanctuary of better life.
But tho' the seas of sorrow flood his heart,
Some silent spring of roses blossoms there.
His spirit-wounds a precious balsam bleed.
The loveliest ministrants that visit him,
Rise veiled when his heart-fountains spring in tears.
And when this misty life hath rolled away
The turmoil husht; all foolish voices still;
The bonds that crusht his great heart shattered down,
And all his nature shines sublimely bare;
Death whitens many a stain of strife and toil,
And careful hands shall pluck away each weed
Around the spring that wells melodious life.

Many are called, Aurelia replied,
But few are crowned. I knew a Poet once;
One of the world's most marvellous might-have-beens;
A strange wild harper upon human heart-strings.
Life's morning-splendour round him prophesied
That he should win his garland in the game.
But he was lost for lack of that sweet thing,
A Wife, to live his love's dear dream of beauty,
And wandered darkling in his dazzling dream.
Life's waters—troubled till that Angel comes—
Never grew calm above the jewel he sought,
Till in Death's harbour all their surges slept.

He was betrothed to Beauty ere his birth—
That silent Spirit of the universe,
Which seeks interpreters of her dumb shows,
'Mong human lovers whom she may not wed!

This Spirit arose from many things, as soars
The soul of Harmony from many sounds.
She beckoned him for her Evangelist,
Out of the byeway of his lonely life,
And straightway he arose and followed her,
And in the shadow of her loveliness,
Or in her wake of glory, walkt the world.

That shining Shape, in her sweet mystery, seemed
Some beauteous miracle of silent love.
Thro' smiles, and tears, he saw his visioned Bride,
With gorgeous grace, and twinkling limbs of light,
Aye dancing on in her delightsomeness.
His love-dream glided silent thro' his life,
Like rosy-handed Day 'twixt Earth and Night,
And came betwixt his mind and all its glooms;
Her sandals wet and fragrant with Heaven's dew.
She set the barren thorns in jewelled glow,
And sowed the furrows of his life with flowers.
He followed with wild looks and heart a-fire,
And that rich mist of feeling in the eyes,
Whose alchymy half-creates the thing we see.

She rose at dawn in sparkling clouds of dew,
And kept the Morning's ruddy golden gates;
Stood high in sunrise on the mountain-top;
Or in her bower of the silvery air
Sat, shedding her rich beauty on the sea,
Which of her likeness took some trembly tints;
Voyaged like Venus in her car of cloud
About the sapphire heaven's lake of love,
Or danced on sunset streams to harp of gold:
Then twilight mists would robe more faint and fair
Her dim, delicious, dreamy loveliness.

The Flowers that startle at the voice of May
And open gamesome eyes, had been with her;
Their subtle smile said what they could reveal.
Among the boughs of balm rainbowed with bloom;

The coloured clouds that kindle and richly rise
From out the bosom of Earth's emerald sea;
Hedge-roses set in dewy radiance green;
The lush Laburnums, all a rain of gold;
She seemed to have fled and left her robe afloat.
An Ariel, soft she murmured in the pines;
He heard, but knew no magic word or wand.
A wavy Naiad, she rippled the cool brooks
That round her dallied, babbling in their dreams.
The fragrant feeling of the languorous air
Was as the soft endearment of her touch,
And wound him in a tremulous caress.

Not by appointment do we meet Delight
And Joy; they heed not our expectancy;
But round some corner in the streets of life,
They, on a sudden, clasp us with a smile.
So on him rose his visitant divine,
From many a magic mirror of the mind;
With elfin evanescence came and went.

When, thronged with life, the Year in beauty burst,
Lifted her lids, and blossomed from the trees,
She smiled in all the gateways of the spring.
In burnisht bark swam down the summer-tide
That floods the vallies, breaks o'er all the hills,
In sparkling spray of flowers, and leafy life.
She rooft the Autumn forests with the wealth
Of melted rainbows, caught from summer heaven.
And winter trees stretcht fingers weird to win
Her perfect pearl, and her white purity.
Where'er she went Earth lookt up with a smile.

Thro' Music's maze she glode at hide-and-seek;
Played with the Storm, then in her rainbow-shape
Laught from the purple skirts of Heaven, as laughs
Some radiant Child from Mother's hiding robe.
Adown dim forest-windings he would peer;

Surprise his Beautiful at her woodland bath,
And in a solemn hush of heart stand still
Like fixéd flame! for lo, how softly glowed
Her dainty limbs in depths of dissolved pearl!
Then swift as runs a wind-wave over grass,
He saw her garments gleam in leafy light.
Were those love-whisperings among the leaves,
Or elvish laughters twitting thro' the trees?
Sometimes the boughs let in her haunting face;
But the old forest kept the secret still,
And husht it round with grave unconscious look.

In vernal nights so tender, calm, and cool,
When eerie Darkness lays its shadowy hands
On Earth, and reads her sins with searching eyes,
Like a Confessor o'er a kneeling Nun;
He stood in God's wide whispering gallery,
And breathed his worship: down from visible heaven
Her influence fell, and thrilled in music thro'
The silences of space, and soothed his soul,
Till life was folded up brimfull of beauty,
As the flower folds its pearl and droops to dream.

At times, from out the curtains of the dark,
Her face would meet him thro' the glowing gloom.
Sometimes she passed; her rippling raiment toucht
His brows, and sphered him with diviner air,
Like honeysuckles brusht at dewy dusk.
The fragrance of her breath made old earth young
From mystery to mystery, like a Bride,
The dainty-waisted darling led him on,
And dropt love-tokens in his pilgrim path.
The red Rose peering from its cool green leaves
Like warm Love lifting half its hiding veil,
Symbolled her soft red mouth held up to him.
A virgin whiteness in a dream of bloom,

Gave to her tender cheeks their taking tint.
Her eyes were orbs of thought that on him burned
Fervent as Hesper in the brow of Eve.

He walkt as in a clime of golden eves.
The vineyard of his life reeled lusty ripe;
He ached to press the wine upon her lips,
But aye she melted from his love's embrace,
To float him far away in faëry lands.
The wooing wind would murmur of her fairness,
And round him breathe in many whispers sweet;
Bring dews of healing as from Hermon hill;
Creep to his burning heart with drink of life,
And cool him with her kisses. Oft he husht,
As one who pauses on a midnight heath,
To catch the footfall felt on Fancy's ear.

When he awoke in Dreamland, 't was to find
He had been floated thro' some starry dark,
Far from earth's shore, on an enchanted sea:
And he lay pillowed 'twixt her white warm breasts,
In glowing arms of glorifying love:
A light of love-dreams on her features shone,
And she had laid her daylight mask aside;
All the sweet soul of things lay bare, as lies
The mirrored moon in silver sleeping seas.

A shimmering splendour from the By-gone broke,
As the Ship leaves a luminous wake behind;
And, looking back, his Childhood's world she ringed
With rich auroral hues of summer dawns.
When weird, dark shapes of sorrow hunted nigh
With their slow solemn eyes, and silent aim,
She dropt the gold cloud of her tresses round him.
When o'er him hung the night of adverse fate,
She was a light along his perilous path,
And thro' the darkness of his soul there broke
A heaven of worlds all tenderness and peace.

At times he walkt with glad and dauntless step,
As inner wings to heroic music moved;
And men who read his lighted look might deem
His life a summer story told in flowers.
But often he would falter weeping-weak,
With claspéd hands, and very lowly heart.
Then she rose radiant in finer light,
Seen thro' the altar-smoke and mist of tears.
So his life grew to beauty silently,
And shaped his soul into an orb of song.
He sang of Her his beautiful Unknown!
And to his music she would coyly come;
He ceased—to look on her—and she was gone.
He sang of Her his beautiful Unknown,
Heart-wild, as some glad bird that sings of spring,
And all Earth's voices rang a rich refrain.
He would have made the world her worshipper:
The sceptic world that flung him Christ's old crown.
One day our passionate pilgrim sat him down
By the wayside of life, and thus he sang.

"Like a tree beside the river
  Of her life that runs from me,
Do I lean me, murmuring ever
  In my love's idolatry.
Lo, I reach out hands of blessing;
  Lo, I stretch out hands of prayer;
And, with passionate caressing,
  Pour my life upon the air.
In my ears the syren river
  Sings, and smiles up in my face;
But for ever, and for ever,
  Runs from my embrace.

"Spring by spring the branches duly
  Clothe themselves in tender flower;
And for her sweet sake as truly
  All their fruit and fragrance shower.
But the stream, with careless laughter,
  Runs in merry beauty by,
And it leaves me yearning after,
  Lorn to droop, and lone to die.

In my ears the syren river
  Sings, and smiles up in my face;
But for ever, and for ever,
  Runs from my embrace.

"I stand mazéd in the moonlight,
  O'er its happy face to dream;
I am parchéd in the noonlight
  By that cool and brimming stream:
I am dying by the river
  Of her life that runs from me,
And it sparkles by me ever,
  With its cool felicity.
In my ears the syren river
  Sings, and smiles up in my face;
But for ever, and for ever,
  Runs from my embrace."

"O THOU Belovéd! O thou Beautiful!
On our perfection, throned for pedestal:
O spirit as the lightning wild and bright,
Come from thy palace of the purple light.
Come down to mortal arms a living form,
With heavenly height of brow, and bosom warm.
Glow human from the mist, thou Shape of Grace;
Thou tender wonder, fold me face to face.
Art thou not mine, thou delicate Delight?
Hast thou not visited me noon and night?
Freighted with my dead Hopes I follow thee,
Like some Norse sea-king flaming out to sea.
Say, are the pleasant bowers far away,
Deckt by thy dear hands for our marriage-day,
Where we the gardens of delight shall roam
In endless love? When wilt thou lead me home,
To find our bliss in heaven's honied heart;
Live secret soul to soul, never to part?

"O awful Glory, felt, but never found;
I have but seen thy Shadow on life's ground.
I know thee now, Immortal! show the way
To thine Elysium, I could die to-day.
Break into wings this chrysalis of my life,
That I may soar to thee my spirit-wife.
Thy dark bower-door, the Grave, gives me no fear;
When I emerge beyond, thou wilt be near."

O'er all his face the sudden splendour smiled,
Sweet as first love, and sad as wailing winds.
His soul had rent the veil 'twixt life and life.
Slowly the shining vapours orb a Star,
By fine degrees before his fixéd eyes.
The Spirit he had sought thro' all the world,
Turned full upon him face to face at last.
She laid her hand upon his throbbing harp;
She prest her lips upon his passionate life;
And both stood still. He found his Bride in death.

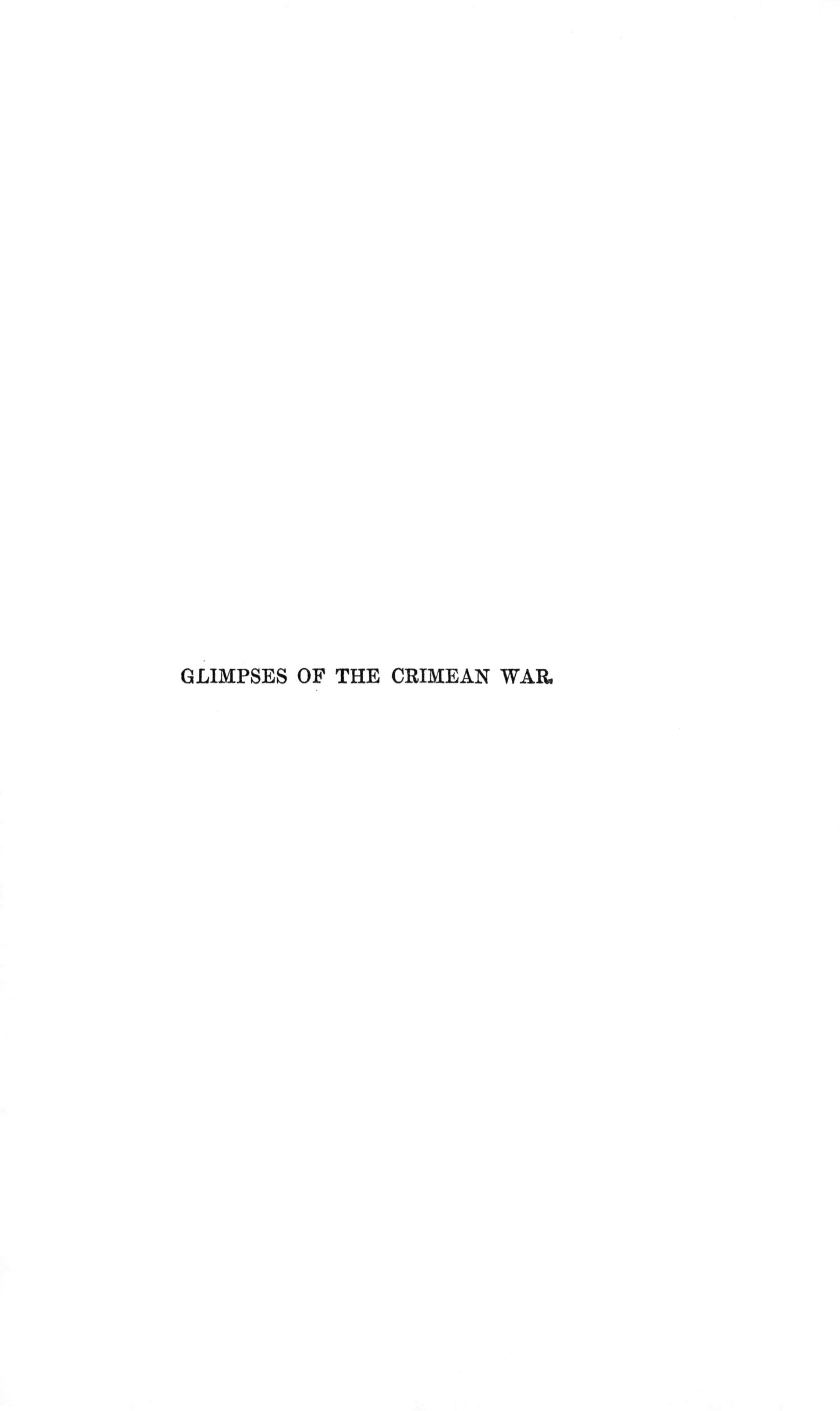

GLIMPSES OF THE CRIMEAN WAR.

GLIMPSES OF THE CRIMEAN WAR.

LIKE peeping Children down some distant lane,
What time with pealing pomp and pageant shows
The Battle in its bravery blazons by,
We peered into the passing world of War —
Its crowning Heaven a-glow with starry hopes —
Its crowded Hell of red and writhing pain;
With hearts that ached or burned, as kindled cheeks
Flamed up in reddening shame, or bloom of pride,
And told the story as the pictures rose.
How England swooned beneath the kiss of Peace,
And languisht in her long voluptuous dream,
While weed-like creatures crept along her path.
Where leapt of old proud waves of glorious life,
The sluggish channels choked with golden sand.
The hills of light rose shining far away,
Where she should stand and touch the hem of Heaven;
But, day by day she darkened deeper down.
The cold, grim Shadow stretcht o'er half the earth,
Came freezing round her watchfire's dying flame,
While spirit-finger-pointings signalled her,
And spirit-rustlings stirred the air in vain.

A tearless anguish flamed from Poland's eyes
When the red Deluge closed above her head:
Sodden with suffering and unwept tears,
The heart of Hungary pled in silence stern:
Poor Italy lay in her guarded grave,
Her life all crouching in one listening sense,

To catch aught stirring in the upper world:
Out of the North the brute Colossus strode,
With grimly solemn pace, proud in the might
That moves not but to crush, and terribly towered
Its growing shape thro' Battle's bloody gap
Where Nations fell; and like a Cyclop's eye
Its one idea lit it to the prey:
While pale Expediency paltered for
Our peaceful chance of being eaten last.

And England slumbered in the lap of Peace,
Beneath her grand old Oak, which, hale and strong,
Rode down the storm, and wrestled with the winds,
To rise in pomp of bloom, and pæan of song,
Green with the sap of many hundred springs;
And tossed its giant arms in wanton life,
Like Victory smiling in the sun of Glory.
She saw not how the worms eat out its heart.
Life deftly masks the hiding-place of death;
And Ruin leads his Bride in a garland green
For sacrifice. So England slept in peace.
And in the glamour of her dream she saw
Brave fancies foot it holding Freedom's pall,
Waving their funeral links for bridal lights.

Came Nemesis, her lightnings stabbed the dark,
To show the way, and startled England woke!
Behold the glorious creature leaping from
Delilah's lap, to the battle-chariot,
Like Sternness stript for strife. Grim-wooing War
Mirrors his terrible beauty in her face;
On fire to bring the death-strokes hand to hand.
Her heart is dancing to a loftier tune.
Ah, God hath called His Chosen once again,
And the Old Guard of Freedom takes the field.
Rejoicing in the glory of her strength,
Like some proud cataract she shouts for the strife,

And hurls her hurrying waves of valour down.
The glorious shudder of intrepid blood
Hurtles thro' all her veins, and Victory's voice
Cries from the inmost oracle of her soul.
Her swift avenging armaments shall flame
O'er land and sea, sublime as when of old
With a colossal calm she rode the waves
Of war, that heaved magnificent in storm.
The noble prophecy of ripened age
Was on her youthful brow; fulfilment comes.
She lifts the Ark of Freedom in her arms,
Safe thro' the deluge of a warring world.

ENGLAND GOES TO BATTLE.

Now, glory to our England,
  She arises, calm and grand,
The ancient spirit in her eyes, —
  The good Sword in her hand!
Our royal right on battle-ground
  Was aye to bear the brunt:
Ho! brave heart! for one passionate bound,
  And take thy place in front!
Now glory to our England,
  As she rises, calm and grand,
The ancient spirit in her eyes —
  The good Sword in her hand!

Who would not fight for England?
  Who would not fling a life
I' the ring, to meet a Tyrant's gage,
  And glory in the strife?
Her stem is thorny, but doth burst
  A glorious Rose a-top!
And shall our dear Rose wither? First
  We 'll drain life's dearest drop!

Who would not fight for England ?
  Who would not fling a life
I' the ring, to meet a Tyrant's gage,
  And glory in the strife ?

To battle goes our England,
  All as gallant and as gay
As Lover to the Altar, on
  A merry marriage-day.
A weary night she stood to watch
  The battle-dawn up-roll'd ;
Her spirit leaps within, to match
  The noble deeds of old.
To battle goes our England,
  All as gallant and as gay
As lover to the Altar, on
  A merry marriage-day.

Now, fair befall our England,
  On her proud and perilous road :
And woe and wail to those who make
  Her foot-prints red with blood !
Up with our red-cross banner, — roll
  A thunder-peal of drums !
Fight on there, every valiant soul,
  And courage ! England comes !
Now fair befall our England,
  On her proud and perilous road :
And woe and wail to those who make
  Her foot-prints red with blood !

Now, victory to our England !
  And where'er she lifts her hand
In Freedom's fight, to rescue Right,
  God bless the dear Old Land !
And when the Storm has pass'd away,
  In glory and in calm,
May she sit down i' the green o' the day,
  And sing her peaceful psalm !

Now, victory to our England!
And where'er she lifts her hand
In Freedom's fight, to rescue Right,
God bless the dear Old Land!

TROOPS LEAVING EDINBURGH.

For Freedom's battle march auld Scotland's brave,
And Edinburgh streets are piled with life to-day.
High on her crags the royal City sits,
And sees the files of war far-winding out,
And with the gracious golden Morning smiles
Her proudest blessing down. Old Arthur's Seat
Flings up his cap of cloud for brave success;
But the old Castle standeth staidly stern,
As some scarred Chief who sends his boys to battle:
While the Sea flashes in the sun, our Shield,
So rich in record of heroic names!

The gay Hussars come riding thro' the town,
A light of triumph sparkling in their eyes;
The Music goeth shouting in their praise,
Like a loud people round the Victor's car;
And Highland plumes together nod as though
There went the Funeral Hearse of a Russian Host:
The bickering bayonets flutter wings of fire,
And gaily sounds the March o' the Cameron Men.

The War-steeds sweeping — men to battle going —
The wave of Beauty's hand — meed of her eyes —
The banners with old battle-memories stirred —
The thrilling Pibroch, and the wild war-drum,
The stern sword-music of our grand Hurrah,
And answering cheer for death or victory —
All make me tingle with a triumph of life,

And I could weep that I am left behind,
To see the tide ebb where I may not follow.
And there they march afield, those gallant men;
To win proud death, or larger life, they leave
Home's rosy circle ringed with blessings rich,
For the far darkness, and the battle-cloud,
Where many have fall'n, and many yet must fall,
In spurring their great hearts up to the leap,
For such brave dashes at unconquered heights.
The shadow of solemn Sorrow falls behind,
Where sobbing Sweethearts look their loving last,
And weeping Wives hold up the little ones.
The sun sets in their faces, life grows grey,
And sighs of desolation sweep its desert.
The winter of the heart aches in the eyes
Of Mothers who have given their all, their all.

And yet methinks the Heroic Time returns,
Such look of triumph lit the meanest face
To-day: there seemed no heart so earthly but
Had some blind gropings after nobler life,
With hands that reacht toward God's Gate Beautiful.
Our England bright'ning thro' the battle-smoke,
Had toucht them with her glory's lovelier light.
And though their darlings fall, and tho' they die
In this death-grapple in the night with Wrong;
The memory of their proud deeds cannot die.
They may go down to dust in bloody shrouds,
And sleep in nameless tombs. But for all time,
Foundlings of Fame are our beloved Lost.
For me, this day of glorious life shall be
One of the starry brides of Memory,
Whose glittering faces light the night of soul.

DOWN IN AUSTRALIA.

QUAFF a cup, and send a cheer up for the Old Land!
We have heard the Reapers shout,
For the Harvest going out,
With the smoke of battle closing round the bold Land;
And our message shall be hurled
Right across the ringing world,
There are true hearts beating for you in the Gold Land.

We are with you in your battles, brave and bold Land!
For the old ancestral tree
Striketh root beneath the sea,
And it beareth fruit of Freedom in the Gold Land!
We shall come, too, if you call,
We shall fight on if you fall;
Cromwell's land shall never be a bought and sold Land.

The standard of the Lord wave o'er the Old Land!
For the waiting world holds breath
While she treads the den of Death,
With the peaceful sleeve stript up from her bare bold hand;
And her rose in blood shall bloom
On the bosom, and the tomb
Of her many heroes fallen for the Old Land.

O, a terror to the Tyrant is that bold Land!
He remembers how she stood,
With her raiment roll'd in blood,

When the tide of battle burst upon the Old Land;
And he looks with darken'd face,
For he knows the hero race
Strike the Harp of Freedom — draw her Sword with bold hand.

Let thy glorious voice be heard, thou great and bold Land!
Speak the one victorious word,
And fair Freedom's wander'd Bird
Shall wing back with leaf of promise from the Old Land;
And the peoples shall come out
From their slave-land with a shout
For the spring that greeneth in the Future's Gold Land.

When the smoke of Battle rises from the Old Land,
You shall see the Tyrant down!
You shall see the ransom'd crown
On the brow of prisoned peoples won with bold hand:
She shall thresh her foes like corn,
They shall eat the bread of scorn,
And we'll sing her song of triumph in the Gold Land.

Quaff a cup, and send a cheer up for the Old Land.
We have heard the Reapers shout,
For the harvest going out,
Seen the smoke of Battle closing round the bold Land;
And our answer shall be hurl'd
Right across the ringing world, —
There are true hearts beating for you in the Gold Land.

THE LILIES OF FRANCE AND OUR OWN RED ROSE.

Like a stern old friend, War grimly comes
  To the temple of peaceful Life;
With the well-known nod of his beckoning plumes
  He hurries us into the strife.
And we meet once more, in the fields of fate,
  With our chivalrous Enemy,
Who knows, by the grip of our hands in hate,
  What the strength of our love may be.
O! the Lilies of France and our own Red Rose
  Are twined in a Coronal now;
At War's bloody bridal it glitters and glows
  On Liberty's beautiful brow.

We have dasht together like waves and rocks!
  We have fought till our shirts grew red!
We have met in the shuddering battle-shocks,
  Where none but the freed soul fled!
Now side by side, in the fields of fate,
  And shoulder to shoulder, are we;
And we know, by the grip of our hands in hate,
  What the strength of our love may be.
O! the Lilies of France and our own Red Rose
  Are twined in a Coronal now;
At War's bloody bridal it glitters and glows
  On Liberty's beautiful brow.

Then gather ye, gather to battle, ye Braves,
  In the might of your old renown!
And follow ye, follow ye, over the waves,
  Where Liberty's sun went down!
By the bivouac-fire, in the battle-shower,
  Remember your destiny grand,
To set in the thrones of their olden power
  The peoples of many a land!

For the Lilies of France and our own Red Rose
  Are twined in a Coronal now;
At War's bloody bridal it glitters and glows
  On Liberty's beautiful brow.

Till the last fetter'd nation that calls us is free,
  Let us fall upon Tyranny's horde!
Brave Italy, Poland, and Hungary, see,
  With their praying hands seek for a Sword!
Till the Storm-God is roused in each suffering land,
  Let us march thro' the welcoming world;
And till Freedom and Faith shall go hand-in-hand,
  Let us keep the war-standard unfurl'd!
For the Lilies of France and Old England's Red Rose
  Are twined in a Coronal now;
At War's bloody bridal it glitters and glows
  On Liberty's beautiful brow.

AFTER ALMA.

OUR old War-banners on the wind
  Were dancing merrily o'er them;
The hope of half the world behind —
  The sullen Foe before them!
They trode their march of battle, bold
  As death-devoted freemen;
Like those Three Hundred Greeks of old,
  Or Rome's immortal Three Men.
Ah, Victory! joyful Victory!
  Like Love, thou bringest sorrow;
But, O! for such an hour with thee,
  Who could not die to-morrow?

With towering heart and lightsome feet
  They went to their high places;
The fiery valour at white heat
  Was flashing in their faces!
Magnificent in battle-robe,
  And radiant, as from star-lands,
That spirit shone which girds our globe
  With glory, as with garlands!
Ah, Victory! joyful Victory!
  Like Love, thou bringest sorrow;
But, O! for such an hour with thee,
  Who could not die to-morrow?

They saw the Angel Iris o'er
  Their deluge of grim fire;
And with their life's last tide they bore
  The Ark of Freedom higher!
And grander 't is i' the dash of death
  To ride on Battle's billows,
When Victory's kisses take the breath,
  Than sink on balmiest pillows!
Ah, Victory! joyful Victory!
  Like Love, thou bringest sorrow;
But, O! for such an hour with thee,
  Who could not die to-morrow?

Brave Hearts, with noble feeling flusht,
  In ripe and ruddy riot
But Yesterday! how are ye husht
  Beneath the smile of Quiet!
For us they pour'd their blood like wine,
  From life's ripe-gather'd clusters;
And far thro' History's night shall shine
  Their deeds with starry lustres.
Ah, Victory! joyful Victory!
  Like Love, thou bringest sorrow;
But, O! for such an hour with thee,
  Who could not die to-morrow?

We laid them not in Churchyard home,
  Beneath our darling daisies:
But to their rude mounds Love will come,
  And sit, and sing their praises.
And soothly sweet shall be their rest
  Where Victory's hands have crown'd them;
To Earth our Mother's bosom prest,
  And Heaven's arms around them.
Ah, Victory! joyful Victory!
  Like Love, thou bringest sorrow;
But, O! for such an hour with thee,
  Who could not die to-morrow?

Yes, there they lie 'neath Alma's sod,
  On pillows dark and gory, —
As brave a host as ever trod
  Old England's fields of glory.
With head to home and face to sky,
  And feet the Tyrant spurning,
So grand they look, so proud they lie,
  We weep for glorious yearning.
Ah, Victory! joyful Victory!
  Like Love, thou bringest sorrow;
But, O! for such an hour with thee,
  Who could not die to-morrow?

They in Life's outer circle sleep,
  As each in death stood Sentry!
And with our England's Dead still keep
  Their watch for kin and country.
Up Alma, in their red footfalls,
  Comes Freedom's dawn victorious;
Such graves are courts to festal halls!
  They banquet with the Glorious.
Ah, Victory! joyful Victory!
  Like Love, thou bringest sorrow;
But, O! for such an hour with thee,
  Who could not die to-morrow?

Our Chiefs who matcht the men of yore,
And bore our shield's great burden, —
The nameless Heroes of the Poor, —
They all shall have their guerdon.
In silent eloquence, each life
The Earth holds up to heaven;
And Britain gives for Child and Wife,
As those dear hearts have given.
Ah, Victory! joyful Victory!
Like Love, thou bringest sorrow;
But, O! for such an hour with thee,
Who could not die to-morrow?

The spirits of our fathers still
Stand up in battle by us;
And in our need, on Alma hill,
The Lord of Hosts was nigh us.
Let Joy or Sorrow brim our cup,
'T is an exultant story,
How England's Chosen Ones went up
Red Alma's hill to glory.
Ah, Victory! joyful Victory!
Like Love, thou bringest sorrow;
But, O! for such an hour with thee,
Who could not die to-morrow?

BEFORE SEBASTOPOL.

Hurrah! we grip the Tyrant now!
And there 's no heart so lowly
But burns to strike a battle-blow,
And win a cause so holy!
The Brave look fearless in the eyes
Of Death, nor cry him quarter;
And grand promotion waits them, Boys,
Who fall by land or water!

Sing O! but a jubilant carouse
  Awaits us in our far land,
When we shall thrust up conquering brows,
  And take our Country's garland.

O, think how happy eyes will brim
  To greet us on the beaches,
With blissful looks of love that swim
  Thro' long luxurious reaches!
They watch us now from out the West,
  But all too proud to sorrow
For us who rest on Victory's breast,
  Or wear her wreath to-morrow.
Sing O! but a jubilant carouse
  Awaits us in our far land,
When we shall thrust up conquering brows,
  And take our Country's garland.

We 'll seek the bed of Death, to win
  Fair Freedom's dream of beauty,
Or wrest her from the Tyrant, in
  The loving arms of duty.
Then gaily thro' the ocean foam
  Shall sail our nobler Argo,
And proudly to our Island-home
  We 'll bear the precious cargo.
Sing O! but a jubilant carouse
  Awaits us in our far land,
When we shall thrust up conquering brows,
  And take our Country's garland.

To-day the ancient valour starts;
  The spirit of old story
Shall flash from out heroic hearts,
  And kindle England's glory.
Wild voices wail across the sea, —
  They cry from many a woe-land, —
Revenge! remember Sinope!
  Revenge! remember Poland!

Sing O! but a jubilant carouse
  Awaits us in our far land,
When we shall thrust up conquering brows,
  And take our Country's garland.

Now Soldiers up to conquest stride,
  Let not one spirit falter:
For Victory is your plighted Bride,
  The breach your solemn altar!
Thro' all this bloody cemet'ry
  Behold what seed lies sleeping;
God! but thy sun should stand while we
  Our harvest field are reaping.
Sing O! but a jubilant carouse
  Awaits us in our far land,
When we shall thrust up conquering brows,
  And take our Country's garland.

Now, Sailors, fight your Ships to-day
  As Grenville fought the Spaniard!
If Battle's bloodiest game they play,
  Have at them grip-and-poignard.
One thrilling shout for England, Ho!
  Then, naked for the fight, men,
Dash in like fire upon the foe,
  And God defend the Right, men!
Sing O! but a jubilant carouse
  Awaits us in our far land,
When we shall thrust up conquering brows,
  And take our Country's garland.

TWINE A GARLAND FOR THE GRAVE.

Twine a garland for the grave
Of our Beautiful! our Brave!
And their names in glory grave
  Who have died for us.

High the battle-banner wave!
They have perisht but to save,
They have leapt a Curtian grave
In their pride for us.

How they conquer, gallant guarders, with the red wet sword in hand!
How thy life, at their brave ardours, crimsons high with health, Old Land!
How they run the race of glory! how they light these darkened years!
In our land's heroic story, 't is the proudest tale of tears.

In the Alma's vineyards ruddy, did they toil for our increase;
In the fields of battle bloody, they shall plant our palms of Peace.
They may rest by Alma river; they may die in deserts drear:
But for ever, and for ever, shall our country hold them dear.

With her smile the Angel Duty lit their brows as with a crown;
And for love of her dear beauty they to death go daring down.
Eyes may weep the unreturning; hearts will break with Mother and Bride:
But, on Britain's front no mourning glooms for those who thus have died.

Twine a garland for the grave
Of our Beautiful! our Brave!
And their names in glory grave
Who have died for us.
High the battle-banner wave!
They have perisht but to save,
They have leapt a Curtian grave
In their pride for us.

THE DEATH-RIDE.

SIT stern in your saddles! grip tighter each blade
We charge thro' their guns, or thro' blood we shall wade!
To-day win a glory that never shall fade.
Old England for ever! Hurrah!

O the lightning of life! O the thunder of steeds!
Great thoughts burn within us like fiery seeds,
Swift to flame out a red fruitage of deeds.
Old England for ever! Hurrah!

O the wild joy of Warriors going to die,
All Sword, and all Flame, with our brows lifted high!
Ride on, happy band, for thy glory swims nigh.
Old England for ever! Hurrah!

Chariots of fire in the dark of death stand;
To crown all who die for their own dear land:
My God, what a time ere we come hand to hand!
Old England for ever! Hurrah!

The Sea of Flame wraps us now! take one long breath,
And plunge for the prize of Immortals, beneath.
Silence the cannonade, shouting to Death:
Old England for ever! Hurrah!

Spring to now! dash thro' now! and cleave crest and crown!
For each foe round you strown now, a wreath of renown!
In a red rain of Sabres ride down, dash them down.
Old England for ever! Hurrah!

Charge back! once again we must ride the death-
 ride,
You Victor-few smiling in terrible pride!
Charge home! smoking hell of horse, grim, glori-
 fied!
 Old England for ever! Hurrah!

Now cheer for the living! now cheer for the dead
Now cheer for the deed on that hill-side red!
The glory is gathered for England's head.
 Old England for ever! Hurrah!

OUR HEROES.

Ah, weep not for the Heroes whom we never more
 shall see;
Ah, weep we were not with them in their ruddy
 revelry!
God of Battles! but 't were glorious to have
 mounted Victory's Car,
When the Chivalry of Europe smote the squadrons
 of the Czar!

'T is brave, while banners wave, to be where Free-
 dom's Champions are,
And burst upon the Enemy like Gods from clouds
 of war!
Our Old Land beauteous leans above her darlings
 as they die,
And, bosom'd in her arms of love, her slain ones
 richly lie.

We blessed them for the Battle, who but marcht to
 the Bier;
Some were riper for the Bridal—some were Fa-
 thers gray and sere;

With a kiss for Child and Wife, some went out in
War's red wrack;
And to the land that gives us life, who'd grudge
to give it back?

I had a gallant Brother, loved at home, and dear
to me —
I have a mourning Mother, winsome Wife, and
Children three —
He lies with Balaklava's dead. But let the Old
Land call,
We would give our living remnant, we would follow one and all!

We speak a few weak words; but, the great hearts
gone to God,
They have fought with their Swords — won our
battles red wet-shod!
While we sat at home, brave laurels for our Land
they went to win;
And with smiles Valhalla lightens as our Heroes
enter in.

They bore our Banner fearless to the death, as to
the fight,
They lifted England peerless to the old heroic
height.
We weep not for the Heroes whom we never more
shall see, —
We weep we were not with them in their ruddy
revelry.

OUR ENGLISH NIGHTINGALE

"You brave, you bonny Nightingale,
 You are no summer Bird;
Your music sheathes an Army's wail
 That pierces like a Sword."
All night she sings, brave Nightingale,
 With her breast against the thorn;
Her saintly patience doth not fail,
 She keepeth watch till morn.

"Ah, sing, you bonniest Bird of God,
 The night is sad and long;
To dying ears—to broken hearts—
 You sing an Angel's song!"
She sings, she sings, brave Nightingale,
 And weary warrior souls
Are caught up into Slumber's heaven,
 And lapped in Love's warm folds.

"O sing, O sing! brave Nightingale,
 And at your magic note
Upon Life's sea victoriously
 The sinking soul will float.
O sing, O sing! brave Nightingale,
 And lure them back again,
Whose path is lost and spirit crost,
 In dark wild woods of Pain."

She sings, she sings, brave Nightingale,
 She breathes a gracious balm;
Her presence breaks the waves of war,
 She smiles them into calm.
She sings, she sings, brave Nightingale,
 Of auld Langsyne and Home;
And life grows light, the world grows bright,
 And blood runs rich with bloom.

Day unto day her dainty hands
  Make Life's soiled temples clean,
And there 's a wake of glory where
  Her spirit pure hath been.
At midnight, thro' that shadow-land,
  Her living face doth gleam;
The dying kiss her shadow, and
  The Dead smile in their dream.

Brave Bird of Love, in Life's sweet May,
  She rose up from the feast,
To shine above our Banner,
  Like God's Angel in the East.
"Brave Bird of Life, wave healing wings
  O'er that gray Land o' the Dead;
God's heaven lie round you like a shield,
  Earth's blessings on your head."

The Rose did lift her veil, and blush
  At her bower-door like a Bride;
The shy brown birds came back with Spring,
  In our merry green woods to hide.
But there she sang, our Nightingale!
  Till War's stern heart grew mild;
And, nestling in the arms of Peace,
  He slumbered like a Child.

INKERMAN.

'TWAS Midnight ere our Guns' grim laugh o'er
    their wild work did cease,
And at the smouldering fires of War we lit the pipe
    of peace.

At Four, a burst of Bells went up thro' Night's Cathedral dark,
It seemed so like our Sabbath-chimes, we could but lie, and hark!
So like the Bells that call to prayer in the dear land far away;
Their music floated on the air, and kist us—to betray.
Our camp lay on the rainy hill, all silent as a cloud,
Its very heart of life stood still—and the white Mist brought its shroud;
For Death was walking in the dark, and smiled His smile to see
How all was ranged and ready for a sumptuous jubilee.

O wily are the Russians, and they came up thro' the mirk—
Their feet all shod for silence in the best blood of the Turk!
While in its banks our fiery tide of War serenely slept,
Their subtle serpentry unrolled, and stealthily they crept!
In the Ruins of the Valley do the Birds of Carnage stir?
A rustle in the gloom like wheels! feet trample—bullets whir—
Blessed God! the Foe is on us. Now the Bugles with a start
Thrill—like the cry of a wrongéd Queen—to the red roots of the heart;
And long and loud the wild war-drums with throbbing triumph roll,—
A sound to set the blood on fire, and warm the shivering soul.

The war-worn and the weary leapt up ready, fresh, and true!
No weak blood curdled white i' the face, no valour turned to dew;
Majestic as a God defied, arose our English Host—
All for the peak of Peril went—each for the fieriest post!
Thro' the mist, and thro' the mire, and o'er the hill-brow scowling grim,
As is the frown of Murder when he dreams his dreadful dream.
No Sun! but none is needed,—Men can feel their way to fight,
The lust of Battle in their face—eyes filled with fiery light;
And long ere dawn was red in heaven, upon the dark earth lay
The prophesying morning-red of a great and glorious day.

As Bridegroom leaves his wedded Bride in gentle slumbers sealed,
Our England slumbered in the West, when her Warriors went a-field.
We thought of her, and swore that day to strike immortal blows,
As all along our leaguered line the roar of battle rose.
Her Banners waved like blessing hands, and we knew it was the hour
For a glorious grip till fingers met in the throat of Russian power.
And at a bound, and with a sound that madly cried to kill,
The Lion of Old England leapt like lightning from the hill.

And there he stood superb, thro' all that Sabbath
of the Sword,
And there he slew, with a terrible scorn, his hunters,
horde on horde.

All Hell seemed bursting on us, as the yelling
legions came —
The Cannon's tongues of quick red fire lickt all
the hills a-flame!
Mad whistling shell, wild sneering shot, with devilish
glee went past,
Like fiendish feet and laughter hurrying down the
battle-blast.
And thro' the air, and round the hills, there ran a
wrack sublime
As tho' the Eternal's Ark were crashing on the
shores of Time.
On Bayonets and Swords the smile of conscious
victory shone,
As down to death we dasht the Rebels plucking at
our Throne.
On, on they came with face of flame, and storm of
shot and shell —
Up! Up! like heaven-scalers, and we hurled them
back to Hell.

Like the old Sea, white-lipped with rage, they dash,
and foam despair
On ranks of rock, and what a prize for the Wrecker
Death was there!
But as 'twere River Pleasaunce, did our fellows
take that flood,
A royal throbbing in the pulse that beat voluptuous
blood:
The Guards went down to the fight in grey, but
now they're gory red —
Christ save them, they're surrounded! Leap your
ramparts of the dead,

And back the desperate battle, for there is but one short stride
Between the Russ and victory! One more tug, you true and tried —
The Red-Caps crest the hill! with bloody spur, Ride, Bosquet, ride!
Down like a flood from Etna foams their valour's burning tide.

Now, God for Merrie England, cry! Hurrah for France the Grand,
And charge the foe together, all abreast, and hand to hand!
He caught a shadowy glimpse across the smoke of Alma's fray
Of the Destroying Angel that shall blast his strength to-day.
We shout and charge together, and again, again, again,
Our plunging battle tears its path, and paves it with the slain.
Hurrah! the mighty host doth melt before our fervent heat;
Against our side its breaking heart doth faint and fainter beat.
And O, but 'tis a gallant show, and a merry march, as thus
We sound into the glorious goal with shouts victorious!

From morn till night, we fought our fight, and at the set of sun
Stood Conquerors on Inkerman—our Soldiers' Battle won.
That morn their legions stood like corn in its pomp of golden grain!
That night the ruddy sheaves were reapt upon the misty plain!

We cut them down by thunder-strokes, and piled the shocks of slain:
The hill-side like a vintage ran, and reel'd Death's harvest-wain.
We had hungry hundreds gone to sup in Paradise that night,
And robes of Immortality our ragged Braves bedight!
They fell in Boyhood's comely bloom, and Bravery's lusty pride;
But they made their bed o' the Russian dead, ere they lay down and died.

We gathered round the tent-fire in the evening cold and gray,
And thought of those who rankt with us in Battle's rich array,
Our Comrades of the morn who came no more from that fell fray!
The salt tears wrung out in the gloom of green dells far away —
The eyes of lurking Death that in Life's crimson bubbles play —
The stern white faces of the Dead that on the dark ground lay
Like Statues of old Heroes, cut in precious human clay —
Some with a smile as life had stopt to music proudly gay —
The household Gods of many a heart all dark and dumb to-day!
And hard hot eyes grew ripe for tears, and hearts sank down to pray.

From alien lands, and dungeon-grates, how eyes will strain to mark
This waving Sword of Freedom burn and beckon thro' the dark!

The Martyrs stir in bloody graves, the rusted armour rings
Adown the long aisles of the dead, where lie the warrior Kings.
To the proud Mother England came the radiant Victory
With Laurels red, and a bitter cup like Christ's last agony.
She took the cup, she drank it up, she raised her laurelled brow:
Her sorrow seemed like solemn joy, she lookt so noble now.
The dim divine of distance died — the purpled Past grew wan,
As came that crowning Glory o'er the heights of Inkerman.

NICHOLAS AND THE BRITISH LION.

CZAR Nicholas called to North and South,
"Come, see the world's great show!
I'll thrust my head in the Lion's mouth,"
And he laught, "Ha! Ha! Ho! Ho!"
"I am the Lion-Tamer dread —
I make the old brute quail!"
The Lion he shook his incredulous head,
And wagged his dubious tail.

O the Lion lay down in the pride of his might;
'T was a brave, magnanimous beast!
O the Lion leapt up to his shaggiest height;
The lord of a bloody feast!
Now hold, now hold, thou desperate man,
Or thy braggart cheek may pale;
Terror is towering up in his mane,
And Vengeance tugs at his tail.

Like a statue of Satan, Nick, alas! stood,
  And he chuckled a low lying laugh:
"The world is my Knoutship's whipping-top:
  Hot blood for wine I quaff!"
He called to North, he called to South,
  "Come, see the old brute quail:
I'll thrust my head in his mumbling mouth:"
  The Lion he wagged his tail.

He thrust his head in the Lion's mouth:
  Ho! Ho! but the sport was rare!
The Lion smelt blood in the giant's breath,
  And his clencht teeth held him there.
Then he cried, from between the gates of death,
  With the voice of a Spirit in bale,
"Now God-a-mercy on my soul!
  Does the Lion wag his tail?"

Then each one strove to say him Yea,
  But each one held his breath;
For the fires of hell lit the Lion's eyes,
  His looks communed with Death!
The Giant's heart melts like snow in his mouth,
  His voice is a woman's wail;
The Avenger knocks at the door of his life,
  In that lash of the Lion's tail.

A low, dread sound, as from underground,
  Now signals the realms of the dead;
And the Tamer lies tamed on the earth full-length;
  That is, except — a head.
And the poor old beast, at whose aspect mild
  The meanest thing dared rail,
Shakes his mane like a Conqueror's bloody plumes,
  And — quietly wags his tail.

A SOLDIER'S WIFE.

"Around us the night closes dense as a wood,
The Stars down the darkness like eerie eyes brood,
While out through the nightfall my fearless thoughts flee
To him who is fighting far over the sea.

"Across the mirk moorland the birds of night cry;
A wind stirs my flesh as of Ghosts gliding by;
Oh, clasp thy hands, pretty one, kneel down with me,
And pray for thy father far over the sea.

"O, brave is my Darling, and gallant and gay
He'll flash through the fight in the wild, bloody day;
He'll crest the high waves upon Valour's red sea;
God shield him! God send him back safely to me!"

He's lying, poor Wife! with the valiant and tried,
Who to-night poured their life on a ruddy hill-side:
And still she sings tenderly, "Over the sea,
Blow, breezes, and bring back my darling to me."

Her soul it sat smiling, all meek as a dove,
In her pure perfect face that was lighted with love;
Her child to the full heart endearing she drew,
And bowed like a Flower 'neath its blessing of dew.

Some luminous Beauty glides over the place,
A white mist of glory! a white spirit-face!
And a starry shape comes slow and sweet from the gloom;
God help thee, poor Widow! thy Husband is home!

She knows not the Presence that hovereth nigh,
Nor whence fell the slumber that healed her
heart's-cry;
But she weeps in her vision, and prayerfully
Still murmurs, "God send him back safely to me!"

A WAR WINTER'S-NIGHT IN ENGLAND.

Wild is the wintry weather!
Dark is the night, and cold!
All closely we crowd together,
Within the family fold.
A mute and mighty Shadow flies
Across the land on wings of Gloom!
And thro' each Home its awful eyes
May lighten with their stroke of doom.
Life's light burns dim — we hold the breath —
All sit stern in the shadow of Death,
Around the household fire —
This Winter's-night in England,
Straining our ears for the tidings of War,
Holding our hearts, like Beacons, up higher,
For those who are fighting afar.

We talk of Britain's glory,
We sing some brave old song,
Or tell the thrilling story
Of her wrestle with the wrong.
Till we clutch the spirit-sword from the strife,
And into our Rest would rather fall
Down Battle's cataract of life,
Than turn the white face to the wall.
Sing, O, for a charge victorious!
And the meekest face grows glorious!
As we sit by the household fire,

This Winter's-night in England, —
Our souls within us like steeds of War!
And we hold our hearts, like Beacons, up higher,
For those who are fighting afar.

And oft in silence solemn
We peer from Night's dark tent,
And see the quivering column
Like a cloud by lightning rent.
For death, how merry they mount and ride!
Those swords look keen for their lap of gore!
Such Valour leaps out Deified!
Such souls must rend the clay they wore!
How proud they sweep on Glory's track!
So many start! so few come back
To sit by the household fire,
On a Winter's-night in England,
And with rich tears wash their wounds of War,
Where we hold our hearts, like Beacons, up higher,
For those who are fighting afar.

We thrill to the Clarion's clangour,
And harness for the fight:
With the Warrior's glorious anger,
We are nobly mad to smite:
No dalliance, save with Hate, hold we,
Where Life and Death keep bloody tryst,
And all the red Reality
Reels on us through a murder-mist!
Wave upon Wave rolls Ruin's flood,
And the hosts of the Tyrant melt in blood,
As we sit by the household fire,
This Winter's-night in England,
And our colour flies out to the music of War,
While we hold our hearts, like Beacons, up higher,
For those who are fighting afar.

Old England still hath Heroes
  To wear her sword and shield!
We knew them not while near us,
  We know them in the field!
Look! how the Tyrant's hills they climb,
  To hurl our gage in his grim hold!
The Titans of the earlier time,
  Tho' larger-limb'd, were smaller-soul'd!
Laurel, or Amaranth, light their brow!
Living or dead, we crown them now!
  As we sit by the household fire,
  This Winter's-night in England:
From the white cliffs watching the storm of War,
  Holding our hearts, like Beacons, up higher,
For those who are fighting afar.

O! their brave love hath rootage
  In the Old Land, deep and dear,
And Life's ripe, ruddy fruitage
  Hangs summering for them here!
And tender eyes, tear-luminous,
  Melt thro' the dark of dreamland skies,
While, pleading aye for home and us,
  The heart is one live brood of cries!
Old feelings cling! O how they cling!
And sweet birds sing! O how they sing
  Them back to the household fire,
  This Winter's-night in England,
Where we wait for them weary and wounded from
    War,
  Holding our hearts, like Beacons, up higher,
For those who are fighting afar!

Ah, me! how many a Maiden
  Will wake o' nights, to find
Her tree of life, love-laden,
  Swept bare in this wild wind!
The Bird of bliss, to many a nest,
  Will come back never, never, never!

So many a goodly, gallant crest
 That waved to victory, low for ever!
We pray for them, we fear for them,
And silently drop a tear for them,
 As we sit by the household fire;
 This Winter's-night in England,
Each life looking out for its own love-star!
 Holding our hearts, like Beacons, up higher,
For those who are fighting afar.

But, there 's no land like England,
 Wherever that land may be!
Of all the world 't is king-land
 Crown'd, by its Bride, the Sea!
And they shall rest i' the balmiest bed,
 Who battle for it, and bleed for it!
And they shall be head of the Glorious Dead,
 Who die in the hour of need for it!
And long shall we sing of their deeds divine,
In songs that warm the heart like wine,
 As we sit by the household fire,
 On a Winter's-night in England,
And the tale is told of this night of War,
 How we held our hearts, like Beacons, up higher,
For those who were fighting afar.

THE MARTYRS' HILL.

Sitting in her sorrow lone,
Still our Mother makes her moan
For the Lost; and to the Martyrs' Hill our thoughts in mourning go.
O, that desert of the Dead,
Who lay down in their death-bed,
With their winding-sheet and wreath of winter snow!

Into glory had they rode
When the tide of triumph flowed,
Not a tear would we shed for the heroes lying low.
But our hearts break for the Dead,
In their desolate death-bed,
With their winding-sheet and wreath of winter snow.

Praying breath rose white in air,
Eyes were set in a stern stare,
Hands were stretcht for help that came not as they sank in silence low:
Our grand, our gracious Dead,
Who lay down in their death-bed,
With their winding-sheet and wreath of winter snow.

Now the winter snows are gone,
And Earth smiles as though the Dawn
Had come up from it in Flowers—such a light of grace doth glow
All about our darkened Dead,
Who lay down in their death-bed,
With their winding-sheet and wreath of winter snow.

But, never, never more,
Comes the Spring that will restore
To their own love, their own land, the dear ones lying low
On the Martyrs' Hill, our Dead
Who lay down in their death-bed,
With their winding-sheet and wreath of winter snow.

Till with victory God replies,
Shall our Battle storm the skies,
And our living heroes think, as they grapple with the foe,

Of our perisht, peerless Dead,
Who lay down in their death-bed,
With their winding-sheet and wreath of winter snow.

Through a hundred battles red,
Shall their fame float overhead:
Into everlasting flowers shall their martyr memories blow.
So we crown our glorious Dead,
Who lay down in their death-bed,
With their winding-sheet and wreath of winter snow.

THE AUSTRIAN.

How shall I help thee, Mother, in thy need?
I cried, and lookt my life out thro' mine eyes,
Across the smoke of thy great Sacrifice.
Give me some perilous post, or daring deed.
O might I breathe in Song heroic breath,
And strike my harp, as Lightning smites his wires,
To bear God's message with celestial fires!
Sing how the Glory of our land hath risen;
Sing midnight pæans by the Martyrs' graves
Walk War's red highways, voyage grim wide waves:
Or in an English cheer go down to death,
Where the soul bursts in wings on Battle's wind!
No! England waves her Minstrels forth to find
Our Lion Heart again in Austria's prison.

THE EXILE TO HIS COUNTRY.

How dimmed is all thy glory, and how dark the shadow falls!
And wild the sorrow waileth thro' thy hamlets and thy halls!
Thy banner burns no longer on the mountain and the lea,
And O! the dead are blessed who thy suffering may not see.
How are thy brave ones scattered on many an alien strand!
Thy darlings leal and true to the dear old Motherland.

They have bound thee in the grave-clothes, but we watch with tears and sighs,
Till Freedom comes like Christ, and thou like Lazarus shalt rise.
Thy pale, pale face, my Country, yet shall flush with ripening bloom,
As Nature's color kindles when the breath of Spring doth come.
O! come thou Spring of promise; mighty Hope, put forth thy hand,
And build thy arch of triumph for the dear old Motherland.

The Birds that follow Summer, they come and they depart,
For the Land of my love, and the home of my heart:
And, like a wounded Bird, my spirit trembles in the wind,
And flutters down: and they are gone, and I am left behind!

O my Dovelets in the nest! O the spoiler's bloody hand!
And I so far away from the dear old Motherland.

Sometimes when life is darkest, a glory bursts its glooms,
As Lightning thro' the startled night, the face of things illumes;
A sudden splendour smites me, and ere the thunders roll,
I see thy face look radiant thro' the darkness of my soul!
And thou art sitting at the feet of Freedom, great and grand,
Thy children happy in thy smile, thou dear old Motherland.

O thou among the nations, for thy might shalt yet be themed,
Thy fatal curse of Beauty by Love's blessing all redeemed!
The red wounds where they pierced thee, shall to scars of glory turn,
And in thy tearful eyes the light of boundless life shall burn!
The heavens are filled with Martyrs, but the earth still holds a band
Who will meet in battle yet for the dear old Motherland.

O! many are the gallant hearts will never answer when
Thy clarion-cry shall call us up to the field again!
And many are the tears must fall, and prayers go up to God,
But swift the vintage ripens, and the wine-press shall be trod!

The Harvest reddens rich for death, the Reapers
clench the hand,
And Victory comes to claim his Bride, thou dear
dear Motherland.

CATHCART'S HILL.

They have died, our true and tried, ere our flag
victorious flew
O'er the burning battle-hell, we must ride to con-
quest through.
But they died, our Glorified! on the field of their
renown;
And they died when the pride of the Foeman's
power went down.
Bury them on Cathcart's Hill, 't is a famous grave!
Bury them on Cathcart's Hill with our bravest
Brave!

A proud flame in the Death-wind waved the War-
rior's soaring plume:
Stern in his shroud of fire, the Foe glared from his
burning tomb!
Victory's shouts were ringing as they flasht from
out the strife,
To meet God's angels bringing garlands for the
Kings of Life.
Bury them on Cathcart's Hill, 't is a famous
grave!
Bury them on Cathcart's Hill with our bravest
Brave!

Bear them to that grave in a solemn march and
slow,
Let Music talk in tears o'er the great ones lying
low;

They will sleep calm and deep when the battle-bugles blow;
And ye shall build their monument when next ye meet the Foe!
Bury them on Cathcart's Hill, 't is a famous grave!
Bury them on Cathcart's Hill with our bravest Brave!

We quaff our cup o' the vintage, and from darkened depths arise
The bubbles, like the tears that plead in Desolation's eyes;
Yet there 's glory in our grief, — 't is a glory that shall grow
When our Sorrow hath no morrow, and 't was centuries ago.
Bury them on Cathcart's Hill, 't is a famous grave!
Bury them on Cathcart's Hill with our bravest Brave!

Bury them on Cathcart's Hill, — their glory from its crest
Shall flame, a terror to the North, a watchfire to the West!
Cross their hands and lay their brands upon the martial breast,
They have done with their work, lay them down to their rest.
Bury them on Cathcart's Hill, 't is a famous grave!
Bury them on Cathcart's Hill with our bravest Brave!

THE COALITION AND THE PEOPLE.

O SUFFERING people, this is not our fight,
Who called a holy crusade for the right.
The Despot's bloody game our tricksters play,
And stake our future, chance by chance, away.
O darkened hearts in desolate home-stead!
O wasted bravery of our mighty dead!
The flower of men fall stricken from behind:
The Knaves and Cowards stab us bound and blind.
With faces turned from Battle, they went forth:
We marcht with ours set stern against the North.
They shuffled lest their feet should rouse the dead:
We went with resurrection in our tread.
They trembled lest the world might come to blows:
We quivered for the tug and mortal close.
They only meant a mild hint for the Czar:
We would have bled him through a sumptuous war.
While they were quenching Freedom's scattered fires,
We kindled memories of heroic Sires.
They'd have this grand old England cringe and pray,
"Do n't smite me, Kings; but if you will, you may:"
We'd make her as in those proud times of old,
When Cromwell spoke, and Blake's war-thunders rolled.
They to the passing powers of darkness fawn:
With warrior joy we greet this crimson Dawn.
To crowned Bloodsuckers they would bind us slaves:
We would be free, or sleep in glorious graves.

State-Spiders, Here or There, weave webs alike;
These hold the victims, while the others strike.
The Dwarfs drag our great Banner in the mire:
We ask for men to bear it high and higher.
O stop their fiddling over War's grim revel,
And pitch them from your shoulders to — the
Devil.

ALL OVER.

FADES the New Aurora
That so glorious shone afar,
We but saw its fair face smiling
In the ruddy waves of war.
The peace-fool to his pillow
Now may sneak, and sleep:
But a glory gone for ever,
We must weep; let us weep.

Sleep the buried thunders;
Their reverberations cease:
And the grim old War-God
Must smile — a painted Peace.
Wild eyes are mad-house windows
Of Souls that plead in vain!
Over their old dark sorrow
Greeneth the soft spring-rain.

Had we struck for Freedom
One immortal battle-blow,
Like the men who rose for England,
Two hundred years ago, —
The dead Nations lying
Where they fought and fell of old,
Would have risen from their prison,
And their buried flags unrolled.

Cowards in the Council!
  Heroes in the field!
Is our short sad story
  By the blood of Martyrs sealed.
On those lone Crimean ridges
  In the night our dead arise;
Hear the Norland winds come wailing
  With their curses, and their cries.

Sublime in all her suffering!
  In the fight so brave!
Poor old England's victories
  Bow her to the grave.
And the world may see her yet
  Low and lonely lie
Upon her rock, while Tyrants mock
  As they go riding by.

MISCELLANEOUS.

MISCELLANEOUS.

HOOD,

WHO SANG THE SONG OF THE SHIRT.

'T WAS the old story! — ever the blind world
Knows not its Angels of Deliverance
Till they stand glorified 'twixt earth and heaven.
It stones the Martyr; then, with praying hands,
Sees the God mount his chariot of fire,
And calls sweet names, and worships what it spurn'd.
It slays the Man to deify the Christ:
And then how lovingly 't will bind the brows
Where late its thorn-crown laught with cruel lips —
Red, and rejoicing from grim Murder's kiss!
To those who walk beside them, great men seem
Mere common earth; but distance makes them stars.
As dying limbs do lengthen out in death,
So grows the stature of their after-fame;
And then we gather up their glorious words,
And treasure up their names with loving care.
So Hood, our Poet, lived his martyr-life:
With a swift soul that travell'd at such speed,
And struck such flashes from its flinty road,
That by its trail of radiance through the dark,
We almost see th' unfeatured Future's face, —
And went uncrown'd to his untimely tomb.
Certes, the World did praise his glorious Wit —
The merry Jester with his cap and bells!
And sooth, his wit was like Ithuriel's spear:
But 't was mere lightning from the cloud of his life,

Which held at heart most rich and blessed rain
Of tears melodious, that are worlds of love;
And Rainbows, that would bridge from earth to heaven;
And Light, that would have shone like Joshua's sun
Above our long death-grapple with the Wrong;
And thunder-voices, with their Words of fire,
To melt the Slave's chain, and the Tyrant's crown.
His wit? — a kind smile just to hearten us! —
Rich foam-wreaths on the waves of lavish life,
That flasht o'er precious pearls and golden sands.
But, there was that beneath surpassing show!
The starry soul, that shines when all is dark! —
Endurance, that can suffer and grow strong —
Walk through the world with bleeding feet, and smile! —
Love's inner light, that kindles Life's rare colours,
Bright wine of Beauty for the longing soul;
And thoughts that swathe Humanity with such glory
As limns the outline of the coming God
In him were gleams of such heroic splendours
As light this cold, dark world up as a star
Array'd in glory for the eyes of heaven:
And a great heart that beat according music
With theirs of old, — God-likest kings of men!
A conquering heart! which Circumstance, that frights.
The Many down from Love's transfiguring height,
Aye mettled into martial attitude.
He might have clutcht the palm of Victory
In the world's wrestling-ring of mightiest deeds;
But he went down a precious Argosy
At sea, just glimmering into sight of home,
With its rare freightage from diviner climes.
The world may never know the wealth it lost,
When Hood went darkling to his tearful tomb,
So mighty in his undevelopt force!

With all his crowding unaccomplished hopes!
Th' unuttered wealth and glory of his soul!
And all the music ringing round his life,
And poems stirring in his dying brain.
O! blessings on him for the songs he sang —
Which yearn'd about the world till then for birth!
How like a bonny bird of God he came,
And pour'd his heart in music for the Poor;
Who sit in gloom while sunshine floods the land,
And feel through darkness, for the hand of Help!
And trampled Manhood heard, and claimed his crown,
And trampled Womanhood sprang up ennobled!
The human soul lookt radiantly through rags!
And there was melting of cold hearts, as when
The ripening sunlight fingers frozen flowers.
O! blessings on him for the songs he sang!
When all the stars of happy thought had set
In many a mind, his spirit walkt the gloom
Clothed on with beauty, as the regal Moon
Walks her night-kingdom, turning clouds to light.
Our Champion! with his heart too big to beat
In bonds, — our Poet in his pride of power!
Ay, we 'll remember him who fought our fight,
And chose the Martyr's robe of flame, and spurn'd
The gold and purple of the glistering slave.
His Mausoleum is the People's heart,
There he lies crown'd and glorified, — our King
In state, with singing robe wrapt richly round.
But 't is not meet, my England, his dear dust
Should lie where splendid flatteries flaunt on tombs,
As treachery serves to brighten wanton tears —
With not a line of letter'd love to tell
What mighty heart lies quencht and broken there.
So let us build our Poet's monument!
With passionate hearts of love for corner-stones,
And tears that temper for immortal fame.

And it were well, my England, shouldst thou
come
To weep some honest drops above his grave.
Our Hood is worthy of eternal praise
And blessings, and dear heart-amenities,
As warrior Wellington, who rode to fame
On Death's white horse, by Battle's crimson path

SIR ROBERT'S SAILOR SON.

Our country has no need to raise
The ghosts of glories gone;
Such heroes dying in our days,
Still pass the live torch on.
Brave blood as bright a crimson gleams,
Still burns as goodly zeal;
The old heroic radiance beams
In men like William Peel.

With beautiful bravery clothed on,
And such high moral grace,
The flash of rare soul-armour shone
Out of his noble face!
So mild in peace, so stern in war,
He walkt our English way,
Just one of Shakespeare's Warriors for
A weary working day.

His Sailors loved him so on deck,
So cheery was his call,
They leapt on land, and in his wake
Followed him, guns and all.
For, as a battle-brand red-hot,
His Spirit grew and glowed,
When in his swift war-chariot
The Avenger rose and rode.

Sleep, Sailor Darling, true and brave,
  With our dead Soldiers sleep!
That so the land you lived to save,
  You shall have died to keep.
You may have wished the dear Sea-blue
  To have folded round your breast,
But God had other work for you,
  And other place of rest.

We might have reacht you with our wreath
  If living; but laid low,
You grow so grand! and after death
  The dearness deepens so!
To have gone so soon, so loved to have died,
  So young to wear that crown,
We think. But with such thrills of pride
  As shake the last tears down.

God rest you, gallant William Peel,
  With those whom England leaves,
Scattered as still she plies her steel,
  But God gleans up in sheaves.
We 'll talk of you on land, on board,
  Till Boys shall feel as Men,
And forests of hands clutch at this Sword
  Death gives us back again.

Our old Norse Fathers speak in you,
  Speak with their strange sea-charm,
That sets our hearts a-beating to
  The music of the storm.
There comes a Spirit from the deep,
  The salt wind waves its wings,
That rouses from its Inland sleep
  The blood of the old Sea Kings.

THE OLD LAND.

O LEAL high hearts of England,
  The evil days are near;
When ye, with steel in heart and hand,
  Must strike for all that's dear!
And better tread the bloodiest deck,
  And fieriest field of fame,
Than break the heart and bow the neck,
  And sit in the shadow of shame.
Let Despot, Death, or Devil come,
  United here we stand:
We'll safely guard our Island-Home,
  Or die for the dear old Land.

O, Warriors of Old England,
  You'll hurry to the call;
And her good ships shall sail the storm,
  With their merry mariners all.
In words she wasteth not her breath,
  But be the trumpet blown,
And in the Battle's dance of death,
  She'll dance the bravest down.
Let Despot, Death, or Devil come,
  United here we stand:
We'll safely guard our Island-Home,
  Or die for the dear old Land.

Success to our dear England,
  When dark days come again;
And may she rise up glorious
  As the rainbow after rain.
A thousand memories warm us still,
  And, ere the old spirit dies,
The purple of each wold and hill
  From English blood shall rise.

Let Despot, Death, or Devil come,
  United here we stand:
We'll safely guard our Island-Home,
  Or die for the dear old Land.

God strike with our dear England!
  Long may the old land be
The guiding glory of the world,
  The home of the fair and free!
Old Ocean on his silver shield
  Shall lift our little Isle
Unvanquisht still by flood or field,
  While the heavens in blessing smile.
Let Despot, Death, or Devil come,
  United here we stand:
We'll safely guard our Island-Home,
  Or die for the dear old Land.

THE FIGHTING TEMERAIRE TUGGED TO HER LAST BERTH.

It is a glorious tale to tell
  When nights are long and mirk;
How well she fought our fight, how well
  She did our England's work;
  Our good Ship Temeraire!
  The fighting Temeraire!
She goeth to her last long home,
  Our grand old Temeraire.

Bravely over the breezy blue
  They went to do or die;
And proudly on herself she drew
  The Battle's burning eye!
  Our good Ship Temeraire!
  The fighting Temeraire!

She goeth to her last long home,
  Our grand old Temeraire.

Round her the Glory fell in flood,
  From Nelson's loving smile,
When, raked with fire, she ran with blood
  In England's hour of trial!
  Our good Ship Temeraire!
  The fighting Temeraire!
She goeth to her last long home,
  Our grand old Temeraire.

And when our darling of the Sea
  Sank dying on his deck,
With her revenging thunders she
  Struck down his foe — a wreck.
  Our good Ship Temeraire!
  The fighting Temeraire!
She goeth to her last long home,
  Our grand old Temeraire.

Her day now draweth to its close
  With solemn sunset crowned;
To death her crested beauty bows,
  The night is folding round.
  Our good Ship Temeraire!
  The fighting Temeraire!
She goeth to her last long home,
  Our grand old Temeraire.

No more the big heart in her breast
  Will heave from wave to wave.
Weary and war-worn, ripe for rest,
  She glideth to her grave.
  Our good Ship Temeraire!
  The fighting Temeraire!
She goeth to her last long home,
  Our grand old Temeraire.

In her dumb pathos desolate
  As night among the dead!
Yet wearing an exceeding weight
  Of glory on her head.
  Our good Ship Temeraire!
  The fighting Temeraire!
She goeth to her last long home,
  Our grand old Temeraire.

Good bye! good bye! Old Temeraire,
  A sad and proud good bye!
The stalwart spirit that did wear
  Your sternness, shall not die.
  Our good Ship Temeraire!
  The fighting Temeraire!
She goeth to her last long home,
  Our grand old Temeraire.

Thro' battle blast, and storm of shot,
  Your Banner we shall bear;
And fight for it like those who fought
  Our good Ship Temeraire.
  The fighting Temeraire!
  The conquering Temeraire!
She goeth to her last long home,
  Our grand old Temeraire.

A DAY AT CRAIGCROOK CASTLE.

I.

LIFE is at most a Meeting and a Parting;
A glimpse into the world of Might-have-been.
And standing rapt on some new-trodden height,
We long to build a tabernacle there.

A sudden glorious glimpse, a nestling face,
Will bid the kingly moment live for ever.
Ah, could we paint their picture in the mind,
And breathe the blessèd breath of Beauty back!

We think how on some heavenly day the Sun
Gathered his glory for a grand repose;
And with her folding stillness Eve came down,
So meek and shadowy, bringing healing dews,
While Angels walkt our garden of the soul.
How on a summer morn the dewy lanes
In sunny England took us in cool arms.
Or, in a wondrous Moonlight long ago,
The face of early Love upturned to us
Two human stars that swam in bridal dew;
With brow of virgin white, and cheek's warm touch;
The full heart's sweetness parting young red lips;
And, caught by some surprise o' the tender time,
Our Deity half forgot her veiling cloud,
And pure soul all in silent beauty smiled.

So Memory maketh rich the house of life,
Where our great moments come as gorgeous guests;
At Fancy's touch the walls with pictures bloom,
And rosy recollections rise around.

Even so I linger o'er my perfect day,
Whose fruitful round of ripe and crowded life
In its sole glory summed a golden age;
Whose whispering memory cometh like an air
Of heaven wafting warm immortal breath;
Then leaves me softly as the Dove of Day,
That shakes down dews of freshness as it goes.

II.

In that sweet season when the Year is green,
And hearts grow merry as spring-groves full of birds,

And young Earth putteth forth the lovely things
She hath been dreaming through long winter
nights;
Taking the May-tide in a golden swim,
Her blithe heart singing for the flooding cheer;
While life for pleasure ripples as it runs;
With dainty colour the kindling country dawns;
Death lieth low; his hidden footprints bloom;
Upon his grave Life danceth all in flowers:
And lying shell-like on our shore o' the world,
We are caught up to listening ear of Heaven,
That leaneth down maternal meek to hear
Our inner murmurs of the eternal sea:
Then Craigcrook puts its budding glory on.
An emerald Eden nestling in the North:
To which the mariner worn on life's salt wave,
Might point his prow and find a conqueror's home,
And storm-tost Love up-fold his wearied wings.

A happy island in a sea of green,
Smiling it lies beneath the changing sky,
Well pleased, and conscious that each wave and
wind
Is tempered kindly or with blessing rich:
And all the quaint cloud-messengers that come
Voyaging the blue Heaven's summer sea,
Soft, shining, sumptuous, blown by languid breath,
Touch tenderly, or drop with ripeness down.
Spring builds her leafy nest for birds and flowers,
And folds it round luxuriant as the Vine
When grapes are filled with wine of merry cheer:
The Summer burns her richest incense there,
Swinging the censers of her thousand flowers:
Brown Autumn comes o'er seas of glorious gold:
And there old Winter keeps some greenth of heart,
When on his head the snows of age are white.

Mid glimpsing greenery at the hill-foot stands
The castle with its tiny town of towers:

A smiling Martyr to the climbing strength
Of Ivy that will crown the old bald head,
And Roses that will mask him merry and young,
Like an old Man with Children round his knees.
With cups of colour how the Roses rise
On walls and bushes, red and yellow and white;
A dance and dazzle of Roses range all round.

The path runs down and peeps out in the lane
That loiters on by fields of wheat and bean,
Till the white-gleaming road winds city-ward.
Afar, in floods of sunshine blinding white,
The City lieth in its quiet pride,
With castled crown, looking on Towns and Shires,
And Hills from which cloud-highlands climb the
 heavens:
A happy thing in glory smiles the Firth;
Its flowing azure winding like an arm
Around the warm waist of the yielding land.

III.

I ROSE betimes upon my day of days;
Through faëry forests of the lady fern,
Went up the wooded height to see the Dawn,
That new, eternal Picture fresh from God,
Quicken and colour into perfect life.
Quietly, quietly slept the world beside
The sepulchre of the dark, till Light awoke.
The haunting spirit of each lonely place
Seemed passing through the still and solemn wood.
What breath of life the breeze of morning blew!
What dewy smell and after-sense of showers
Came wooing like rich airs from secret shores
To those who sail into the eternal dawn!
Bird after bird the waking stillness stirred,
As Earth were warbling some new tune of joy
With which her heart gusht, and its radiance fired

Her face, as she arrayed to meet the morn.
The meek and melting amethyst of dawn
Blusht o'er the blue hills in the ring o' the world;
Up emerald twilights came the shining sea
Of sunlight, breaking in a silent surge,
Whence Morning like the birth of Beauty rose;
And, at a rosy touch, the clouds that lay
In sullen purples round the hills of Fife,
Adown her pathway spread their cloaks of gold:
The silvery-green-and-violet sheen o' the sea
Changed into shifting opal tinct with gold:
And like an Alchymist with furnace-face,
The Sun smiled on his perfect work, pure gold.

The breath of Dawn brought God's good-morning kiss
To bud and leaf and flower, and human hearts
That like pond-lilies open heavenward eyes.
Sweet lilies of the valley, tremulous fair,
Peep through their curtains claspt with diamond dew
By faëry jewellers working while they slept:
The Pansies, pretty little puritans,
Come peering up with merry eyes to see
How sleeping Beauty wakens as the sun
Doth kiss her in the sly green secrecies!
And arch Laburnum droops her budding gold
From emerald fingers, with such taking grace.
The Lilac is alight with all her stars:
Wall-flowers in fragrance burn themselves away
With the sweet Season on her precious pyre;
Pure passionate aromas of the Rose,
And purple perfume of the Hyacinth,
Come like a colour thro' the golden day.
A summer soul is in the Limes; they stand
Low murmuring honied things that wing forth Bees;
Their busy whisperings done, the Poplars hush!
But lo, a warm wind winnowing odour-rain

Goes breathing by, and there they curtsey meek,
Or toss their locks in frolic wantonness,
And a great gust of joy runs shivering thro' them;
All the leaves thrill and sparkle wild as wings.
Voluptuously ripening in the sun,
The Meadows swell their bosom plump with life.
The Buttercups spread tiny laps to take
The warm gold showering down from heaven, and oft
Each to its crownèd likeness nods and smiles.
The Birds low-crooning o'er their sweet Spring-tunes
Still touch them with a riper luxury:
That Blackbird with the wine of joy is mellow,
And in his song keeps laughing, he's so jolly,
To think how summer pulps the fruit for him.
The Apple-tree hath felt the ruddying breath
Of May upon her yielding leafy lips,
Look how she flushes over! warm in white!

Deep after deep the generous heart of Spring,
Full of glad days, hath opened into bloom,
Ripe with all sweetness.
Crown us, lusty leaves!
Shake down your gathered coolness, O green leaves!

IV.

At Craigcrook Castle all that bounteous day
Rare talk we had and sweet society,
To floating filled with bright Olympian life.
Under the tender trees, where rippled grass
Caressed us with its smiles, we sat, and watcht
The rich World in her blooming airy nest,
Warm-burnishing her colours like a Bird
O' the Sun, to soar on silent wings of light;
And Heaven brooding down with golden eye,
Where Sunlight, seeking hidden Shadow, toucht

The green leaves all a-tremble as they played.
While One whose looks were mild as they had drawn
A Christ-like sweetness from the face of Babes, —
His brow the triumph-arch of royal soul —
A Prodigal of Freedom whose great heart,
Big as the world it floods with wealth to-day,
Must eat to-morrow of the Stranger's husks —
Prometheus on his rock of exile — told
The vision passing solemn thro' his soul.

Ah! how they drank the breath of Battle, won
Its swarthy bloom, those spirits fiery-fine!
O, gallant hearts, how stalwartly they stood;
How fought the faithful, how the deathless died!
And there in saviour sepulchres they sleep,
Crowned with the diadem o' the kingly Dead;
Green graves on earth, — high memories in heaven.
And how the night came down with treachery dark,
But reddened with the light of burning homes,
That lit the Hangman while he knit his noose:
Then silence, at the hush of Death, above;
Nought but a ghastly Golgotha below.

And O, but hearts flew out, like Freedom's bird,
To flap their wings upon the flag of war.
And fierce looks flasht, and prayers went up to God,
In fiery chariots of our fervent hearts.
And eyes were veiled with noble tears to see
That Exile by the hounds of torture trackt;
Who, while they tore his stricken life, still drank
His cup of trembling, smiling very calm.

Fight on, thou Hero! Heaven's glooming look
Frowns only on the wrong. This dark shall break
In resurrection hour. The chariot wheels
Of coming Vengeance spin too swift for sight.

The Nemesis of Nations only waits,
Until the glass of Destiny runs out,
To wake the Murderers with her whip of fire,
Caught by the hair in sudden hands of Hell!
While in a ruddy rain old Earth laughs up.
O, we shall see a sight ere England's sun
Goes down behind her hills of gathered gold!
The time of times, the year of years is nigh!
When Spring's young hopes lie dead, and her sweet buds
Are low in dust, our Autumn fruitage comes.
Princes shall meet thee in thy Country's gate;
Thy Banner yet shall crown her topmost height,
And all the world shall see it waving there.

V.

In the green quiet of a neighbouring knoll
There sat and sang a beauteous company.
Aurelia with the royal brows, and breast
Bounding with hurrying heart, wave-wanton, for
A rich repose on some Elysian shore:
A gorgeous passion-flower of Womanhood
Come, golden-natured, to its summer throne:
Her eyes, the stars of burning dreams, so rapt
The spirit moth-like for their fire, you might
Have gone to death by sword-light for their smile.
And sullen beauty of her mouth's ripe bloom.
And Mabel, saintly sweet and fairily fine
As maiden rising from enchanted mere;
Pale as a lily crowned with moonlight calm:
A queenly creature with her quiet grace,
And dazzling white hand veined cerulean:
Upon her warm-waved hair the rippled light
Played soft, and fleckt it into cloudy gold;
Her eyes of violet-grey were coloured rich
With gloom of tender thought, and mirrored large
Within them, starry futures swam and shone:

Ah! what a smile to fill a life with light,
And make the waking heart to sing in sleep!
How precious in some costly cup of love,
The perfect pearl of her star-purity!
And stately CHARMIAN with her grander calm,
Like a Greek Goddess Statue that had raised
The veil of being in some diviner dawn,
And yearning Love did woo her into Woman.
With merry melting mouth and subtle eyes,
And warm heart glowing her white silence through
She rose up in her crown the Queen of Smiles
With all the old majesty, unweeting of
The old worship conscious hearts in silence pay;
Our English vesture cannot mask her mould.
And She, with dancing sparkle in her eyes,
Like sun-kist waters twinkling sapphirine,
Our SEERESS with whose soul the Spirits walk:
Who told strange mysteries in Waking Sleep,
And held your hand and read your Book of life;
Whose presence weirdly took the throbbing heart
Bird-like, as it were caught in spirit-figures;
Whose visioned face would shine so glorified,
You lookt with heavenward instinct up to see
Whence came such beauty as brake thro' Raphael's
dream.
They sang those wailing old Scotch songs that set
The heart-strings all a-tremble for their harp:
In which melodious Passion breaks its heart
For evermore, and finds no spousal words.
And mingling oft in Music's airy storm,
Spirit with spirit crossed in tingling touch;
Till every nerve seemed an immortal sense,
For Life to draw the hovering heaven down.

VI.

SOME played at bowls upon unwrinkled sward,
And drank old ale with ruby flame in it,

Where sunny laurels twinkled silver lights;
While others traced the footprints of grey Time,
Long fossilized: some by the Sea — that glowed
In living azure and inviolate calm —
Peered in the portal of its wonder-world.
Some showered playful palms down in the path,
And deckt with flowers the marriage-robe of One
Who brought his beauteous Bride in triumph home:
A jolly Briton, princely to the poor.
His rich heart-warming ruddiness of look
Might make an east wind reel off mellow and mild:
So sunnily his inner ripeness smiled:
And stalwart stood the sheltering wall of his life,
For climbing flower and fruit to bud and bear.
Her fragrant weight of warm and loving life,
That dwined with tender want of folding arms,
Half-sad with sweetness like a dew-droopt flower,
Stirs in his smile and rises ruddy and white,
With breath that maketh dim his dallying eyes:
Glowing imperial as the sun-toucht Rose!
A young Aurora of the Bridal-Dawn.
Her eyes wide-wakened by Love's quickening kiss, —
Sweet-drunken with the wine of tears, — foreshow
How Love hath hived his honey in her heart.
And there they walk their rosy marriage time,
With gracious words that brighten listening brows
Like crowns of splendour, as the first pair walkt
Their morning of the world in Paradise.

Our Poet, Rubens, scoffed at Wedded Love,
And drew a piteous picture of our friend
In harness, drawing the matrimonial car,
Heavily laden, along the ruts of life.
But in his voice there hissed a thirsty sound,
As when the dry leaves rustle for the rain.
With longing eyes he mockt the laughing grapes,

And six weeks after held out eager hands,
To take the bonds that bind for evermore:
And quietly joined the herd of pastured Slaves,
Where nuptial Love thro' sweet tears on him smiled.

Up spoke our Host. A sunny life was his
Among his children, breathing blooms of health,
He, like a rennet Apple wrinkle ripe,
Hived full of sweetness, fragrant to the taste,
Tho' Sorrow's tooth should strike the brave heart's core —
He had the happy soul which, like the Bee,
Rocks with delight upon a thistle-top,
Or finds voluptuous honey on wild moors.
And cheerily he chirpt of Wedded Love,
And Home our refuge from the mad-world-strife,
Where we may keep the spirit-sandals clean,
We soil so on our treadmill of a world;
And open heaven in the shut up heart:
Where Love may help us hand-in-hand across
The dark stream of Eternity, as Life
Goeth on starry stepping-stones to God.
Ah! how it made him turn to his dear nest,
And proudly yearn o'er his dear marriage guest,
Who made their little world so bright with bliss,
It drew God's Angels blessing-laden down.
And as he spoke, the dead flowers in our hearts
All pressed and precious, softly stirred with life;
Bloomed on our brows, and shed a fragrance round.
In silence sat our Crimean Hero, he
Who told us how they fought at Inkerman:
His heart swam up in tears at thoughts of Home.
The roar and rack of Battle over and gone;
No more surprises in the bloody trench,
Where midnight swarmed with visions horrible,
And earth was like a fiery coast of hell!
All that long aching wintriness of soul,

Warm-melted in the arms of Wedded Love,
That drew him from the bloody battle-press,
And claspt him safe in their serene of heaven,
Where Past and Future crown him as they kiss.
And with dumb eloquence his poor armstump moved,
As it were dreaming of a dear embrace.

VII.

A silvered Sage like some old pictured Saint,
Smilingly took the crucial hand of Doubt,
And thrust stern fingers in his spirit-wounds;
And told us how he hunted shadows once,
And felt his spiritual pulse ten times an hour,
With thoughts of Self fatal as Herod's worms.
And how the Child rose up and led the Man
Back very lowly to their Mother's knee:
Worshipping God as in the dear old days.
"'They wrought in faith,' and not 'They wrought in doubt,'
Is the proud epitaph inscribed above
Our glorious Dead who in their grandeur lie,
Crowned with the garland of eternity.
Because they did believe, and conquered Doubt,
They lived great lives and did their deathless deeds,
Who in the old time walkt their perilous way,
With the grey hairs of kingly sorrow crowned:
Who laid their heads upon the bloody block
For their last pillow: who amid the flames
Bore witness still, and with their quivering hands
Sowed every wind with sparks of fiery thought.
Because they did believe, we kneel to read
Where men and angels mingle tears of joy.
Because he did believe, Columbus sailed
For that new world his inner eyes had seen.
He found: so Faith its new worlds yet shall find,

While Doubt shakes its wise head and stays be-
hind.
Newton believed for many a year before
The Hand in heaven shook the Apple down.
Because we have believed, our knowledge comes:
Belief, not Doubt, will touch the secret spring.
Belief is that soul-attitude which sees
How the pure distance of some infinite sea
Relieves the dark ground of our inland life,
And feels the fresh spray make its colour bloom.
But Doubt turns from the light, and only sees
The Shadow that it casts, and follows it;
For Doubt is ever its own Deity:
The Shadow still dilates on darkened eyes,
And lengthens as the awful night comes down.

"Life is a maze, but God i' the centre sits.
I wailed and wandered in the winding ways;
Against the thorns with bleeding bosom beat,
And vainly shouted to the passing stars, —
Those silent spirit-vanishing-points of space, —
That voyaged Ship-like on nor saw my wreck.
I shriekt out with the scorners, 'There 's no God!'
Sat in the womb o' the world like Babe unborn,
And blindly said, 'There is no life to come.'
Then my Beloved came, and drew me in
A little nearer to the heart of light.
A lightning-glimpse from out the cloud of Death
Stern revelation rifted, and I fell
Prone on my face, heart-broken in the dust.
Her vase of love was broken at my feet,
And all the precious perfume filled my life.
Breathed thro' the dark a still voice low and
sweet:
'Let Faith but climb the tree of prayer, and watch
And wait, the Lord will surely pass that way,'
And down a dream of peace a spirit hand
Slid into mine, and at its dewy touch
Existence melted in the dawning heaven,

And human flowering of divine delight.
It led me to my kneeling-place among
The pilgrims of the world who sought in vain,
And closed their eyes in tears, to suddenly find
God sitting in his temple of the soul."

There was strange glory in the old Man's eyes,
Which, with life's setting splendour shone aglow
Like windows lighted by the sinking sun
That paints fair morrow; and a soul of sweetness
Smiled from each wrinkle! pleasant was the sight,
For he had reacht the shining Sunset Isles
That fade into the eternal Heavens, and lo!
The Hesper of a happy memory smiles.

Now Sunset burns. A sea of gold on fire
Serenely surges around purple isles:
O'er billows and flame-furrows Day goes down.
Far-watching clouds with ruby glimmer bloom
A scattered crowd that on its face still wears
The splendid light and life of some brave show.
Dews swarm upon the flowers like silent bees.
Afar and faintlier sounds retiring life;
Husht woods grow solemn dark; the blue peaks fade;
Weird mists rise white, and gracious Twilight comes;
Sweet is the mystery of her loveliness;
And all things feel her dim Divinity.

We gathered all within the house, and there
Shook off the purple silence of the night.
Cried one: "Come let us a Symposium hold,
And each one to the banquet bring our best
In song or story; all shall play a part."
So, for a leader simple and grand, we chose
Our Miracle-worker in Midwifery, He
Who wrestled with the fiend of corporal pain,
And stands above the writhing Agony,

Like Michael with the Dragon 'neath his heel:
Who is in soul — Love riding on a Lion;
In body — a Bacchus crowned with head of Jove:
The keen life looks out in his lighted face
So fulgent that the gazer's brightens too:
He bravely towers above our fume and fret,
Like the old Hills whose feet are in the surge,
And on their lifted brows the eternal calm:
For he is one of those prophetic spirits
That are a World's night-dreams of things to come.
Bravely he broacht the sparkling Hyppocrene,
And round and round the chalice went till morn.

NEW YEAR'S EVE IN EXILE.

1854.

The flower and chivalry of many lands
Betrothed to Martyrdom as to a Bride, —
Warriors of Freedom who for heritage
Wear on their brows a mark as curst as Cain's, —
Had met together, a strange companie!
But brothers, battling in one sacred cause.
They were heroic souls who had lain life's all
On Freedom's hungry Altar, and gone forth
Clad in the spirit of self-sacrifice,
To roam a thankless world with homeless hearts, —
Men who had tost on Danger's wildest waves,
For whom a radiant Victory ever shone,
Like Hero on her watch-tower with her torch,
Lighting her lover through the shadow of death, —
Men who had broken Battle's burning lines,
Dealing life with their looks, death with their hands,
And strode like Salamanders through War's flame;
And in the last stern charge of desperate valour,

On Death's scythe dasht with force that turn'd its
edge.
Some were but youths, yet with such manhood
flusht,
By eager leaps to catch at lordlier life,
They had attain'd the old heroic stature.
Some had grown grey with battle, some with years,
And there were ancient Sorrows grand as kings
Of an old peerless line. Such silent Griefs
And Sufferings crown'd for immortality.
Earnest as fire they sate, and reverent
As though a God were present in their midst;
Stern, but serene and hopeful, prayerful, brave,
As Cromwell's Ironsides on a battle-eve;
Each individual life as clencht and knit,
As though beneath their robes their fingers clutcht
The weapon sworn to strike a Tyrant down,
That would not flash except to light his fall.
Such proud Belief did lift their kindling brows,
Such glowing purpose hunger'd in their eyes,
With fire enough to set a world in flames.
No servile souls, that at your fixéd look,
Like meek worms, writhe into their darkening
holes.
And One up-rose to word the Thought that ran
Hot to their hearts and glittering to their brows;
An old man, with the mournfull'st, thin, grey hair;
The lines of suffering in his face seem'd drawn
Tight with the mortal tug of Agony;
But with sad majesty he smiled, and splendour
Broke sweetly from the furrows of his face,
As wrinkles on the waters laugh with light.
Dilating as a Prophet's wings of flame
Flutter'd within him — all his aspect burn'd
With an unearthly fire. He was caught up
The mount Transfiguration, with eyes fixt
On air, as though he talkt with one beyond.
He stood there looking down the unseen time,
Like some hoar Hill that lifts its solemn peak

To catch the unrisen Morn, while all the plains
Are drowsed and darkling. He already sunn'd
Him in the glory of the coming day.
And his words swept their yielding, springing hearts,
As strong winds take a field of billowing corn.
"The merry bells are jubilant To-night
Through all the land of Exile; blithe wine laughs
Its bubbling laughter,— winking gem-like eyes,
And leaps up in the beaker like red lips
Whose kisses storm the inner gates of bliss.
But not with mirth, and song, and dainty feast,
We meet to hold our solemn festival.
We wait the wine of Freedom: when it runs,
We shall wax merry, too,— perchance grow drunken —
They keep it ripening to such mellow age!
And we shall banquet like Immortals fed
By Hebe's hand at the Ambrosial feasts.
The New Year flashes on us sadly grand,
Leaps in our midst with ringing armour on,
Strikes a mail'd hand in ours, and bids us arm
Ere the first trumpet sound the onset hour.
Dense darkness lies on Europe's winter-world.
Stealthy and grim the Bear comes creeping on,
Out of the North, and all the Peoples sleep
By Freedom's smouldering watch-fire: there is none
To snatch the brand, and dash it in his face.
Old England sleeps, and still the Bear creeps on.
Ah! she forgetteth how, in the old years,
The great hearts of her glorious Commonwealth
Sent thunder-throbbings through the lands, and gave them
Such a new pulse of nobler life: and when
Their sumless Venture wreckt, and o'er them roll'd
The wormwood waters of defeat and death,
How in their pleading hands they held the Babe
And Orphan Liberty, and bade her rear it
For love of them, and for its own sweet sake.

And England slinks behind the nations now.
Dim is her Beacon Despots paled to see
Burn on them through the dark, like God's stern
eye.
Her battle-armour rusteth in her halls,
And the old mighty arm that struck such blows
For Right and Freedom, hangeth listless now.
A dry-rot eats her life: her God is Mammon!
God Mars no longer leaps into her heart,
As in a chariot driving down to battle.
Her ancient fame and valour have become
A tale that 's told us of forgotten times —
Some fabled Kraken slumbering in its sea!
O! for the voice of Milton once again,
To make the lion-eyes lighten, and her heart
As tremblingly alive as is a Star,
Till in her naked strength majestical
She walkt the sun-road of her glorious way.
But England sleeps — the Ruin still rolls on.
Earth crouches 'neath the shuddering wings of
Fear.
Silent, and very calm, Freedom lies husht,
And listens like a panting thing pursued,
Heark'ning, heart-stifled, for the stealthiest tread
Of One that hunts like Tarquin for Lucrece.
'T is midnight now, and all the creeping things,
And Birds of Darkness, ply their ghastly work
Life gropes and stumbles among gaping graves,
And Freedom's worshippers fall headless, while
They bend to give their hearts up at her shrine!
But God 's in heaven, and yet the day shall dawn—
Break from the dark upon her golden wings,
Her quick, ripe splendours rend and burn the
gloom,
Her living tides of glory burst, and foam,
And hurry along the darksome streets of night.
Cloud after cloud shall light a rainbow-roof,
And build a Triumph-Arch for conquering Day
To flash her beauty — trail her grandeurs through,

And take the world in her white arms of light.
And Earth shall fling aside her mask of gloom,
And lift her tearful face. O there will be
Blood on it thick as dews! The Children's blood
Splasht in the Mother's face! And there must be
A red sunrise of retribution yet!
A mighty future is about to break
The hush o' the world — the waiting gloom in heaven.
The New Year cometh with a magic key,
To ope some radiant chamber in Time's palace.
Our Martyrs have not sown such seed in vain!
Beneath old Winter's snows a world of hope
Lies ripening, and shall richly run to flowers,
When earth shall kindle as a countenance
Alive with love, and all the soul alight!
O come, thou Spring of God, and at thy voice
The balmy blood shall beat in bud and leaf!
And come, thou mellow rain, fall on it warm,
And fondle it with kisses, drop rich tears;
And blow, thou sweet Spring-wind, and make it stir
With secret rapture — budding tenderly,
With all the glory of its folded bloom,
And all its fragrance striving for the light.
God, what a Spring and Harvest yet shall crown
The dark, dern Deluge of Calamity!
Then come, thou grand New Year, in silence come
Across the white snows, and the winter-land.
Come, great Deliverer, call the peoples up, —
Up from the Egypt of their slavery!
Ring out the death-knell of old Tyranny —
'T is rotten ripe, and the heart of half the world
Doth beat and burst to hurry it into hell.
Stride o'er the Present, grand as some huge wave
Should rush across Panama at a leap,
And make two Seas one perfect world of waters.
So link our great Past to a nobler Future,
And set our new world singing on its way,

With sunshine freighted, like a heart of bliss,
Her Life's rich tide at Glory's high flood-mark.
A little while, and we shall yet return
Each to the Fatherland, like kings to conquest.
Light breaks there! in the East: it grows, and soon
Shall Freedom's sun roll up the Heaven of Life.
We may not see God's face, yet at our side
He combats for us, with his vizor down.
But no more words — like weeds they sap the soul
Of richness that should fill the fruit of deeds.
Henceforth let lips be dumb, as Bravery —
Her parley done — had shut her gates, to ope not
Save for the shouts that chariot Victory forth.
We are all ready! We have waited long!
God strike the hour, Ho! let the trumpets ring!"
He ceased. One shout ran thro' the night, and struck
Heaven's boss of stars, and like a ship went down
In the lone sea of silence flowing round.
In touching majesty the Stars lookt down,
As tho' they yearn'd to them with answering pulse,
And with invisible speed the world roll'd on.

THE DISTANT.

Stars deep in Midnight's blue abyss,
Moving in heaven seem to kiss;
But, darling, they are far apart,
And close not beating heart to heart.

And high in glory many a Star
Shines, lighting other worlds afar,
That holds within the dust and dearth,
And darkness of a fireless hearth.

PEGASUS IN HARNESS.

THEY pity Pegasus because
The Matrimonial Car he draws
  Along the ruts of life:
And hot and dusty is the road,
And heavy is the living load
  Of leaning weans and wife.

Poor Pegasus! to turn the Mill,
And grind, and pull the plough, until
  The work his withers wrings!
Why not? 't is he should do it best,
And tread his measure easiest,
  Or where 's the use of wings?

EPITAPH FOR A PAINTER OF STILL-LIFE WHO WAS VERY FOND OF WHISKEY.

HE was a poor old doited body,
Whom Satan took in his cussed toddy;
And here he lies as in his ill life,
Making a picture still of still-life.

LIFE AND DEATH.

THIS butterfly of human breath
Is followed fast and far by Death;
Some flower of life it settled on
He clasps and crushes, but, 't is gone!

IMPATIENCE.

To see what gems lie hidden where it grows,
Would'st pluck the tree of life up by the root?
Wait till the unseen into flower blows;
Wait till the jewels hang in precious fruit.

ON A VERY EARLY RISER.

At the Last Day while all the rest
Are soundly sleeping underground,
He will be up, clean shaved, and dressed,
An hour before the Trumpet sound.

THE THREE SPIRITS.

They were three Spirits fresh from God's own hand,
And beautifuller ne'er took mortal mould,
They had worn vestures of the undefiled,
At spirit-spousals sang the nuptial song,
Sat down with Gods and Heroes, held high converse
With Milton and the mighty men of old,
Divine old Socrates and deathless sages,
The martyr'd Prophets and the warrior-saints,
Who fought as we do now, and wrestled down
Doubt's grim despairs, with pangs and quenchless faith.
Glory tiara'd their immortal brows,
Their lips were yet alive with seraph-fire,

And locks bedropt rich dews of Paradise:
They lookt a fore-taste and fore-feel of heaven.
Christ-like they came to wear old Earth's life-harness,
And yoke their fiery sun-steeds in her furrows.
They came to battle, toil in tears, and pray,
" Our Father," with the family of Men.
'T was midnight in the husht and moonlit land,
The heavens had on their silver robe of stars,
And earth had on her silver robe of dew,
When they first lookt like smiles of God, through eyes
Where struggling heaven-light shone half-drown'd in tears,
As rainy sunbeams strike a watery world.
They grew sweet babes, where fond hearts set Love's throne,
Heaven breathed about them, Angels sang to them,
And joy was with them in their innocence.
Their dawn of being broaden'd into day,
And they had sprung to Manhood unawares.
The lusty blood ran brave fire in their veins,
Life's surging waves, with them, were at mad-plunge,
And plough'd the passionate heart with tempest-beat.
Then high thoughts burst like battle on their souls,
Rousing and stern as in the noon of night
The clarion's clangour smites a sleeping host!
And gorgeous Visions, glory-clad, swept by.
And one went down to moil in Mammon's mine,
For love of Gold; thenceforth in his warpt heart,
The Devil at death-grips set himself to God,
And day by day worm'd out some trace divine!
Day unto day, Gold rotted out the soul.
Still he toil'd on for Gold, sweet! damning Gold!
The poor man's sweat, and tears, and blood, congeal'd;
And he waxt wealthy! all around him rose

The hoarded heaps, like trophies after battle,
Or tribute-treasure flung at Monarchs' feet.
He turn'd to what he fed on, dust to dust;
The angel-plumes once moulted, grew no more!
The God dwarft in him, and his heart was hoary
Before Time's silver mark had blancht his brow.
And one up-rear'd a fame which stood apart
In the world's gaze, as 'mid old Tadmor's ruins
Some column loometh in the eye of sunset.
He crown'd with beacon-fire the reef which wreckt
The mighty of all time. His marvellous name
Moved men's tongues regally as Euroclydon,
The storm-wind! wakes the voices of old ocean.
Leviathan of blood! what crimson seas
He spilt to revel in; his path to empire
Was wasted hearts and desolated lands.
The other trode the world's face poor as Christ,
Drank gall and wormwood; lived Gethsemane,
In many a midnight solitude of heart!
Loved, hoped, and nurst large faith in human-kind,
Wept glorious tears that telescope the soul,
And bring heaven nearer to the eyes of Faith!
The hounds of hell bay'd at him, hoary Evil
Breathed blighting influences on his heart,
To turn it to a Upas-tree, and kill
All nestling birds of love. With tears and travail
He walkt the furnace, trode Earth's stony ways,
And beat his rugged path with bleeding feet.
Yet nought bore down his heart, or blencht his faith,
And many a cloud-rift radiantly rent,
Dropt blessing dear as parted lips of Love.
From suffering he won strength to throw the world;
And when the fight ran sorest, his roused spirit
Went forth a Conqueror! wrapt in victory's robes.
Amid the mirk and mire, he kept his heart
A temple for the Beautiful! all warm
And bright, with blessed light of Love, that window

Of our dim life, which ever opes on God!
He trimmed Love's lamp in poor men's hearts and homes,
And in the world's waste places his life blossom'd.
So each built up a life. Time's scaffolding
Fell from them, and they stood in God's eye bare!
Into the silent land, they pass'd, the Grave,
Which Spring had made a beautiful gate of flowers;
On wings of wonder won the starry threshold
Of God, where like to like is gauged and garnered.
They stood where Paradise uprear'd its portals,
And shook down splendours, palpitated bliss,
Like a town full of triumph,—heart of love.
O in that hour how shook the rich man's soul!
He stood there beggar'd, poorest of the poor!
Gold would not purchase heaven; and if it might,
Eternity ran 'twixt him and his riches;
And he went wailing with his world of woe.
The other had gambled for a life, and lost;
Let slip his chance for an Eternity!
For fame, had barter'd an immortal birthright;
For name on Earth had sold Heaven's heritage;
And there the gates of glory on him closed.
The poor man came, and his meek tearful eyes
Grew luminous, as lit with sudden sun.
Divinity leapt up full-statured, when
His life burst its worn manacle of clay,
And wore God's splendour round it as a raiment.
Throbbing with glory like a midnight star,
All heaven was husht to hear the Lord's "Well done."
Then shining hosts and choiring orbs sang "Welcome,"
And angels crown'd him in their Capitol.
For in his heart he kept God's image bright.
Love was his life-blood. Thro' the long work-day —
The dark and terrible night-time — aye, to death,

He nurst his love: and God himself is love.
And there be none of all the poorest poor
That walk the world, worn heart-bare, none so poor
But they may bring a little human love
To mend the world. And God himself is love.

LINES INSCRIBED TO THE REV. F. D. MAURICE.

GOD bless you, Brave One, in our dearth,
 Your life shall leave a trailing glory;
And round the poor Man's homely hearth
 We proudly tell your suffering's story.

All Saviour-souls have sacrificed,
 With nought but noble faith for guerdon;
And ere the world hath crown'd the Christ,
 The man to death hath borne the burden!

The Savage broke the glass that brought
 The heavens nearer, saith the legend!
Even so the Bigots welcome aught
 That makes our vision starrier-region'd!

They lay their Corner-stones in dark
 Deep waters, who up-build in beauty,
On Earth's old heart, their Triumph-Arc
 That crowns with glory lives of duty.

And meekly still the Martyrs go
 To keep with Pain their solemn bridal!
And still they walk the fire who bow
 Not down to worship Custom's idol.

In fieriest forge of martyrdom,
  Their swords of soul must weld and brighten:
Tear-bathed, from fiercest furnace, come
  Their lives, heroic-temper'd — Titan !

And heart-strings sweetest music make
  When swept by Suffering's feeling fingers !
And thro' soul-shadows starriest break
  The glories on God's brave light-bringers.

Take heart ! tho' sown in tears and blood,
  No seed that 's quick with love, hath perisht,
Tho' dropt in barren byeways — God
  Some glorious flower of life hath cherisht.

Take heart ; the rude dust dark To-day,
  Soars a new-lighted sphere To-morrow !
And wings of splendour burst the clay
  That clasps us in Death's fruitful furrow.

THE MEN OF FORTY-EIGHT.

They rose in Freedom's rare sunrise,
  Like Giants roused from wine ;
And in their hearts and in their eyes
  The God leapt up divine !
Their souls flasht out naked as swords
  Unsheathed for fiery fate !
Strength went like battle with their words —
  The Men of Forty-eight,
                Hurrah !
  For the Men of Forty-eight.

Dark days have fall'n, yet in the strife
  They bate no hope sublime,
And bravely works the exultant life,
  Their hearts pulse thro' the time :

As grass is greenest trodden down,
So suffering makes men great,
And this dark tide shall richly crown
The work of Forty-eight,
Hurrah!
For the Men of Forty-eight.

Some in a bloody burial sleep,
Like Greeks to glory gone,
But in their steps avengers leap
With their proof-armour on:
And hearts beat high with dauntless trust
To triumph soon or late,
Tho' they be mould'ring down in dust—
Brave Men of Forty-eight!
Hurrah!
For the Men of Forty-eight.

O when the world wakes up to worst
The Tyrants once again,
And Freedom's summons-shout shall burst,
Rare music! on the brain,—
All Truehearts still, in many a land,
Ye'll find them all elate—
Brave remnant of that Spartan-band,
The Men of Forty-eight.
Hurrah!
For the Men of Forty-eight.

THE PATRIOT.

Ay, Tyrants, build your Babels! forge your fetters! link your chains!
As brims your guilt-cup fuller, ours of grief ebbs to the drains;

Still, as on Christ's brow, crowns of thorn for Freedom's Martyrs twine;
Still batten on live hearts, and madden, o'er the hot blood-wine.
Murder men sleeping, or awake,—torture them dumb with pain,
And tear, with hands all bloody red, the vesture of the slain!
Your feet are on us, Tyrants—strike! and hush Earth's wail of sorrow:
Your sword of power, so red to-day, shall kiss the dust to-morrow.
O! but 't will be a merry day, the world shall set apart,
When Strife's last brand is broken in the last crown'd Tyrant's heart!
And it shall come,—despite of Rifle, Rope, and Rack, and Scaffold,
Once more we lift the earnest brow, and battle on unbaffled.

Our hopes ran mountains high, we sang at heart, wept tears of gladness,
When France, the bravely beautiful, dasht down her sceptred madness;
And Hungary her one-hearted race of mighty heroes hurl'd
In the death-gap of nations, as a bulwark for the world.
O Hungary! gallant Hungary! grand and glorious thou wert,
The World's soul feeding, like a river, gushing from God's heart;
And Rome,—who, while her Heroes bled, felt her old breast heave higher,—
How her eyes redden'd with the flash of all their Roman fire!
Mothers of children, who shall live the Gods of future story!

Your blood shall blossom from the dust, and crown
the world with glory.
Ye 'll tread them down yet, curse and crown! uplift the trodden Slave,
And Freedom shall be sovran in the courts of fool
and knave.

Wail for the hopes that have gone down! the young
life vainly spilt!
Th' Eternal Murder still sits crown'd, and throned
in damning guilt:
Still in God's golden sun the Tyrants' bloody banners burn,
And Priests,—Hell's midnight Thugs!—to their
soul-strangling work return!
See how the oppressors of the poor with serpents
hunt our blood;
Hear, from the dark, the groan and curse go maddening up to God.
They kill and trample us poor worms, till earth is
dead men's dust;
Death's red tooth daily drains our hearts, but end,
ay, end it must.
The herald of our coming Christ leaps in the womb
of Time;
The poor's grand army treads the Age's march with
step sublime.
Ours is the mighty future! and what marvel, brother
men,
If the devoured of ages should turn devourers then?

O! brothers of the bounding heart, I look thro'
tears and smile,
The World is rife with sound of fetters snapping
'neath the file;
I lay my hand on England's heart, and in each life-throb mark,
The pealing thought of freedom ring its Tocsin in
the dark.

I see the Toiler hath become a glorious Christ-like preacher,
And, as he wins a crust, stands proudly forth, the great world-teacher;
He still toils on, but, Tyrants, 't is a mighty thing when slaves,
Who delve their lives into their work, know that they delve your graves.
Anarchs! your doom comes swiftly! brave and eagle spirits climb,
To ring Oppression's death-knell from the old watch-towers of time;
A spirit of Cromwellian might is stirring at this hour,
And thought is burning in men's eyes with more than speechful power.

Old England, cease the mummer's part! wake, Starveling, Serf, and Slave!
Rouse in the majesty of wrong, great kindred of the brave!
Speak, and the world shall answer, with her voices myriad-fold,
And men, like Gods, shall grapple with the giant-wrongs of old.
Now, Mothers of the people, give your babes heroic milk;
Sires, soul your sons for daring deeds, no more soft words of silk;
Great spirits of the mighty dead take shape, and walk our mind,
Their glory smites our upward look, we seem no longer blind;
They tell us how they broke their bonds, and whisper, "So may ye:"
One sharp, stern struggle, and the slaves of centuries are free!
The people's heart, with pulse like cannon, panteth for the fray,
And, brothers, gallant brothers, we 'll be with you in that day.

OUR FATHERS ARE PRAYING FOR PAUPER-PAY.

SMITTEN stones will talk with fiery tongues,
And the worm, when trodden, will turn;
But, Cowards, ye cringe to the cruellest wrongs,
And answer with never a spurn.
Then torture, O Tyrants, the spiritless drove,
Old England's Helots will bear:
There's no hell in their hatred, no God in their love,
Nor shame in their dearth's despair.
For our Fathers are praying for Pauper-pay,
Our Mothers with Death's kiss are white;
Our Sons are the rich man's Serfs by day,
And our Daughters his Slaves by night.

The Tearless are drunk with our tears: have they driven
The God of the poor man mad?
For we weary of waiting the help of Heaven,
And the battle goes still with the bad.
O but death for death, and life for life,
It were better to take and give,
With hand to throat, and knife to knife,
Than die out as thousands live!
For our Fathers are praying for Pauper-pay,
Our Mothers with Death's kiss are white;
Our Sons are the rich man's Serfs by day,
And our Daughters his Slaves by night.

Fearless and few were the Heroes of old,
Who play'd the peerless part:
We are fifty-fold, but the gangrene Gold
Hath eaten out Hampden's heart.
With their faces to danger, like freemen they fought,
With their daring, all heart and hand:

And the thunder-deed follow'd the lightning-thought,
When they stood for their own good land.
Our Fathers are praying for Pauper-pay,
Our Mothers with Death's kiss are white;
Our Sons are the rich man's Serfs by day,
And our Daughters his Slaves by night.

When the heart of one half the world doth beat
Akin to the brave and the true,
And the tramp of Democracy's earthquake feet
Goes thrilling the wide world through, —
We should not be living in darkness and dust,
And dying like slaves in the night;
But, big with the might of the inward "*must*,"
We should battle for Freedom and Right!
For our Fathers are praying for Pauper-pay,
Our Mothers with Death's kiss are white;
Our Sons are the rich man's Serfs by day,
And our Daughters his Slaves by night.

THEY ARE BUT GIANTS WHILE WE KNEEL.

GOOD People! put no faith in Kings, nor in your Princes trust,
Who break your hearts for bread, and grind your faces in the dust!
The Palace Paupers look from lattice high, and mock your prayer:
The Champions of the Christ are dumb, or golden bit they wear!
O but to see ye bend no more to earth's crime-cursèd things!
Ye are God's Oracles: stand forth! be Nature's Priests and Kings!

Ye fight and bleed, while Fortune's darlings slink in splendid lair;
With lives that crawl, like worms through buried Beauty's golden hair! —
A tale of lives wrung out in tears their Grandeur's garb reveals,
And the last sobs of breaking hearts sound in their Chariot-wheels!
O league ye — crush the things that kill all love and liberty!
They are but Giants while we kneel: ONE LEAP, AND UP GO WE.

Trust not the Priests, whose tears are lies, and hearts are hard and cold;
Who lead ye to sweet pastures, where they fleece the foolish fold!
The Church and State are linkt and sworn to desolate the land.
Good people, 'twixt these Foxes' tails, We'll fling a fiery brand!
Up, if ye will be free, to golden calves no longer bow:
The Nations yearn for liberty — the world is earnest now!
Your bent-knee is half-way to hell! — Up, Serviles, from the dust!
The Harvest of the free red-ripens for the sickle-thrust.
They're quaking now, and shaking now, who've wrought the hurtling sorrow,
To-day the desolators, but the desolate To-morrow!
Loud o'er their murder's menace wakes the watch-word of the Free:
They are but Giants while we kneel: ONE LEAP, AND UP GO WE!

Some bravest patriot-hearts have gone, to break beyond the Sea,

And many in the dungeon have died for you and
me!
And still we glut the Merciless — give all Life's
glory up,
That stars of flame, and winking eyes, may crown
their revel-cup!
Back, tramplers on the Many! Death and Danger
ambusht lie;
Beware ye, or the blood may run! the patient
people cry:
Ah! shut not out the light of hope, or we may
blindly dash,
Like Samson in his strong death-grope, and whelm
ye in the crash.
Think how they spurred the People mad, that old
Régime of France,
Whose heads, like poppies, from Death's Scythe fell
in a bloody dance.
Ye plead in vain, ye bleed in vain, ah! Blind!
when will ye see
They are but Giants while we kneel? ONE LEAP,
AND UP GO WE.

The merry flowers are springing from our last-year
Martyrs' mould,
As their dreams had taken blossom telling what
they would have told;
Of all our rainbowed Future: and what this earth
shall be
When we have bartered blows and bonds for life
and liberty.
Ah! what a face of glory shall the weary world
put on,
When Love is crownèd, and shall king the heart
its royal throne!
O we shall see our darlings smile, — who meet us
tearful now, —
Ere the Eternal morn breaks gray, on the Beloved's
brow:

And Love shall give the kiss of Death no more to
those we love,
And pride, not shame, shall flush the face of our
heart-nestling Dove.
Rouse, Titans, scale th' Olympus where the hindering Tyrants be:
They are but Giants while we kneel: ONE LEAP,
AND UP GO WE.

EIGHTEEN HUNDRED AND FORTY-EIGHT.

PEOPLE of England, rouse ye from your dreaming!
Sinew your souls for Freedom's glorious leap:
Look to the Future, where our day-spring's gleaming:
Lo! a pulse stirs that never more shall sleep
In the world's heart. Men's eyes flash wide with
wonder!
The Robbers tremble in their mightiest tower,
Strange words roll o'er their souls with wheels of
thunder,
The leaves from Royalty's tree fall hour by
hour, —
Earthquakes leap in our Temples, crumbling
Throne and Power.

Vampyres have drain'd the human heart's best
blood,
Kings robb'd, and Priests have curst us in God's
name:
Out in the midnight of the Past we've stood —
While fiends of darkness plied their hellish game.
We have been worshipping a gilded crown,
Which drew heaven's lightning-laughter on our
head;

Chains fell on us as we were bowing down;
We deem'd our Gods divine, but lo! instead —
They are but painted clay, — with morn the charm has fled!

And this is merry England, — cradling-place
Of souls self-deified and glory-crown'd!
Where smiles made splendour in the Peasant's face,
And Justice reign'd — Her awful eyes close-bound!
Where Toil with open brow went on light-hearted,
And twain in love Law never thrust apart?
How is the glory of our life departed
From us, who sit and nurse our bleeding smart;
And slink, afraid to break the laws that break the heart!

Husht be the Herald on the walls of fame,
Trumping this People as their Country's pride;
Weep rather, with your souls on fire with shame:
See ye not how the palaced knaves deride
Us flatter'd fools? how priestcraft, strong and stealthy,
Stabs at our freedom through its veil of night,
And grinds the poor to flush its coffers wealthy?
Hear how the land groans in the grip of Might,
Then quaff your cup of Wrongs, and laud a Briton's "Right."

There 's not a spot in all this flowery land,
Where Tyranny's cursed brand-mark has not been:
O! were it not for its all-blasting hand,
Dear Christ, what a sweet heaven this might have been!
Has it not hunted forth our spirits brave, —
Kill'd the red rose of health that crown'd our daughters,

Wedded our living hopes unto the grave,—
  Filled happy homes with strife, the world with slaughters,
  And turn'd our thoughts to blood—to gall, the heart's sweet waters?

Where is the spirit of our ancient Sires,
  Who, bleeding, wrung their Rights from tyrannies olden?
God-spirits have been here, for Freedom fires
  From out their ashes, to earth's heart enfolden;
The mighty dead lie slumbering around,—
  Whose names thrill thro' us as Gods were in the air;
Life leaps from where their dust makes holy ground:
  Their deeds spring forth in glory,—live allwhere,—
  But we are traitors to the trust they bade us bear.

Go forth, when Night is husht, and heaven is clothèd
  With stars that in God's smiling presence roll,
Feel the stirr'd spirit leap to them betrothèd,
  As Angel-wings were fanning in the soul;
Feel the hot tears flood in the eyes upturning,
  The tide of goodness heave its brightest waves,—
Then suddenly crush the grand and God-ward yearning
  With the mad thought that ye are bounden slaves!
  O! how long will ye make your hearts its living graves?

Immortal Liberty! we see thee stand
  Like Morn just stept from heaven upon a mountain
With beautiful feet, and blessing-laden hand,
  And heart whence welleth Love's most living fountain!

O! when wilt thou string on the People's lyre
  Joy's broken chord? and on the People's brow
Set Empire's crown? light up thy beacon-fire
  Within their hearts, with an undying glow;
  Nor give us blood for milk, as men are drunk
    with now?

Old Poets tell us of a golden age,
  When earth was guiltless, — Gods the guests of
    men,
Ere sin had dimm'd the heart's illumined page, —
  And Sinai-voices say 't will come again.
O! happy age! when Love shall rule the heart,
  And time to live shall be the poor man's dower,
When Martyrs bleed no more, nor Exiles smart, —
  Mind is the only diadem of power. —
  People, it ripens now! awake! and strike the
    hour.

Hearts, high and mighty, gather in our cause;
  Bless, bless, O God, and crown their earnest
    labour,
Who dauntless fight to win us equal laws,
  With mental armour, and with spirit-sabre!
Bless, bless, O God! the proud intelligence,
  That like a sun dawns on the People's fore-
    head, —
Humanity springs from them like incense,
  The Future bursts upon them, boundless — star-
    ried —
  They weep repentant tears, that they so long
    have tarried.

THEY WHO FELL FOR HUNGARY AND ROME.

1850.

They are gone!
When on earthquake-edge they slumbered,
Who have man accurst;
And Hope's blossoms, many-numbered,
Into flower burst;
When our hearts, like throbbing drums,
Beat for Freedom; sang, She comes!
God! they stumbled among tombs.

They are gone!
Freedom's strong ones, young and hoary,
Beautiful in faith!
And her first dawn-blush of glory
Gilds their camp of death!
There they lie in shrouds of blood;
Murder'd, where for Right they stood —
Murder'd, Christ-like, doing good.

They are gone!
Yet 't is good to die up-giving
Valour's vengeful breath,
To make Heroes of the living, —
Thus divine is death.
One by one, dear hearts! they 've left us,
Yet Hope hath not all bereft us:
Still we man the breach they cleft us.

They are here!
Here, where life ran ruddy rain,
When power from God seem'd wrencht:
Here, where tears fall — molten brain!
And hands are agony-clencht!

Look, Love lifts the veil; ah! now
There's a glory, where the glow
Of their fire-crown seam'd each brow.

They are here!
In the Etna of each heart,
Where Vengeance makes hell-mirth,
In the silent tears that start
O'er their glorious worth!
Tears? ay, tears of fire, proud Weepers!
For these soul-sepultured sleepers:
Fire! to smite Death's blood-seed reapers.

They are here!
With us in the march of time,
Beating at our side!
Let us live their lives sublime,
Die as they have died!
Wait: these Martyrs yet shall come,
Myriad-fold, from their heart-tomb!
In the Tyrants' day of doom.

A CRY OF THE PEOPLES.

Like a strong man in torture, the weary world turneth,
To clutch Freedom's robe round her slavery's starkness:
With shame and with shudder, poor Mother! she yearneth
O'er wrongs that are done in her dearth and her darkness.
O gather thy strength up, and crush the Abhorréd,
Who murder thy poor heart, and drain thy life-springs, —

And are crownéd to hide the Cain-brand on their forehead :
  O let them be last of the Queens and the Kings!

By the lovers and friends we have tenderly cherisht,
  Who made the Cause soar up like flame at their breath,
Who struggled like Gods met in fight, and have perisht
  In poverty's battle with grim daily death:
O, by all dear ones that bitterly plead for us —
  Life-flowers tied up in the heart's breaking strings —
Sisters that weep for us — mothers that bleed for us —
  Let these be last of the Queens and the Kings!

Sun and Rain kindle greenly the graves of our Martyrs,
  Ye might not tell where the brave blood ran like rain!
But there it burns ever! and heaven's weeping waters
  And branding suns never shall whiten the stain!
Remember the hurtling the Tyrants have wrought us,
  And smite till each helm bravely flashes and rings!
Life for life, blood for blood, is the lesson they've taught us,
  And be these the last of the Queens and the Kings!

Ho! weary Nightwatch, is there light on the summit?
  Yearner up through the Night, say, is there hope?

For deeper in darkness than fathom of plummet,
Our Bark thro' the tempest doth stagger and grope!
"To God's unforgiven, to caitiff and craven —
To Crown and to Sceptre, a cleaving curse clings:
Ye must fling them from deck, would ye steer into haven,
For Death tracks the last of the Queens and the Kings!"

HOPE ON, HOPE EVER.

Hope on, hope ever! though to-day be dark,
The sweet sunburst may smile on thee to-morrow:
Tho' thou art lonely, there 's an eye will mark
Thy loneliness, and guerdon all thy sorrow!
Tho' thou must toil 'mong cold and sordid men,
With none to echo back thy thought, or love thee,
Cheer up, poor heart! thou dost not beat in vain,
For God is over all, and heaven above thee —
Hope on, hope ever.

The iron may enter in and pierce thy soul,
But cannot kill the love within thee burning:
The tears of misery, thy bitter dole,
Can never quench thy true heart's seraph yearning
For better things: nor crush thy ardour's trust,
That Error from the mind shall be uprooted,
That Truths shall dawn as flowers spring from the dust,
And Love be cherisht where Hate was embruted
Hope on, hope ever.

I know 't is hard to bear the sneer and taunt, —
With the heart's honest pride at midnight wrestle,
To feel the killing canker-worm of Want,
While rich rogues in their stolen luxury nestle;
For I have felt it. Yet from Earth's cold Real
My soul looks out on coming things, and cheerful
The warm Sunrise floods all the land Ideal,
And still it whispers to the worn and tearful,
Hope on, hope ever.

Hope on, hope ever! after darkest night,
Comes, full of loving life, the laughing Morning;
Hope on, hope ever! Spring-tide, flusht with light,
Aye crowns old Winter with her rich adorning.
Hope on, hope ever! yet the time shall come,
When man to man shall be a friend and brother
And this old world shall be a happy home,
And all Earth's family love one another!
Hope on, hope ever.

THE PEOPLE'S ADVENT.

'T is coming up the steep of Time,
And this old world is growing brighter!
We may not see its dawn sublime,
Yet high hopes make the heart throb lighter.
We may be sleeping in the ground,
When it awakes the world in wonder;
But we have felt it gathering round,
And heard its voice of living thunder.
'T is coming! yes, 't is coming!

'T is coming now, the glorious time,
Foretold by Seers, and sung in story;
For which, when thinking was a crime,
Souls leapt to heaven from scaffolds gory!

They pass'd, nor see the work they wrought,
  Now the crown'd hopes of centuries blossom!
But the live lightning of their thought
  And daring deeds, doth pulse Earth's bosom.
    'T is coming! yes, 't is coming!

Creeds, Empires, Systems, rot with age,
  But the great People 's ever youthful!
And it shall write the Future's page,
  To our humanity more truthful!
The gnarliest heart hath tender chords,
  To waken at the name of "Brother;"
And time comes when brain-scorpion words
  We shall not speak to sting each other.
    'T is coming! yes, 't is coming!

Out of the light, ye Priests, nor fling
  Your dark, cold shadows on us longer!
Aside! thou world-wide curse, call'd King!
  The People's step is quicker, stronger.
There 's a Divinity within
  That makes men great, whene'er they will it.
God works with all who dare to win,
  And the time cometh to reveal it.
    'T is coming! yes, 't is coming!

Freedom! the tyrants kill thy braves,
  Yet in our memories live the sleepers;
And, tho' doom'd millions feed the graves,
  Dug by Death's fierce, red-handed reapers,
The world shall not for ever bow
  To things which mock God's own endeavour;
'T is nearer than they wot of now,
  When flowers shall wreathe the sword for ever
    'T is coming! yes, 't is coming!

Fraternity! Love's other name!
  Dear, heaven-connecting link of Being!
Then shall we grasp thy golden dream,
  As souls, full-statured, grow far-seeing.

Thou shalt unfold our better part,
  And in our Life-cup yield more honey;
Light up with joy the poor man's heart,
  And Love's own world with smiles more sunny
    'T is coming! yes, 't is coming!

Ay, it must come! The Tyrant's throne
  Is crumbling, with our hot tears rusted;
The Sword earth's mighty have leant on
  Is canker'd, with our heart's blood crusted.
Room! for the men of Mind make way!
  Ye robber Rulers, pause no longer;
Ye cannot stay the opening day:
  The world rolls on, the light grows stronger,—
    The People's Advent 's coming!

OUR LAND.

'T IS the Land that our stalwart fore-sires trode,
    Where the brave and heroic-soul'd
Implanted our freedom with their best blood,
    In the martyr-days of old.
The huts of the lowly gave Liberty birth,
    Their hearts were her cradle glorious,
And wherever her foot-prints letter'd the earth,
    Great spirits up-sprang victorious,
In our rare old Land, our dear old Land,
    With its memories bright and brave,
And sing hey for the hour its sons shall band
    To free it of Tyrant and Slave.

John Hampden's sword and Shakespeare's thought
    Beking us, all crowns above!
And Freedom's dear faith a fresh splendour caught
    From our grand old Milton's love!

And we should be marching on gallantly,
    On the track of the famous in story,
For the Right with our Might striking valiantly,
    And striding from glory to glory —
For our rare old Land, our dear old Land,
    With its memories bright and brave,
And sing hey for the hour its sons shall band
    To free it of Tyrant and Slave.

On Naseby-field of the fight sublime,
    Our old red Rose doth blow!
Would to God that the soul of that earlier time
    Might marshal us conquering now!
On into the Future's fair clime the world sweeps,
    And the time trumpets true men to freedom:
At the heart of our helots the mounting God leaps,
    But O for the Moses to lead 'em!
For our rare old Land, our dear old Land,
    With its memories bright and brave!
And sing hey for the hour its sons shall band
    To free it of Tyrant and Slave.

What do we lack, that the ruffian Wrong
    Should starve us 'mid heaps of gold?
We have brains as broad, we have arms as strong,
    We have hearts as big and as bold!
Will a thousand years more of meek suffering school
    Our lives to a sterner bravery?
No! down and down with their robber rule,
    And up from the land of slavery!
For our rare old Land, our dear old Land,
    With its memories bright and brave!
And sing hey for the hour its sons shall band
    To free it of Tyrant and Slave.

THE CRY OF THE UNEMPLOYED.

'Tis hard, 't is hard to wander on through this bright world of ours,
Beneath a sky of smiling blue, on velvet paths of flowers,
With music in the woods, as there were nought but joyaunce known,
Or Angels walkt earth's solitudes, and yet with want to groan,
To see no beauty in the stars, nor in God's radiant smile,
To wail and wander misery-curst! willing, but cannot toil.
There 's burning sickness at my heart, I sink down famishéd!
God of the wretched, hear my prayer: I would that I were dead!

Heaven droppeth down with manna still in many a golden show'r,
And feeds the leaves with fragrant breath, with silver dew the flow'r.
There 's honey'd fruit for bee and bird, with bloom laughs out the tree,
And food for all God's happy things; but none gives food to me.
Earth, deck'd with Plenty's garland-crown, smiles on my aching eye,
The purse-proud, — swathed in luxury, — disdainful pass me by:
I 've eager hands, and earnest heart — but may not work for bread!
God of the wretched, hear my prayer: I would that I were dead!

Gold, art thou not a blessed thing, a charm above
all other,
To shut up hearts to Nature's cry, when brother
pleads with brother ?
Hast thou a music sweeter than the voice of loving-
kindness ?
No ! curse thee, thou 'rt a mist 'twixt God and men
in outer blindness.
"Father, come back !" my children cry ; their voices,
once so sweet,
Now quiver lance-like in my bleeding heart ! I can-
not meet
The looks that make the brain go mad, for dear
ones asking bread —
God of the wretched, hear my prayer : I would that
I were dead !

Lord ! what right have the poor to wed ? Love's
for the gilded great :
Are they not form'd of nobler clay, who dine off
golden plate ?
'T is the worst curse of Poverty to have a feeling
heart :
Why can I not, with iron-grasp, tear out the tender
part ?
I cannot slave in yon Bastille ! ah no, 't were bit-
terer pain,
To wear the Pauper's iron within, than drag the
Convict's chain.
I 'd work but cannot, starve I may, but will not beg
for bread :
God of the wretched, hear my prayer : I would that
I were dead !

SONG OF THE RED REPUBLICAN.

Fling out the red Banner! its fiery front under,
Come, gather ye, gather ye, Champions of Right!
And roll round the world, with the voice of God's thunder,
The Wrongs we've to reckon, oppressions to smite.
They deem that we strike no more like the old Hero-band,
Victory's own battle-hearted and brave:
Blood of Christ! brothers mine, it were sweet but to see ye stand,
Triumph or Tomb welcome, Glory or Grave!

Fling out the red Banner in mountain and valley!
Let Earth feel the tread of the free once again;
Now soldiers of Freedom, for love of God, rally,
Old Earth yearns to know that her children are Men.
We are nerved by a thousand wrongs, burning and bleeding,
Bold Thoughts leap to birth, but the bold Deeds must come;
And wherever Humanity's yearning and pleading,
One battle for Liberty strike we heart-home.

Fling out the red Banner! achievements immortal
Have yet to be won by the hands labour-brown;
And few, few may enter the proud promise-portal,
Yet wear it in thought like a glorious Crown!

And O joy of the onset! sound trumpet, array us
True hearts would leap up were all hell in our path;
Up, up from the Slave-land; who stirreth to stay us,
Shall fall, as of old, in the Red Sea of wrath.

Fling out the red Banner, O Sons of the morning!
Young spirits abiding to burst into wings, —
We stand shadow-crown'd, but sublime is the warning,
All heaven's grimly husht, and the Bird of Storm sings!
"All 's well," saith the Sentry on Tyranny's tower,
While Hope by his watch-fire is grey and tear-blind;
Ay, all 's well! Freedom's Altar burns, hour by hour,
Live brands for the fire-damp with which ye are mined.

Fling out the red Banner! the patriots perish,
But where their bones whiten the seed striketh root:
Their blood hath run red the great harvest to cherish:
Then gather ye, Reapers, and garner the fruit.
Victory! victory! Tyrants are quaking!
The Titan of Toil from the bloody thrall starts;
The slaves are awaking, the dawn-light is breaking,
The foot-fall of Freedom beats quick at our hearts!

PRESS ON.

Press on, press on, ye Rulers, in the roused world's forward track:
It moves too sure for ye to put the clock of Freedom back!
We're gathering up from near and far, with souls in fiery glow,
And Right doth bare its arm of might to bring the spoilers low.
Kings, Priests, ye're far too costly, and we weary of your rule;
We crown no more "Divinity," where Nature writeth "Fool!"
Ye must not bar our glorious path as in the days agone;
We know that God made Men, not Princes, Kings, or Priests.—Press on!

Press on, press on, ah! "Nobles!" ye have play'd a daring game;
But your star of strength is falling, fades the prestige of your name:
Too long have ye been fed and nurst on human blood and tears;
The naked truth is known, and Labour leaps to life, and swears
His pride of strength to bloated Ease he will no longer give:
For all who live should labour; "Lords," then all who work might live!
The combat comes! make much of what ye've wrung from Fatherland!
Press on, press on! To-day we plead, To-morrow we'll command.

Press on! a million pauper-foreheads bend in Misery's dust;
God's champions of the golden Truth still eat the mouldy crust:
This damning curse of Tyrants must not kill the nation's heart;
The spirit in a million Slaves doth pant, on fire to start
And strive to mend the world, and walk in Freedom's march sublime;
While myriads sink heart-broken, and the land o'erswarms with crime.
"O God!" they cry, "we die, we die, and see no earnest won!"
Brothers, join hand and heart, and in the work press on, press on!

ANATHEMA MARANATHA.

DEEPER and deeper the Tyrant's lash flayeth,
Swifter and swifter fierce Misery slayeth;
Tighter and tighter the grip of Toil groweth,
Nearer and nearer the dark Ruin floweth.
And still ye bear on, and ye faint heart and breath,
Till ye creep, scourgéd hounds, to your kennel of death:
O down to the dust with ye, cowards and slaves,
Plague-stricken cumber-grounds, slink to your graves!

Love is the crown of all life, but ye wear it not;
Freedom, Humanity's palm, and ye bear it not;
Beauty spreads banquet for all, but ye share it not;
Grimmer the blinding veil glooms, and ye tear it not.

Weaving your life-flowers in Wrong's robe of glory,
Ye stint in your starkness with hearts smitten hoary:
O down to the dust with ye, cowards and slaves,
Plague-stricken cumber-grounds, slink to your graves!

They have broken our hearts for their hunger, and trod
The wine-press for Death, with the grapes of our God;
And ye lick their feet, red with your blood, like dumb cattle:
Ah! better and braver to meet them in battle!
The bow that Tell drew hath lost none of its spring,
But ye nerve not with daring the arrow and string:
Then down to the dust with ye, cowards and slaves,
Plague-stricken cumber-grounds, slink to your graves!

There 's a curse on the Mammonites fiery and fell,
Whose hearts gold hath turned into hearthstones of hell;
And there 's wringing of hands with the Knave and the Tyrant,
For God's graven autograph 's on their death-warrant.
While lordlier manhood 'neath Freedom's heart yearneth,
Up now! while before ye the fire-pillar burneth!
Or down to the dust with ye, cowards and slaves,
Down, down for ever, and slink to your graves!

THE LORDS OF LAND AND MONEY

Sons of Old England, from the sod,
  Up-lift the noble brow!
Gold apes a mightier power than God,
  And wealth is worshipt now!
In all these toil-ennobled lands
  Ye have no heritage;
They snatch the fruit of youthful hands,
  The staff from weary age.
O tell them in their Palaces,
  These Lords of Land and Money!
They shall not kill the poor like bees,
  To rob them of Life's honey.

Thro' long dark years of blood and tears,
  We 've toil'd like branded slaves,
Till Wrong's red hand hath made a land
  Of paupers, prisons, graves!
But our long-sufferance endeth now;
  Within the souls of men
The fruitful buds of promise blow,
  And Freedom lives again!
O tell them in their Palaces,
  These Lords of Land and Money!
They shall not kill the poor like bees,
  To rob them of Life's honey.

Too long have Labour's nobles knelt
  Before exalted "Rank;"
Within our souls the iron is felt—
  We hear our fetters clank!
A glorious voice goes throbbing forth
  From millions stirring now,
Who yet before these Gods of earth
  Shall stand with unblencht brow.

O tell them in their Palaces,
These Lords of Land and Money!
They shall not kill the poor like bees,
To rob them of Life's honey.

THE DESERTER FROM THE CAUSE.

He is gone: better so. We should know who stand under
Our Banner: let none but the trusty remain!
For there 's stern work at hand, and the time comes shall sunder
The shell from the pearl, and the chaff from the grain!
And the heart that thro' danger and death will be dutiful —
Soul that with Cranmer in fire would shake hands,
With a Life, like a palace-home built for the Beautiful —
Freedom of all her Beloved demands!

He is gone from us! Yet shall we march on victorious,
Hearts burning like Beacons — eyes fixt on the Goal!
And if we fall fighting, we fall like the Glorious;
With face to the Stars, and all heaven in the soul!
And aye for the brave stir of battle we 'll barter
The sword of life sheatht in the peace of the grave:
And better the fieriest fate of the Martyr,
Than live like the Coward, and die like the Slave!

ALL'S RIGHT WITH THE WORLD.

SWEET Phosphor makes the brow of heaven smile,
Dawn's golden springs surge into floods of day,
Lush-leavy woods break into singing, Earth
From dewy dark rolls round her balmy side,
And all goes right, and merrily, with the world.

Spring with a tender beauty clothes the earth,
Happy, and jewell'd like a sumptuous Bride,
As tho' she knew no sorrow—held no grave:
No glory dims for all the hearts that break,
And all goes right, and merrily, with the world.

Birds sing as sweetly on the blossom'd boughs,
Suns mount as royally their sapphire throne,
Stars bud in gorgeous gloom, and harvests yield,
As tho' man nestled in the lap of Love:·
All, all goes right, and merrily, with the world.

But slip this silken-folded mask aside,
And lo, Hell welters at our very feet!
The Poor are murder'd body and soul, the Rich
In Pleasure's chalice melt their pearl of life!
Ay, all goes right, and merrily, with the world.

Lean out into the looming Future, mark
The battle roll across the night to come!
"See how we right our Wrongs at last," Revenge
Writes with red radiance on the midnight heaven
Yet, all goes right, and merrily, with the world.

So Sodom, grim old Reveller! went to death.
Voluptuous Music throbb'd thro' all her courts,
Mirth wanton'd at her heart, one pulse before
Fire-tongues told out her bloody tale of wrong,—
And all went right, and merrily, with the world.

THE AWAKENING OF THE PEOPLE.

O SWEET is the fair face of Nature, when Spring
 With living flower-rainbow in glory hath spann'd
Hill and dale; and the music of birds on the wing
 Makes earth seem a beautiful faëry land!
And dear is our first-love's young spirit-wed bride,
 With her meek eyes just sheathing in tender eclipse,
When the sound of our voice calls her heart's ruddy tide
 Up in beauty to break on her cheeks and her lips.
But Earth has no sight half so glorious to see,
As a People up-girding its might to be free.

O to see men awake from the slumber of ages,
 With brows grim from labour, and hands hard and tan,
Start up living heroes, the dreamt-of by Sages!
 And smite with strong arm the oppressors of man:
To see them come dauntless forth 'mid the world's warring,
 Slaves of the midnight-mine! serfs of the sod!
Show how the Eternal within them is stirring,
 And never more bend to a crownèd clod:
Dear God! 't is a sight for Immortals to see,—
A People up-girding its might to be free.

Battle on bravely, O sons of humanity!
 Dash down the cup from your lips, O ye Toilers!
Too long hath the world bled for tyrants' insanity—
 Too long our weakness been strength to our spoilers.

For Freedom and Right, gallant hearts, wrestle
 ever,
 And speak ye to others the proud words that won
 ye:
Your rights conquer'd once, shall be wrung from
 you never;
 Battle on! battle aye! Heaven's eyes are on ye
And Earth has no sight half so glorious to see,
As a People up-girding its might to be free!

THE WORKER.

I CARE not a curse though from birth he inherit
 The tear-bitter bread and the stingings of scorn,
If the man be but one of God's nobles in spirit, —
 Though penniless, richly-soul'd, — heartsome,
 though worn —
And will not for golden bribe lout it or flatter,
 But clings to the Right aye, as steel to the pole:
He may sweat at the plough, loom, or anvil, no
 matter,
 I'll own him the man that is dear to my soul.

His hand may be hard, and his raiment be tatter'd,
 On straw-pallet nightly his weary limbs rest;
If his brow wear the stamp of a spirit unfetter'd,
 I'm mining at once for the gems in his breast.
Give me the true man, who will fear not nor falter,
 Though Want be his guerdon, the Workhouse
 his goal,
Till his heart has burnt out upon Liberty's Altar:
 For this is the man I hold dear to my soul.

True hearts, in this brave world of blessings and
 beauty,
 Will scorn the poor splendour of losel and lurker;

Toil is creation's crown, worship is duty,
  And greater than Gods in old days is the Worker.
For us the wealth-laden world laboureth ever;
  For us harvests ripen, winds blow, waters roll;
And him who gives back in his might of endeavour,
  I'll cherish, — a man ever dear to my soul.

GOD'S WORLD IS WORTHY BETTER MEN.

Behold! an idle tale they tell,
  And who shall blame their telling it?
The rogues have got their cant to sell,
  The world pays well for selling it!
They say the world 's a desert drear, —
  Still plagued with Egypt's blindness!
That we were sent to suffer here, —
  What! by a God of kindness?
That since the world hath gone astray
  It must be so for ever,
And we should stand still, and obey
  Its Desolators. Never!
We'll labour for the better time,
  With all our might of Press and Pen;
Believe me, 't is a truth sublime,
  God's world is worthy better men.

With Paradise the world began,
  A world of love and gladness:
Its beauty may be marr'd by man
  With all his crime and madness.
Yet 't is a brave world still. Love brings
  A sunshine for the dreary;

With all our strife, sweet Rest hath wings
To fold o'er hearts a-weary.
The Sun in glory, like a God,
To-day in heaven is shining,
The flowers upon the jewell'd sod
Are sweet love-posies twining,
As radiant of immortal youth
And beauty, as in Eden; then
Believe me, 't is a noble truth,
God's world is worthy better men.

O! they are bold, knaves over-bold,
Who say we are doom'd to anguish:
That men in God's own image soul'd,
Like hell-bound slaves, must languish.
Probe Nature's heart to its red core,
There 's more of good than evil;
And man, down-trampled man, is more
Of Angel than of Devil.
Prepare to die? *Prepare to live!*
We know not what is living:
And let us for the world's good give,
As God is ever giving.
Give Action, Thought, Love, Wealth, and Time,
To win the primal age again;
Believe me, 't is a truth sublime,
God's world is worthy better men.

NEBRASKA: OR, THE SLAVERY-ABOLITIONIST TO HIS BRIDE.

SAD I come for thy caresses, bonny bride, bonny bride,
And my nestling brow is bound with crown of thorn;

And the more thy leal heart presses, bonny bride,
bonny bride,
Is thy true and tender bosom pierced and torn.

I have gloom'd thy girlish gladness, bonny bride,
bonny bride,
Made thee tearful in thy Wifehood's dewy
dawn,
Given thy voice a soul of sadness, bonny bride,
bonny bride,
Set thy dainty cheek's ripe beauty waxing wan.

The wild light of wilder'd sorrows, bonny bride,
bonny bride,
Is the lustre that comes flashing to thine eyes,
As of hopes that know no morrows, bonny bride,
bonny bride,
Or from sunken suns that set no more to rise.

My poor heart hath put on mourning, bonny bride,
bonny bride,
For the death of sweet and saintly Liberty;
It was down the Traitor's Turning, bonny bride,
bonny bride,
That they smote her in the Country of the Free.

Where the Ark of Freedom rested, bonny bride,
bonny bride,
When the May-Flower rode so bravely o'er the
Flood,
Where the Bird of Freedom nested, bonny bride,
bonny bride,
In the land our Fathers bought with precious
blood.

They have broken every promise, bonny bride,
bonny bride,
False as hell to League, and Covenant, and
vow;—

Torn the Babes of Freedom from us, bonny bride,
bonny bride,
Grim as Herod! and like Herod they shall bow.

In the mire our Banner's trailing, bonny bride,
bonny bride;
It but symbols bloody stripes and bitter tears,
To a world of Tyrants hailing, bonny bride, bonny
bride,
And a world of Slaves that groans, a Hell that
cheers.

Our good Bark is heavily wearing, bonny bride,
bonny bride,
And the hungry sharks they track us thro' the
sea,
With their cruel keen eyes glaring, bonny bride,
bonny bride,
For the burial of embalméd Liberty.

How the darkness round us presses, bonny bride,
bonny bride!
By the dying watch-fire hearts sit dark and
dumb;
And we strain and make blind guesses, bonny bride,
bonny bride,
Of the morning and the morrow that shall
come.

O, 't will be a fearful waking, bonny bride, bonny
bride,
Should the faces of our Brothers dawn in view,
With the light above us breaking, bonny bride,
bonny bride,
And the earth beneath us wet with crimson dew.

We are weak, and win derision, bonny bride, bonny
bride,
All too weak to crush the Serpents that we clasp;

But I see in solemn vision, bonny bride, bonny bride,
The young Heroes who shall kill them in their grasp.

See — the Flag of Freemen dancing, bonny bride, bonny bride,
On the Tyrants' towers, and Ruins of old Wrong —
See — the Slave's proud eyes up-glancing, bonny bride, bonny bride,
With the heart that breaks no more, save into song.

See — the hills of earth that whiten, bonny bride, bonny bride,
With the feet of angels coming down to men!
See — the homes of earth that brighten, bonny bride, bonny bride,
With the beautiful that vanisht, come again.

There 's a long road, wild and dreary, bonny bride, bonny bride,
Thro' the winding ways of Sorrow's wilderness!
And a many will fall weary, bonny bride, bonny bride,
And but few the honeyed Land of Promise press.

Yet we 'll battle on with bravery, bonny bride, bonny bride,
We shall battle on as sabbathless as Doom;
And we 'll leave the land of Slavery, bonny bride, bonny bride,
Tho' the wreath of Victory crown the Martyr's tomb.

IT WILL END IN THE RIGHT.

NEVER despair! O, my Brother in sorrow!
I know that our mourning is ended not. Yet,
Shall the vanquisht to-day be the Victors to-morrow,
Our Star shall shine on when the Tyrant's sun 's set.
Hold on! tho' they spurn thee, for whom thou art living
A life only cheer'd by the lamp of its love:
Hold on! Freedom's hope to the bounden ones giving:
Green spots in the waste wait the worn spirit-dove.
Hold on,—still hold on,—in the world's despite,
Nurse the faith in thy heart, keep the lamp of God bright,
And, my life for thine! it shall end in the Right.

What, tho' the Martyrs and Prophets have perisht?
The Angel of Life rolls the stone from their graves:
Immortal 's the faith, and the freedom they cherisht,
Their lone Triumph-cry stirs the spirits of slaves!
They are gone,—but a Glory is left in our life,
Like the day-god's last kiss on the darkness of Even—
Gone down on the desolate seas of their strife,
To climb as star-beacons up Liberty's heaven.
Hold on,—still hold on,—in the world's despite,
Nurse the faith in thy heart, keep the lamp of God bright,
And, my life for thine! it shall end in the Right.

Think of the Wrongs that have ground us for ages,
Think of the Wrongs we have still to endure!

Think of our blood, red on History's pages;
  Then work, that our reck'ning be speedy and
    sure.
Slaves, cry unto God! but be our God reveal'd
  In our lives, in our works, in our warfare for
    man;
And bearing—or borne upon—Victory's shield,
  Let us fight battle-harness'd, and fall in the van.
Hold on,—still hold on,—in the world's despite,
Nurse the faith in thy heart, keep the lamp of God
    bright,
And, my life for thine! it shall end in the Right.

A WELCOME TO LOUIS KOSSUTH.

Ho! Patriots of old England, wake!
  And join ye heart and hand,
To welcome him for Freedom's sake
  To our free fatherland!
He needs no proud triumphal arch,
  Nor banners on the wind:
In hearts that beat his triumph-march,
  Is Kossuth fitly shrined!
We meet him here, we greet him here—
  With Love's wide arms caress him!
And Kings have no such welcome here,
  As Kossuth hath: *God bless him.*

He rose like Freedom's morning star,
  Where all was darkling, dim—
We saw his glory from afar,
  And fought in soul for him!
Brave Victor! how his radiant brow
  King'd Freedom's host like Saul!
And in his crown of sorrow now
  He 's royallest heart of all.

We meet him here, we greet him here —
  With Love's wide arms caress him!
And Kings have no such welcome here,
  As Kossuth hath: *God bless him.*

Ay, English hearts thro' proud tears gush
  With glory at his name —
Whose brave deeds made the roused blood rush
  Along our veins like flame:
We cheer'd him thro' his hero-strife —
  And, in his presence met,
We 'll show the world that noble life
  Lives in Old England yet!
We meet him here, we greet him here —
  With Love's wide arms caress him!
And Kings have no such welcome here,
  As Kossuth hath: *God bless him.*

He cometh dim with glorious dust,
  From out his wrestling ring:
But, blessings — praises — deathless trust —
  Like armies round him cling!
And Freedom runs her radiant round,
  Tho' clouds shut out the sky;
And yet the World's great heart shall bound
  To Kossuth's conquering cry.
We meet him here, we greet him here —
  With Love's wide arms caress him!
And Kings have no such welcome here,
  As Kossuth hath: *God bless him.*

His Hungary billows o'er with graves
  Of Martyrs not in vain:
A rising ripening harvest waves
  Its fruit of that red rain!
And once again the Hapsburgh Star
  His flaming Sword shall dim;
And palsy strike the arm that dare
  Not strike a blow for him!

We meet him here, we greet him here —
  With Love's wide arms caress him!
And Kings have no such welcome here,
  As Kossuth hath: *God bless him.*

Ring out, exult, and clap your hands,
  Free Men and Women brave —
Shout, Britain! shake the startled lands,
  And free the bounden Slave!
Come forth, make merry in the sun,
  And give him welcome due;
Heroic hearts have crown'd him one
  Of Earth's Immortal few!
We meet him here, we greet him here —
  With Love's wide arms caress him!
And Kings have no such welcome here,
  As Kossuth hath: *God bless him.*

EDEN.

There is not a rift in the blue sky now,
  Where a million tempests tore it;
There is not a furrow on Ocean's brow,
  Tho' a million years have past o'er it.
And for all the strife and the storms that have roll'd
  Down the ages, grim and gory;
Earth weareth her pleasant face, as of old,
  And laughs in her morning glory.
And Man — tho' he beareth the brand of Sin,
  And the flesh and the devil have bound him —
Hath a spirit within, to old Eden akin,
  Only nurture up Eden around him.

The cloud may have fall'n on the human face,
  And its lordliest beauty blighted;

For love hath gone out with a dark'ning trace,
  Where its inward glory lighted.
Yet the old world of love liveth still in the heart,
  As we 've many a sweet revealing;
And its rich fossil-jewels in tears will up-start
  With the warm flood of holier feeling.
Ay, Man — tho' he beareth the brand of Sin,
  And the flesh and the devil have bound him —
Hath a spirit within, to old Eden akin,
  Only nurture up Eden around him.

O the terrors, the tortures, the miseries dark —
  That have curst us, and crusht, and cankered!
Yet, aye, from the Deluge, Humanity's Ark
  Hath on some serene Ararat anchored.
The golden chains that link heaven to earth,
  The rusts of all time cannot sever!
Evil shall die in its own dark dearth,
  And the Good liveth on for ever.
Ay, Man — tho' he beareth the brand of Sin,
  And the flesh and the devil have bound him —
Hath a spirit within, to old Eden akin,
  Only nurture up Eden around him.

ONWARD AND SUNWARD.

Tell me the song of the beautiful Stars,
    As grandly they glide on their blue way above
      us,
Looking, despite of our spirit's sin-scars,
    Down on us tenderly, yearning to love us!
This is the song in their work-worship sung,
Down thro' the world-jewelled universe rung:
" Onward for ever, for evermore onward,"
And ever they open their loving eyes Sunward.

"Onward," shouts Earth, with her myriad voices
Of music, aye answering the song of the Seven,
As like a wing'd child of God's love she rejoices,
Swinging her censer of glory in heaven.
And lo, it is writ by the finger of God,
In sunbeams and flowers on the smiling green sod:
Onward for ever, for evermore onward,
And ever she turneth all trustfully Sunward.

The mightiest souls of all time hover o'er us,
Who labor'd like Gods among men, and have gone
Like great bursts of sun on the dark way before us:
They're with us, still with us, our battle fight on,
Looking down victor-brow'd, from the glory-crown'd hill
They beckon, and beacon us, on, onward still:
And the true heart's aspirings are onward, still onward;
It turns to the Future, as earth turneth Sunward.

THE THREE VOICES.

A WAILING voice comes up a desolate road,
Drearily, drearily, drearily!
Where mankind have trodden the by-way of blood,
Wearily, wearily, wearily!
Like a sound from the Dead Sea all shrouded in glooms,
With breaking of hearts, fetters clanking, men groaning,
Or chorus of Ravens, that croak among tombs,
It comes with the mournfullest moaning:

"Weep, weep, weep!
Yoke-fellows, listen,
Till tearful eyes glisten:
'Tis the voice of the Past: the dark, grim-featured Past,
All sad as the shriek of the midnight blast:
Weep, weep, weep,
Tears to wash out the red, red stain,
Where earth hath been fatted
By brave hearts that rotted,
And life ran a deluge of hot, bloody rain:
Weep, weep, weep.

Another voice comes from the millions that bend,
Tearfully, tearfully, tearfully!
From hearts which the scourges of slavery rend,
Fearfully, fearfully, fearfully!
From many a worn, noble spirit that breaks,
In the world's solemn shadows adown in Life's valleys,
From Mine, Forge, and Loom, trumpet-tongued it awakes,
On the soul wherein Liberty rallies:
"Work, work, work!"
Yoke-fellows, listen,
Till earnest eyes glisten:
'Tis the voice of the Present. It bids us, my brothers,
Be Freemen: and then for the freedom of others
Work, work, work!
For the Many, a holocaust long to the Few:
O work while ye may!
O work while 't is day!
And cling to each other, united and true:
Work, work, work.

There cometh another voice sweetest of all,
Cheerily, cheerily, cheerily!
And my heart leapeth up at its glorious call,
Merrily, merrily, merrily!

It comes like the soft touch of Spring-tide, unwarping
The frost of oppression that bound us:
It comes like a choir of the Seraphim, harping
Their gladsomest music around us:
"Hope, hope, hope!"
Yoke-fellows, listen,
Till gleeful eyes glisten:
'Tis the voice of the Future, the sweetest of all,
That makes the heart leap to its glorious call.
Hope, hope, hope!
Brothers, step forth in the Future's van,
For the worst is past,
Right conquers at last,
And the better day dawns upon suffering man:
Hope, hope, hope.

THIS WORLD IS FULL OF BEAUTY.

There lives a voice within me, a guest-angel of my heart,
And its sweet lispings win me, till the tears a-trembling start;
Up evermore it springeth, like some magic melody,
And evermore it singeth this sweet song of songs to me —
This world is full of beauty, as other worlds above;
And, if we did our duty, it might be full of love.

Night's starry tendernesses dower with glory evermore,
Morn's budding, bright, melodious hour comes sweetly as of yore;
But there be million hearts accurst, where no sweet sunbursts shine,

And there be million hearts athirst for Love's immortal wine.
This world is full of beauty, as other worlds above;
And, if we did our duty, it might be full of love.

If faith, and hope, and kindness pass'd, as coin, 'twixt heart and heart,
How, thro' the eye's tear-blindness, should the sudden soul upstart!
The dreary, dim, and desolate, should wear a sunny bloom,
And Love should spring from buried Hate, like flowers o'er Winter's tomb.
This world is full of beauty, as other worlds above;
And, if we did our duty, it might be full of love.

Were truth our uttered language, Angels might talk with men,
And God-illumined earth should see the Golden Age again;
The burthen'd heart should soar in mirth like Morn's young prophet-lark,
And Misery's last tear wept on earth, quench Hell's last cunning spark.
For this world is full of beauty, as other worlds above;
And, if we did our duty, it might be full of love.

Lo! plenty ripens round us, yet awakes the cry for bread,
The millions still are toiling, crusht, and clad in rags, unfed!
While sunny hills and valleys richly blush with fruit and grain,
But the paupers in the palace rob their toiling fellow-men.
This world is full of beauty, as other worlds above;
And, if we did our duty, it might be full of love.

Dear God! what hosts are trampled 'mid this killing crush for gold!
What noble hearts are sapp'd of love! what spirits lose life's hold!
Yet a merry world it might be, opulent for all, and aye,
With its lands that ask for labour, and its wealth that wastes away.
This world is full of beauty, as other worlds above;
And, if we did our duty, it might be full of love.

The leaf-tongues of the forest, and the flow'r-lips of the sod —
The happy Birds that hymn their raptures in the ear of God —
The summer wind that bringeth music over land and sea,
Have each a voice that singeth this sweet song of songs to me —
This world is full of beauty, as other worlds above;
And, if we did our duty, it might be full of love.

A SONG IN THE CITY.

Coining the heart, brain, and sinew, to gold,
  Till we sink in the dark, on the pauper's dole,
Feeling for ever the flowerless mould,
  Growing about the uncrownéd soul!
O, God! O God! must this evermore be
The lot of the Children of Poverty?
  The Spring is calling from brae and bower,
  In the twinkling sheen of the sunny hour,
      Earth smiles in her golden green;
  There 's music below, in the glistering leaves,

There 's music above, and heaven's blue bosom heaves
The silvery clouds between;
The boughs of the woodland are nodding in play,
And wooingly beckon my spirit away —
I hear the dreamy hum
Of bees in the lime-tree, and birds on the spray
And they, too, are calling my thinking away;
But I cannot — cannot come.
Visions of verdant and heart-cooling places
Will steal on my soul like a golden spring-rain,
Bringing the lost light of brave, vanisht faces;
Till all my life blossoms with beauty again.
But O, for a glimpse of the flower-laden Morning,
That makes the heart leap up, and knock at heaven's door!
O for the green lane, the green field, the green wood,
To take in, by heartfuls, their greenness once more!
How I yearn to lie down and just roll in the meadows,
And nestle in leaves, and the sleep of the shadows,
Where violets in the cool gloom are awaking,
There, let my soul out from its cavern of clay,
To float down the warm spring, away and away!
FOR I WAS NOT MADE MERELY FOR MONEY-MAKING.

At this wearisome work I oftentimes turn,
From my bride, and my monitress, Duty,
Forgetting the strife, and the wrestle of life,
To talk with the spirit of beauty.
The multitude's hum, and the chinking of gold,
Grow hush as the dying of day,
For on wings, making music, with joy untold,
My heart is up, and away!
Glad as the bird in the tree-top chanting
Its anthem to Liberty;

With its heart all in musical gratitude panting,
And O, 't is a bliss to be!
Once more to drink in the life-breathing air,
Lapt in luxurious flowers —
To recall again the pleasures that were
In Infancy's innocent hours —
To wash the earth-stains and the dust from my soul,
In nature's reviving tears, once more;
To feast at her banquet, and drink from her bowl
Rich dew, for the heart's hot core.
Ah me! ah me! it is heavenly then,
And hints of the spirit-world, near alway,
Are stirring, and stirr'd, in my heart again,
Like leaves at the kiss of May:
It is but a dream, yet 't is passing sweet,
And when from its spells my spirit is waking,
Dark is my heart, and the wild tears start;
For I was not made merely for money-making.

My soul leaneth out, to the whisperings
Of the mighty, the marvellous spirits of old;
And heaven-ward soareth to strengthen her wings,
When Labour relapseth its earthly hold;
And breathless with awfullest beauty, — it listens,
To catch the Night's deep, starry mystery;
Or in mine eyes, dissolved, it glistens,
Big, for the moan of Humanity.
Much that is written within its chamber,
Much that is shrined in the mind's living amber,
Much of this thought of mine, —
I fain would struggle and give to birth;
For I would not pass away from earth,
And make no sign!
I yearn to utter, what might live on,
In the world's heart, when I am gone.
I would not plod on, like these slaves of gold,
Who darken their souls, in a dusky cave:

I would see the world better, and nobler-soul'd,
  Ere I lay me down in my green turf-grave.
I may toil till my life is filled with dreariness,
Toil till my heart is a wreck in its weariness,
Toil for ever, for tear-steept bread,
Till I go down to the silent dead.
But, by this yearning, this hoping, this aching,
I WAS NOT MADE MERELY FOR MONEY-MAKING.

THE FAMINE-SMITTEN.

IN the tears of the Morning —
  The smiles of the sun,
The green Earth's adorning
  Told spring had begun!
Warm woods donn'd their beauty, wrought
  Through long still nights,
And musical breezes brought
  Flowery delights:
The humming leaves flasht
  Rich in light, with sweet sound,
And the glad waters dasht
  Their starry spray round!
The wood-bines up-climbing,
  Laught out, pink and golden,
And bees made sweet chiming
  In roses half-folden.
But where was that infant-band,
  Wont in spring weather
To wander forth, hand-in-hand,
  Violets to gather?
Ah misery! they slept,
  The dear blossoms of love!
Where the green branches wept,
  And the grass crept above;

Melodious gladness
 Throbb'd thro' the rich air,
But the anguish of madness
 Rent Poverty's lair;
For Famine had smitten
 Its pride of life low,
And agony written
 On heart and on brow.
Sweet from the boughs the birds
 Sang in their mirth,
The lark messaged heaven-wards
 Blessings from earth —
But I turn'd where our gentle Lord's
 Loves lay in dearth.
They heard not, nor heeded,
 The sounds of life o'er them!
They felt not, nor needed,
 The hot tears wept for them!
But earth-flowers were springing
 O'er human flowers' grave,
And, O God! what heart-wringing
 Their tender looks gave!
They died! died of hunger —
 By bitter want blasted!
While wealth for the Wronger
 Ran over untasted —
While Pomp, in joy's rosy bow'rs,
 Wasted life's measure,
Chiding the lagging hours,
 Wearied of pleasure!
They died! while men hoarded
 The free gifts of God:
They died! 't is recorded
 In letters of blood.
Yet the corn on the hills
 Waves its showery gold crown;
Still Nature's lap fills
 With the good heaven drops down.

O! this world might be lighted
With Eden's first smile —
Angel-haunted — unblighted,
With Freedom for Toil:
But they wring out our blood
For their banquet of gold!
They annul laws of God,
Soul and body are sold!
Hark now! hall and palace,
Ring out, dome and rafter!
Ay, laugh on, ye callous!
In Hell there'll be laughter:
But tremble, hell-makers;
The shorn among men —
The world's image-breakers
Grow mighty again;
There be stern times a-coming,
The dark days of reck'ning,
The storms are up-looming —
The Nemesis wak'ning!
On heaven, blood shall call,
Earth quake with pent thunder,
And shackle and thrall
Shall be riven asunder.
It will come, it shall come,
Impede it what may:
Up, People! and welcome
Your glorious day.

PEACE.

Yes, Peace is beautiful; and I do yearn
For her to clasp the World's poor tortured heart,
As sweet spring warmth doth brood o'er coming flowers.
But peace with these Leviathans of blood —

Who pirate crimson seas, devouring men?
Give them the hand of brotherhood — whose fangs
Are in our hearts with the grim blood-hound's grip?
Wouldst see Peace, idiot-like, with smirk and smile,
A-planting flowers to coronal Truth's grave?
Peace, merry-making round the funeral pyre,
Where Freedom, fiery-curtained, weds with death?
Peace, mirroring her form by pools of blood, —
Crowning the Croat in Vienna's fosse,
With all sweet influences of thankful eyes,
For murder of the glorious Burschenschaft?
Peace with Oppression, which doth tear dear friends
And brothers from our side to-day, and comes
To eat OUR hearts and drink OUR blood to-morrow?
Out on 't! it is the Tyrant's cunning cant,
The robe of sheen flung o'er its deadly daggers,
Which start to life, whene'er it hugs to death.
I answer, War! — war with the cause of war, —
War with our misery, want, and wretchedness, —
War with curst Gold, which is an endless war
On Love, and God, and our Humanity!
Brothers, I bid ye forth to glorious war!
Patch fig-leaves o'er the naked truth no more.
The stream of Time runs red with our best blood!
Time's seed-field we have sown with fratricide,
And dragon's teeth have sprung, ay, in our hearts.
O! we have fought and bled on land and sea,
Heapt glory's car with myriads of the brave,
Spilt blood by oceans — treasures by the million,
At every Tyrant's beck. Had we but shed
Such warm and eloquent blood for Freedom's faith,
War's star in heaven had lost its name ere now.
"Brothers!" I cried, — well, Brothers, brother slaves!
O! but to give ye slaves THEIR valiant heart,
Whose dumb, dead dust is worth your living souls —

Dear God! 't were sweet to kiss the scaffold-block!
I 'd proudly leap death's darkness, to let shine
The Future's promise thro' your sorrow's tears!
Sorrow? ah, no! ye feel not sense so holy:
The worm of misery riots in your hearts—
Ye hear your younglings in the drear midnight
Make moan for bread, when ye have none to give!—
Ye drain your life, warm, for the vulture's drink!
The groaning land is choked with living death.
O! ye are mated to the things of scorn.
And I have heard your miserable madness
Belcht forth in drunken pæans to your tyrants,
Pledging your murderers to the hell they 've made!
Ah, Christ! was it for this, thou sudden sun,
Didst light these centuries with thy dying smile?—
Was it for this, so many and so many
Have hackt their spirit-swords against our fetters
And killing cords, that bleed our hearts to death—
Wept griefs might turn the soul grey in an hour—
Broke their great hearts for love, and, in despair,
Dasht their immortal crowns to earth, and died?
Was it for this the countless Host of Martyrs,
Becrown'd and robed in fiery martyrdom,
Beat out a golden-aged Future from
The angel-metal of their noble lives—
Clomb the red scaffold—strain'd their weary eyes,
Across the mists of ages, for one glimpse
Of midnight burning into that bright Dawn
Now bursting golden, up the skies of time?
When will ye put your human glory on?
How long will ye lie darkling desolate,
With barren brain, blind life, and fallow heart?
The hollow yearning grave will kindly close,
And flowers spring where the mould lay freshly dark!
The leaves will burst from out the naked'st boughs,
Fire-ripen'd into glorious greenery,
Waste moor and fen will kindle into spring:

How long will ye lie darkling desolate?
Lord God Almighty! what a spring of freedom
Awaits to burst the winter of our world!
O! if aught moving thrills a brother's love,
Which pleads for utterance in blinding tears,
Then let these words burn living in your souls,
Snatch Fear's cold hand from off your palsied
hearts,
And send the intrepid shudder through your veins.
Helots of Albion! Penury's nurslings! rise,
And swear, in God's name, and in Heaven's or
Hell's,
Ye will bear witness at the birth of Freedom!
Arise, and front the blessed light of Heaven,
With tyrant-quailing manhood in your looks!
Arise, go forth to glorious war for right,
And justice, and mankind's high destiny!
Arise, 't is Freedom's bleeding fight, strike home
Wherever tyrants lift the gorgon-head!
There is a chasm in the coming years,
A-gape for strife's Niagara of blood —
Or to be bridged by brave hearts linkt in love.
The world is stirring with its mighty purpose:
No more be laggards in the march of men.
The Vulture Despotism spreads wide its wings
Right royally, to give ye broader mark!
And the hag Evil sickens unto death,
With her sore travail o'er the birth of Good.
And yet shall War's red-letter'd creed die out;
Where blood is running, shall the wild-flowers
blow;
Where men are groaning, shall their children
sing;
And Peace and Love re-Genesis the world.

A GLIMPSE OF AULD LANG-SYNE.

EARTH, sparkling Bride-like, bares her bosom to the nestling Night,
Who hath come down in glory from the golden halls of light;

Ten thousand tender, starry eyes smile o'er the world at rest,
The weary world — husht like an infant on its mother's breast!

The great old hills thrust up their foreheads in rich-sleeping light:
How humbly-grand, and still they stand, worshipping God to-night!

The flowers have hung their cups with gems of their own sweetness wrought,
And muse and smile upon their stems, in ecstasy of thought:

They have banqueted on beauty, at the fragrant Eve's red lips,
And fold in charmèd rest, with crowns upon their velvet tips.

No green tide sweeps the sea of leaves, no wind-sigh stirs the sod,
While Holiness broods dove-like on the soul, begetting God.

Sweet hour! thou wak'st the feeling that we never know by day,
For angel eyes look down, and read the spirit 'neath the clay:

Even while I listen, music stealeth in upon my
soul,
As though adown heaven's stair of stars, the
seraph-harpings stole —

Or I could grasp the immortal part of life, and
soar, and soar,
Such strong wings take me, and my heart hath
found such hidden lore!

It flings aside the weight of years, and lovingly
goes back,
To that sweet time, the dear old days, that glisten
on its track!

Life's wither'd leaves grow green again, and fresh
with Childhood's spring,
As I am welcomed back once more within its rain-
bow-ring: —

The Past, with all its gather'd charms, beckons me
back in joy,
And loving hearts, and open arms, re-clasp me as a
boy.

The voices of the Loved and Lost are stirring at
my heart,
And memory's miser'd treasures leap to life, with
sudden start, —

As through her darken'd windows, warm and glad
sunlight creeps in,
And Lang-syne, glimpst in glorious tears, my toil-
worn soul doth win.

Thou art looking, smiling on me, as thou hast lookt
and smiled, Mother,
And I am sitting by thy side, at heart a very child,
Mother!

I'm with thee now in soul, sweet Mother, much as
in those hours,
When all my wealth was in thy love, and in the
birds and flowers,

When the long summer days were short, for my
glad soul to live
The golden fulness of the bliss, each happy hour
could give.

When Heaven sang to my innocence, and every
leafy grove
And forest ached with music, as a young heart
aches with love.

When life oped like a flower, where clung my lips,
to quaff its honey,
And joys throng'd like a shower of gold king-cups
in meadows sunny.

I 'll tell thee, Mother! since we met, stern changes
have come o'er me:
Then life smiled like a paradise, the world was all
before me.

O! I was full of trusting faith, and, in my glee and
gladness,
Deem'd not that others had begun as bright, whose
end was madness.

I knew not smiles could light up eyes, like Sunset's
laughing glow
On some cold stream, which burns above, while all
runs dark below;

That on Love's summer sea, great souls go down,
while some, grown cold,
Seal up affection's living spring, and sell their love
for gold;

How they on whom we 'd staked the heart forget
the early vow,
And they who swore to love through life would
pass all coldly now;

How, in the soul's dark hour, Love's temple-veil is
rent in twain,
And the heart quivers thorn-crown'd on the cross
of fiery pain.

And shatter'd idols, broken dreams, come crowding
on my brain,
As speaks the spirit-voice of days that never come
again.

It tells of golden moments lost — heart sear'd —
blind Passion's thrall;
Life's spring-tide blossoms run to waste, Love's
honey turn'd to gall.

It tells how many and often high resolve and pur-
pose strong,
Shaped on the anvil of my heart, have died upon
my tongue.

I left thee, Mother, in sweet May, the merry month
of flowers,
To toil away in dusky gloom the golden summer-
hours.

I left my world of love behind, with soul for life
a-thirsting,
My burning eyelid dropt no tear, although my
heart was bursting.

For I had knit my soul to climb, with poverty its
burden;
Give me but time, O give me time, and I would
win the guerdon.

Ah, Mother! many a heart that all my aspiration
cherisht,
Hath fallen in the trampling strife, and in the life-
march perisht.

We see the bleeding victims lie upon the world's
grim Altar,
And one by one young feelings die, and dark
doubts make us falter.

Mother, the world hath wreakt its part on me, with
scathing power,
Yet the best life that heaves my heart runs for thee
at this hour.

And by these holy yearnings, by these eyes with
sweet tears wet,
I know there wells a spring of love through all my
being yet.

MERRY CHRISTMAS EVE.

Merry Christmas Eve! in the Palace where
knavery
Crowds all the treasures the fair world can ren-
der:
Where spirits grow rusted in silkenest slavery,
And life is out-panted, in sloth, and in splendour
In gladness and glory, Wealth's darlings were
meeting,
And jewel-claspt fingers linkt softly again;
New friendships were twining, and old friends were
greeting,
And twin hearts grew one, in God's golden love-
chain.

Merry Christmas Eve! in a poor man's grim hovel,
  There huddled in silence a famishing family;
Church-bells were laughing in musical revel,
  They heard the loud mockery, with brows throbbing clammily;
All in the merry time there they sat, mourning—
  Two sons — two brothers — in penal chains bleeding;
Their hearts wandered forth to the never-returning
  Who rose on their vision, pale, haggard, and pleading.

Merry Christmas Eve! for the rich, there was music,
  And dancing, and many a wine woo'd on the board;
O Falstaff! you Prince of Lies! 't would have made you sick,
  To hear how they flattered a Mammonite Lord!
Love-kisses sobb'd out 'twixt the rollic and rout,
  And Hope went forth, reaping-in long-promist treasure.
What matter, tho' hearts might be breaking without?
  Their moans were unheard in the palace of pleasure.

Merry Christmas Eve! but the stricken ones heard
  No neighbourly welcome, no kind voice of kin;
They lookt at each other, but spake not a word,
  While through crevice, and cranny, the sleet drifted in.
In a desolate corner, one, hunger-kill'd, lay,
  And the mother's hot tears were a bosom-babe's food.
What marvel, O Statesman, what marvel, I pray,
  Such misery nurseth Crime's dark viper-brood?

O men, angel-imaged in Nature's fair mint,
  And is it for this, ye were fashioned divine?

Ah, where 's the god-stamp — Immortality's print?
  We are tyrants and slaves, knit in one tortured twine:
That a few, like to gods, may stride over the earth,
  Millions, born to be murdered, are given in pawn;
When will the world quicken for Liberty's birth,
  Which she waiteth, with eager wings beating the dawn?

False Priests, dare ye say 't is the will of your God,
  (And shroud the Christ's message in dark sophistry,)
That these millions of paupers should bow to the sod?
  Up, up, trampled hearts, it 's a lie! it 's a lie!
They may carve "State" and "Altar" in characters golden,
  But Tyranny's symbols are ceasing to win;
Be stirring, O people, your scroll is unfolden,
  And bright be the deeds ye emblazon therein.

THE CHIVALRY OF LABOUR EXHORTED TO THE WORSHIP OF BEAUTY.

OUR world oft turns in gloom, and Life hath many a perilous way,
Yet there's no path so desolate and thorny, cold and gray,
But Beauty as a Beacon burns above the dark of strife,
And like an Alchemist aye turns all things to golden life.
On human hearts her presence droppeth precious manna down,

On human brows her glory gathers like a coming crown:
Her smile lights up Life's troubled stream, and Love, the swimmer! lives;
And O 't is brave to battle for the guerdon that she gives!
Then let us worship Beauty with the knightly faith of old,
O Chivalry of Labour toiling for the Age of Gold!

The first-fruits of the Past at Beauty's shrine are offer'd up,
From which a vintage meet for Gods she crusheth in her cup:
And from the living Present doth she press the rare new wine,
To glad the hearts of all her lovers with a draught divine.
Earth's crowning miracle! she comes! with blessing lips, that part
Like mid-May's rose flusht open with the fragrance of her heart:
And life turns to her colour — kindles with her light — like flowers
That garner up the golden fire, and suck the mellow showers.
Come let us worship Beauty with the knightly faith of old,
O Chivalry of Labour toiling for the Age of Gold!

Come let us worship Beauty where the budding Spring doth flower,
And lush green leaves and grasses flush out sweeter every hour;
Or Summer's tide of splendour floods the lap o' the World once more,
With riches like a sea that surges jewels on its shore.
Come feel her ripening influence when Morning feasts our eyes —

Thro' open gates of glory — with a glimpse of Paradise:
Or queenly Night sits crownèd, smiling down the purple gloom,
And Stars, like Heaven's fruitage, melt i' the glory of their bloom.
Come let us worship Beauty with the knightly faith of old,
O Chivalry of Labour toiling for the Age of Gold!

Come from the den of darkness and the city's soil of sin,
Put on your radiant Manhood, and the Angel's blessing win!
Where wealthier sunlight comes from Heaven, like welcome-smiles of God,
And Earth's blind yearnings leap to life in flowers, from out the sod:
Come worship Beauty in the forest-temple, dim and hush,
Where stands Magnificence dreaming! and God burneth in the bush:
Or where the old hills worship with their silence for a psalm,
Or Ocean's weary heart doth keep the sabbath of its calm.
Come let us worship Beauty with the knightly faith of old,
O Chivalry of Labour toiling for the Age of Gold!

Come let us worship Beauty: she hath subtle power to start
Heroic word and deed out-flashing from the humblest heart!
Great feelings will gush unawares, and freshly as the first
Rich Rainbow that up startled Heaven in tearful splendour burst

O blessed are her lineaments, and wondrous are her ways
To re-picture God's worn likeness in the faded human face!
Our bliss shall richly overbrim like sunset in the west,
And we shall dream immortal dreams, and banquet with the Blest:
Then let us worship Beauty with the knightly faith of old,
O Chivalry of Labour toiling for the Age of Gold!

TO MY WIFE.

1852.

Like those Ambassadors of old, that went
To the far Orient land, with kingly gifts
Of gems — from which a subtle spirit lookt —
To nestle richly between Beauty's breasts,
And crown her gorgeous brows with winking flame,
Or clothe her starrily as Queenly Night;
And found that land a garden where they grew,
Lavish, as all the dews were turn'd to gems;
So bring I thee, Sweet Lady of my love,
My jewels, I have garner'd up, to find
How poor they are beside thy peerless wealth.
Th' Elysium where thy tender spirit dwells
Is written o'er with thoughts of beauty, thick
As starry mysteries written on the night.
Thy realm is rich in Memory's golden mines,
And flashing out with harvest-fields of Hope.
My Muse! that moveth swathed with holier light,
Throned on the regnant heights of Womanhood
In all thy summer beauty, warm as when

I lookt out on the sunny side of Life,
And saw thee summering like a blooming Vine,
That reacheth globes of wine in at the lattice
By the ripe armful, with ambrosial smile.
The flying Cares but touch thy Life's fair face,
Lightly as swimming shadows dusk the Lake.
Come sit thee down, dear, by my side, To-night;
The world shut out, our little world shut in!
Where we are happy as the Bird whose nest
Is heaven'd in the hush of purple Hills,
Or region'd in the palmy top of life.
Now shut thine eyes, and see a pageant bloom
Upon the dark, — a Vision sweeping by.
I was a dweller amid shadows grim:
Till FREEDOM toucht my yearning eyes, and lo!
Life in a shining circle, rounding rose,
As heaven on heaven goes up the jewell'd night.
New floods of passionate life swirl'd at my heart,
And FREEDOM was my glittering Bride. For me
She walkt the world as a Divinity,
Sang like a Spirit in Life's darken'd ways,
I' the Rainbow reacht forth girdling arms of love,
To clasp the Unapparent to the Earth, —
Turn'd common things to beauty: as the sun
Kindles a glory in the grass and dust, —
Went forth flame-plumed, in Chariot sublime,
And rode the winds, like him who walks the worlds.
And when the fresh Morn flower'd like a Rose,
Birds sang of her, and all their happy hearts
Rang out in music, Leaves clapt faëry hands,
The flowers for joy stood tearful in her glory,
And World went singing, unto World, of FREEDOM.
And I would blazon her melodious name,
Sing some wild pæan should touch the world to tears,
Or chariot it to battle in her Cause:
For O! her softest breath, that might not stir
The summer gossamer tremulous on its throne,

Makes the crown'd Tyrants start with realmless looks!
I would have given the lustre of my life
To add one jewel to her Diadem!
And then thou cam'st, and LOVE grew lord of all.
Look how the Sun puts out the eyes of fire!
So when Love's royal glance my lattice lit,
The fires of FREEDOM whiten'd on my hearth.
The sleeping Beauty in my heart's charm'd Palace
Woke at Love's kiss. My life was set aflush,
As Roses redden when the Spring moves by,
And the green buds peer out like eyes, to see
The delicate spirit whose sweet presence stirr'd them.
How my heart ripen'd in its flooding spring;
As when the sap runs up the tingling trees,
Till all the sunny life laughs out in leaves,
And lifts its fluttering wings! So my heart felt
With such brave shoots of glory bursting up,
As it had flower'd for Immortality.
The heights of Being came out from their cloud,
As the cliffs kindle when the Morning comes
Swimming the utmost Sea in ruddy haste,
With foam of glory; and the flood of light,
Like mellow wine, runs down remotest hills.
Thou cam'st, my sparkling Bird of Paradise!
With a soft murmuring as of winnowing wings
That fold the nest so Dove-like tenderly!
With brow that parted lovely waves of hair,
And took the gazer's eye like some white Grace!
Eyes, loving large! Lips Houri-like, that light
A soul to glory with their kiss of fire;
And cheeks fresh-misted with the bloom of Morn.
And thou didst move, a Splendour mid Life's Shadows,
Making a Rembrandt Picture. So the Stars
In all their glory pass the shrinking Dark.
O, I was stirr'd as though a Spirit went by;
Or I had met some awful Loveliness,

That haunts the realm of Dreams, or duskly floats
Across the wondering solitudes of Thought.
So Love was lord of all. I touch my lyre,
And Love o'erflows my heart, and floods my hand.
Love makes all dear delights so soothly sweet,
Life pants heart-stifled 'neath its luscious load,
Like young Earth claspt in June's voluptuous arms,
Faint with her fragrance, flooded up in flowers.
Love is divine life, Beauty is its smile.
O, Love will make the killing crown of thorn
Burst into blossom on the Martyr's brow!
Upon Love's bosom Earth floats like an Ark
Through all the Deluge of the solemn dark.
Love rays us round as glory swathes a star,
And, from the mystic touch of lips and palms,
Streams rosy warmth enough to light a world:
And Spirit-eyes, from out the purpling glooms,
Mark how we feed this human Altar-flame,
How speeds this ripening into Deity!
What glittering robes for immortality
Trail starry radiance through our night of Earth
And in our home thy presence maketh Love
A Mortal, who hath died to rise again,
Immortal, in its nobler life with thee.
O Love! make clear my vision, roll thou up
My orb of Song from Passion's misting deeps
To climb the heavens, and win the eternal calm;
And though it shine not mid the Suns of Song,
To set a World sweet-murmuring in its light,
Like Memnon at the radiant touch of Dawn,
I know each Star hath its own perfect place
Above, though it may have no name on Earth.
I hope my hope, and dream my dream, that life
With me shall yet ring out melodious, 'twixt
The silences of heaven and the grave.
O Labour! blind and feeling for the day!
Might I go forth to peer with eagle ken
Into the blessed land of promise, where

The Future like a fruitfuller Summer sits
Ripening HER Eden silently, to bear
The crowning flower of consummated Life,—
Where Freedom's Song-Birds fly, to build their nests,
And warm to life their brood of darling dreams:
Then see thy dark look lighten at my news,
Thy dim eyes dance divinely at the grapes!
To loftier music time thy larger step;
And hearten thee to lift up clearer brows,
Thy face o'erflowing like a shining Sea.
I see a shape behind a mist, that burns
In the flusht distance of some unseen Goal;
It grows with gazing on, like Lovers' beauty.
With beckoning smiles the Glory draws me on;
One hand points up, one holds a glittering crown,
For me to climb and wear with lordlier growth,
And airy Voices call me, bid me leap
In Victory's Car as it goes bickering by.
And Thou, dear Wife! with exultation lit,
Wilt weep proud tears to enrich my wine of joy,—
A costlier cup than ever Anthony's Queen
Magnificent! drank in her voluptuous vein!

DEATH OF HAVELOCK.

EACH day his face grew thinner, and sweeter, saintlier grew;
And day by day they saw the soul fast burning into view:
And higher, each day higher, did the life-flame heavenward climb,
Like sad, sweet sunshine up the wall, that for the sunset time,
Still watches, and the signal that shall call it hence is given,
Even so his spirit kept the watch till beckoned home to heaven.

War-worn and wasted! yet his eyes were soft and satisfied;
His work was done: and in the arms of Victory he died;
Dropping the flesh-robe, with a smile, so gently did he pass, —
Gently as spirits of the flowers from out the new-mown grass:
"*Havelock's dead!*" and darkness fell on every up-turned face;
The Shadow of an Angel going from its earthly place.

They laid it low, the good grey head, not only grey with years;
It had been bowed in Sorrow's lap, and silvered with her tears.
Our England might not crown it, with her heart too full for speech,
The hand that draws into the dark, had borne it beyond reach:
The eyes of far-away heaven-blue, with such keen lustre lit,
As they could pierce the night of death, and star-like fathom it —
They may not swim with sweetness, as the happy children run
To welcome home the Reaper, when the weary day is done:
How would the tremulous radiance round the old man's mouth have smiled!
Our good grey-headed hero, with the heart of a little child!
Nor sleeps he with our noble dead, beneath the Cross-crowned dome:
But now hath resting place more dear within the heart of Home.

Honour to Henry Havelock! tho' not of kingly blood,

He wore the double royalty of being Great and Good.
He leaned a trusting hand on Heaven, a gentle heart on Home;
In secret he grew ready, ere the Judgment-Hour had come.
He rose up in our cruel need, and towering on he trod,
Baring his brow to battle bold as humbly to his God!
He rose, and reached the topmost height, our Hero lowly born!
So from the lowly grass hath grown the proud embattled Corn.
No swerving as he walkt along the roaring earthquake ridge:
He made a way for Victory: his body was her bridge.
One of the Chivalry of Christ! he taught us how to stand
With rootage like the Palm, amid the maddest whirl of sand.

When swarming hell had broken bounds, aye stedfast in that hour,
'Mid the deluge of the devils, as the pillar of our power:
Undaunted while the swarthy storm around him swirled and swirled,
A winding sheet of all white life! a wild Sahara world!
We saw the waves close over him, lost to all human view;
But like an Arrow sent from God, he cleft their twelve hosts thro'.
He battled on in darkness, walking by the inner light,
Majestic as blind Milton 'mid his watches of the night.

He did his work nor thought of nations ringing with his name,
He walkt with God, and talkt with God, nor cared if following Fame
Should find him working in the field, or sleeping underground:
Nor did he mind what resting place, with Heaven embracing round.

In the bloodiest pass of peril, with a fame shall never dim,
Died Havelock, the good Soldier; who would not die like him?
In grandest strength he fell full-length, and now our Hero climbs
To those who stood up in their day and talkt with after-times!
He smileth in his heaven now, the Martyr with his palm:
The weary warrior's tired life is crown'd with starry calm.
His labours done; his rest begun; He only looketh back
To see the blessing flow for those who follow in his track.
On many sailing thro' the storm another Star shall shine,
And they shall look up thro' the dark, and conquer at the sign.
Grand in the mouths of men his fame along the centuries runs,
Women shall read of his brave deed and bear heroic sons.

But while we tell his story, and we talk of his renown,
Above they sing his glory! over us he wears his crown.
His arch of life suspended as it sprang in Heaven, appears

A splendid bow of promise, we may see it thro' our tears.
In the dark hour of duty he had seen God's glory shewn,
And now in all his beauty sees the King upon his throne!
Some Angel-Mute did lead him blind-fold thro' the thorny ways,
Till on a sudden, lo! he stood full in the glory's blaze!
Aloud for all the world to hear God called his servant's name,
And led him forth, where all might see, upon the heights of fame!
And we know not but that England had gone down in that red flood,
If Henry Havelock had not been a chosen Man of God.

THE NORSEMAN.

A swarthy strength with face of light;
As dark sword-iron is beaten bright;
A brave, frank look, with health aglow,
Bonny blue eyes and open brow;
His friend he welcomes, heart-in-hand,
But foot to foot his foe must stand:
A Man who will face, to his last breath,
The sternest facts of life and death:
This is the brave old Norseman

The wild wave-motion weird and strange
Rocks in him! seaward he must range;
His life is just a mighty lust
To wear away with use not rust!
Tho' bitter wintry cold the storm,

The fire within him keeps him warm:
Kings quiver at his flag unfurled,
The Sea-King's master of the world!
And conquering rides the Norseman.

He hides at heart of his rough life,
A world of sweetness for the Wife;
From his rude breast a Babe may press
Soft milk of human tenderness,—
Make his eyes water, his heart dance,
And sunrise in his countenance:
In merry mood his ale he quaffs
By firelight, and his jolly heart laughs:
The blythe, great hearted Norseman.

But when the Battle Trumpet rings,
His soul's a war-horse clad with wings!
He drinks delight in with the breath
Of Battle and the dust of death:
The Axes redden; spring the sparks;
Blood-radiant grow the gray mail-sarks;
Such blows might batter, as they fell,
Heaven's gates, or burst the booms of hell!
So fights the fearless Norseman.

The Norseman's king must stand up tall,
If he would be head over all;
Mainmast of Battle! when the plain
Is miery red with bloody rain!
And grip his weapon for the fight,
Until his knuckles all grow white;
Their banner-staff he bears is best
If double handful for the rest:
When "follow me" cries the Norseman

Valiant and true, as Sagas tell,
The Norseman hated lies like hell;
Hardy from cradle to the grave,
'T was their religion to be brave:

Great, silent fighting men, whose words
Were few, soon said, and out with Swords!
One saw his heart cut from his side
Living, and smiled; and smiling, died:
The unconquerable Norseman.

They swam the flood; they strode in flame;
Nor quailed when the Valkyrie came
To kiss the chosen, for her charms,
With "Rest my Hero, in mine arms."
Their spirits thro' a grim wide wound,
The Norse door-way to heaven found;
And borne upon the battle blast,
Into the hall of Heroes passed:
And there was crowned the Norseman.

The Norseman wrestled with old Rome,
For Freedom in our Island Home;
He taught us how to ride the sea
With hempen bridle, horse of tree:
The Norseman stood with Robin Hood
By Freedom in the merry green wood,
When William ruled the English land
With cruel heart and bloody hand.
For Freedom fights the Norseman.

Still in our race the Norse king reigns;
His best blood beats along our veins;
With his old glory we can glow,
And surely sail where he could row:
Is danger stirring? from its sleep
Our War-dog wakes his watch to keep,
Stands with our Banner over him,
True as of old and stern and grim!
Come on, you'll find the Norseman.

When Swords are gleaming you shall see
The Norseman's face flash gloriously,
With look that makes the foeman reel;

His mirror from of old was steel!
And still he wields, in Battle's hour,
The old Thor's hammer of Norse power
Strikes with a desperate arm of might,
And at the last tug turns the fight:
For never yields the Norseman.

ROBERT BLAKE.

Our Happy Warrior! of a race
To whom are richly given
Great glory and peculiar grace
Because in league with Heaven.
Not that the mortal course they trod
Was free from briar and thorn;
Who bears the arrow mark of God,
Must first the wound have borne.

O like a Sailor Saint was he,
Our Sea-king! grave and sweet
In temper after victory,
Or cheerful in defeat;
And men would leave their quiet home
To follow in his wake,
And fight in fire, or float in foam,
For love of Robert Blake.

Like that drumhead of Zitska's skin,
Thrills his heroic name,
And how the salt-sea-sparkle in
Us, flashes at his fame!
His picture in our hearts' best books
Still keeps its pride of place,
From which a noble spirit looks
With an unfading face;

A face as of an Angel, who
  Might live his Boyhood here!
And yet how deadly grand it grew,
  When Wrong drew darkening near.
All ridged, and ready trench'd for war
  The fair frank brow was bent,
Then flash'd like sudden scimitar,
  The lion lineament.

Behold him, with his gallant band,
  On leaguered Lyme's red beach.
Shoulder to shoulder, see them stand,
  At Taunton in the breach.
Safe through the battle shocks he went,
  With sword-sweep stern and wide;
Strode the grim heaps as Death had lent
  Him his White Horse to ride.

" Give in! our toils you cannot break;
  The Lion is in the net!
Famine fights for us." "No," said Blake,
  " My boots I have not ate."
He smiled across the bitter cup;
  He gripped his good Sword-heft:
" I should not dream of giving up
  While such a meal is left."

Where trumpets blow and streamers flow,
  Behold him, calm and proud,
Bear down upon his bravest foe,
  A bursting thunder-cloud.
Foremost of all the host that strove
  To crowd Death's open door,
In giant mood his way he clove,
  The Man to go before.

And though the battle lightning blazed,
  The thunders roar and roll,
He to Immortal Beauty raised,

A statue with his soul.
And never did the Greeks of old
Mirror in marble rare
A Wrestler of so fine a mould,
An Athlete half so fair.

Homeward the dying Sea-king turns
From his last famous fight,
For England's dear green hills he yearns
At heart, and strains his sight.
The old cliffs loom out grey and grand,
The old War-ship glides on,
With one last wave life tries to land,
Falls seaward, and is gone.

With that last leap to touch the coast,
He passed into his rest,
And Blake's unwearying arms were crossed
Upon his martial breast.
And while our England waits, and twines
For him her latest wreath,
His is a crown of stars that shines
From out the dusk of death.

For him no pleasant age of ease,
To wear what youth could win,
For him no children round his knees,
To get his harvest in.
But with a soul serene, he takes
Whatever lot may come;
And such a life of labour makes
A glorious going home.

Famous old Trueheart, dead and gone,
Long shall his glory grow,
Who never turned his back upon
A friend, nor face from foe.
He made them fear old England's name
Wherever it was heard,

He put her proudest foes to shame,
  For God smiled on his Sword

With lofty courage, loftier love,
  He died for England's sake;
And 'mid the loftiest lights above,
  Shines our illustrious Blake. —
And shall shine! Glory of the West,
  And Beacon for the seas;
While Britain bares its sailor breast
  To battle or to breeze.

Till she forget her old sea-fame,
  Shall England honour him,
And keep the grave-grass from his name,
  Till her old eyes be dim.
And long as free waves folding round,
  Brimful with blessing break,
At heart she holds him, calm and crowned,
  Immortal Robert Blake.

Great Sailor on the seas of strife;
  Victor by land and wave;
Brave liver of a gallant life;
  Lord of a glorious grave;
True Soldier set on earthly hill
  As Sentinel of heaven;
A King who keeps his kingdom till
  The last award be given.

THE ENGLISH OF IT.

It was a gallant stand, Tom:
Give us your hardy hand, Tom:
For love of the Old Land, Tom,
        We grasp it with good will.

Although you heroes of the Fist
May think more of the golden grist
You bring to such a mill.

'T was brave to see you dash on, Tom,
And with your one arm lash on, Tom,
In that true English fashion, Tom,
Which never will wear out:
The only fashion that would do,
At Inkerman and Waterloo,
And many a bloody bout.

Through all that punching time, Tom,
The big heart rode sublime, Tom,
As we have seen it climb, Tom,
On other famous fields:
The temper beaten out with blows,
That when to give in never knows,
And so it never yields.

Valour shall have its crown, Tom,
In your plain way you have shown, Tom,
That we can hold our own, Tom,
Against all comers still;
With not one feather of white in us;
But game, with lots of fight in us;
A heart and a-half up-hill.

The belt with which we are bound, Tom,
Is yon blue ocean round, Tom;
If any foe be found, Tom,
Who thinks to take it, then
He must fight for it till all's dark,
And one shall go down, red and stark,
Never to rise again.

We won our English land, Tom,
And keep it, hand to hand, Tom,
Like you at need can stand, Tom —

Clench hands from shore to shore,
And clasp it. Touch it who so dares!
Our England hath ten thousand Sayers,
And each as brave a doer.

SIR RICHARD GRENVILLE'S LAST FIGHT.

OUR second Richard Lion Heart,
In days of Great Queen Bess,
He did this deed of righteous rage,
And true old nobleness;
With wrath heroic that was nurst
To bear the fiercest battle-burst,
When willing foes should wreak their worst.

Signalled the English Admiral,
"Weigh or cut anchors." For
A Spanish fleet bore down, in all
The majesty of war,
Athwart our tack for many a mile,
As there we lay off Florez Isle,
With crews half sick, all tired of toil.

Eleven of our twelve ships escaped;
Sir Richard stood alone!
Though they were three-and-fifty sail —
A hundred men to one —
The old sea rover would not run,
So long as he had man or gun;
But he could die when all was done.

"The Devil's broken loose, my lads,
In shape of Popish Spain;

And we must sink him in the sea,
  Or hound him home again.
Now, you old sea-dogs, show your paws!
Have at them tooth and nail and claws!"
And then his long, bright blade he draws.

The deck was cleared, the boatswain blew;
  The grim sea-lions stand;
The death-fires lit in every eye,
  The burning match in hand.
With mail of glorious intent
All hearts were clad; and in they went,
A force that cut through where 't was sent.

"Push home, my hardy pikemen,
  For we play a desperate part;
To-day, my gunners, let them feel
  The pulse of England's heart!
They shall remember long that we
Once lived; and think how shamefully
We shook them! — one to fifty-three."

With face of one who cheerly goes
  To meet his doom that day,
Sir Richard sprang upon his foes;
  The foremost gave him way:
His round shot smashed them through and through,
The great white splinters fiercely flew,
And madder grew his fighting few.

They clasp the little ship Revenge,
  As in the arms of fire;
They run aboard her, six at once;
  Hearts beat and guns leap higher.
Through bloody gaps the boarders swarm,
But still our English stay the storm,
The bulwark in their breast is firm.

Ship after ship, like broken waves
  That wash up on a rock,
Those mighty galleons fall back foiled,
  And shattered from the shock.
With fire she answers all their blows;
Again, again in pieces strows
The burning girdle of her foes.

Through all the night the great white storm
  Of worlds in silence rolled;
Sirius with his sapphire sparkle,
  Mars in ruddy gold.
Heaven looked with stillness terrible
Down on a fight most fierce and fell —
A sea transfigured into hell.

Some know not of their wounds until
  'T is slippery where they stand;
Then each one tighter grips his steel,
  As 't were salvation's hand.
Wild faces glow through lurid night
With sweat of spirit shining bright:
Only the dead on deck turn white.

At daybreak the flame-picture fades,
  In blackness and in blood;
There, after fifteen hours of fight,
  The unconquered Sea King stood,
Defying all the power of Spain:
Fifteen Armadas hurled in vain,
And fifteen hundred foemen slain.

Around that little bark Revenge,
  The baffled Spaniards ride
At distance. Two of their good ships
  Were sunken at her side;
The rest lie round her in a ring,
As round the dying lion king
The dogs afraid of his death-spring.

Our pikes all broken, powder spent,
  Sails, masts to shreds were blown;
'And with her dead and wounded crew
  The ship was going down!
Sir Richard's wounds were hot and deep.
Then cried he, with a proud, pale lip,
" Ho, gunner, split and sink the ship!

"Make ready now, my mariners,
  To go aloft with me,
That nothing to the Spaniard
  May remain of victory.
They cannot take us, nor we yield;
So let us leave our battle-field,
Under the shelter of God's shield."

They had not heart to dare fulfil
  The stern commander's word:
With bloody hands and weeping eyes,
  They carried him aboard
The Spaniards' ship; and round him stand
The warriors of his wasted band:
Then said he, feeling death at hand,

" Here die I, Richard Grenville,
  With a joyful and quiet mind;
I reach a soldier's end; I leave
  A soldier's fame behind,
Who for his queen and country fought,
For honour and religion wrought,
And died as a true soldier ought."

Earth never returned a worthier trust
  For hand of Heaven to take,
Since Arthur's sword, Excalibur,
  Was cast into the lake,
And the king's grievous wounds were dressed,
And healed, by weeping queens, who blessed,
And bore him to a valley of rest.

Old heroes who could grandly do,
  As they could greatly dare;
A vesture, very glorious,
  Their shining spirits wear,
Of noble deeds. God give us grace,
That we may see such face to face,
In our great day that comes apace.

THE END.

www.ingramcontent.com/pod-product-compliance
Lightning Source LLC
LaVergne TN
LVHW021124110826
845150LV00005B/937
* 9 7 8 1 4 2 5 5 5 0 8 5 1 *